Teaching World Politics

Teaching World Politics

Contending Pedagogies for a New World Order

EDITED BY
Lev S. Gonick
and Edward Weisband

Routledge
Taylor & Francis Group

LONDON AND NEW YORK

First published 1992 by Westview Press, Inc.

Published 2019 by Routledge
52 Vanderbilt Avenue, New York, NY 10017
2 Park Square, Milton Park, Abingdon, Oxon OX14 4RN

Routledge is an imprint of the Taylor & Francis Group, an informa business

Copyright © 1992 Taylor & Francis

All rights reserved. No part of this book may be reprinted or reproduced or utilised in any form or by any electronic, mechanical, or other means, now known or hereafter invented, including photocopying and recording, or in any information storage or retrieval system, without permission in writing from the publishers.

Notice:
Product or corporate names may be trademarks or registered trademarks, and are used only for identification and explanation without intent to infringe.

A CIP catalog record for this book is available from the Library of Congress.

ISBN 13: 978-0-367-28952-2 (hbk)
ISBN 13: 978-0-367-30498-0 (pbk)

Contents

Acknowledgments vii
About the Contributors viii

Introduction: Framing the Terms of Discourse, 1
Lev S. Gonick and Edward Weisband

Part 1 Realism, Neorealism and Hyperrealism: The Changing Scripts of World Politics

1 The Production and Transmission of Knowledge About International Relations: The Disheveled Discipline, 9
J. Martin Rochester

2 The Westphalian Paradigm: The More It Remains the Same, the More It Changes, Lynn H. Miller 25

3 From the Flows of Power to the Power of Flows: Teaching World Politics in the Informationalizing World System, Timothy W. Luke 39

Part 2 Reality Without Realism: Pedagogical Constructions with a Human Face

4 History and Culture in the Teaching of World Politics, 63
Deborah J. Gerner and Philip A. Schrodt

5   The Pedagogical Is Political: The "Why," the "What" and   83
    the "How" in the Teaching of World Politics,
    Mark Neufeld

6   Undisciplining World Politics: The Personal Is Political,   99
    Anne Sisson Runyan

7   Teaching Concepts and Theory: A View from Denmark,   113
    Georg Sørensen

8   Peace as Pedagogy: The Challenge of Sorting   127
    Fundamental from Transitory Aspects of International
    Politics, *Frederic S. Pearson and Simon Payaslian*

Part 3   Classroom Pegagogics

9   Teaching World Politics (as Well as Teaching for It),   139
    Ralph Pettman

10 Discourse Analysis: Teaching World Politics Through   153
    International Relations, *Bradley S. Klein*

11 Pedagogies on the Edge: World Politics Without   171
    "International Relations," *R.B.J. Walker*

12 The Classroom as Political Arena: The Making of a   187
    World Politics Experience, *Lev S. Gonick*

Part 4   Normative Pedagogies in World Politics: Justice
          and Conviviality

13 Justice and the Challenges of Constructivist Pedagogy: 207
    Normative Perspectives in Teaching Political Economy,
    Edward Weisband

14 Creating a Pedagogy for Convivial Planetary   249
    Community: The Future Challenge of Political Ecology,
    Terrence S. Shea

Acknowledgments

This book is the product of a series of roundtable discussions conducted under the auspices of the Annual Meetings of the International Studies Association. At both the 1991 Meetings in Vancouver and the 1992 Meetings in Atlanta we were extremely gratified by the response to our roundtables on Teaching World Politics in the 1990s. We gauged the exchanges a success, not only because of the large number of colleagues from North America, Europe, Australia, the Middle East, Asia, and Africa who contributed to the spirited discussions, but also because of the encouragement we received, calling on us to keep the discussion on pedagogy at the forefront of our collective reflections. This collection is but the first fruit of our efforts.

We gratefully acknowledge the enthusiasm demonstrated by Jennifer Knerr, Senior Acquisitions Editor of Westview Press. Her continuing support for this enterprise has helped immeasurably.

Finally, we wish to acknowledge the financial support provided by Wilfrid Laurier University's Book Preparation Grants Program.

LSG
EW

About the Contributors

Deborah J. Gerner is Associate Professor of Political Science at the University of Kansas. Her research interests include U.S.-Third World political and economic interactions, foreign policy decision-making, and Middle East politics, particularly the Israeli-Palestinian conflict. She has published a number of articles and book reviews in these areas and is the author of *One Land, Two Peoples: The Conflict Over Palestine*.

Lev S. Gonick is Assistant Professor of Political Science at Wilfrid Laurier University in Waterloo, Ontario. In addition to interests related to pedagogy, he is now engaged in a long-term study on forms of popular resistance to the spread of economic hyperliberalism such as IMF structural adjustment programs. This project is part of a larger study on Democracy, Markets, and Social Protest Movements.

Bradley S. Klein is visiting Assistant Professor of Political Science at Trinity College, Hartford, Connecticut. His studies of discourse and textuality in global strategic relations have appeared in academic books and journals in the U.S., Britain, Germany, and (what was) the Soviet Union.

Timothy W. Luke is Professor of Political Science at Virginia Polytechnic Institute and State University in Blacksburg, Virginia. Much of his work deals with critical political and social theory, international political economy, and comparative state formations. His most recent books are *Social Theory and Modernity: Critique, Dissent, and Revolution* and *Screens of Power: Ideology, Domination, and Resistance in Informational Society*.

Lynn H. Miller is Professor and Chair of the Political Science Department at Temple University. His publications include *Organizing Mankind, Global Order*, and a soon to be published text in international politics co-authored with Lloyd Jensen, *Global Change: An Introduction to World Politics in the Twenty-First Century*.

Mark Neufeld holds a Ph.D. from Carleton University. He is currently Assistant Professor in the Department of Political Studies, Trent University and an External Research Fellow with the Centre for

International and Strategic Studies, York University, Canada. His current research involves a meta-theoretical exploration of the predominance of instrumental reason in the study of world politics.

Simon Payaslian is currently completing his doctorate in Political Science at Wayne State University, where he has also taught courses on World Politics, Comparative Politics, and American Government. His dissertation examines the relationship between U.S. foreign economic and military assistance and human rights concerns.

Frederic S. Pearson is Director of the Center for Peace and Conflict Studies and Professor of Political Science at Wayne State University. He is the author of *The Weak States in International Crisis: The Case of the Netherlands in the German Invasion Crisis of 1939-1940*; co-author (with J. Martin Rochester) of *International Relations: The Global Condition in the Late Twentieth Century;* and author of a number of articles on the international arms trade, military interventions, the international oil crisis, and crisis decision making.

Ralph Pettman is Professor of International Politics at Seinan Gakuin University, Fukuoka, Japan. His most recent publication is a book entitled *International Politics: Balance of Power, Balance of Productivity, Balance of Ideologies*. He is currently engaged in writing another on the politics of globalism. More specifically, it looks at the making (and unmaking) of the modern mind.

J. Martin Rochester is Associate Professor of Political Science and a Fellow in the Center for International Studies at the University of Missouri-St. Louis. A specialist in the international organization field, Professor Rochester has published articles in the *American Political Science Review, International Organization, International Studies Quarterly, Journal of Peace Research*, and other scholarly journals. For many years he was Executive Director of the Consortium for International Studies Education, a nationwide network of universities involved in the development and dissemination of innovative pedagogical materials.

Anne Sisson Runyan is Associate Professor and Chair of Political Science at Potsdam College of the State University of New York, where she teaches undergraduate courses in international relations and feminist political theory. She is active in efforts to diversify the curriculum and has written extensively on integrating gender, race, and class into the study of world politics. She is currently co-authoring a text with V. Spike Peterson entitled *Global Gender Issues*.

Philip A. Schrodt is a Professor of Political Science at the University of Kansas. His research interests include international conflict, foreign policy decision-making, and mathematical models of political behavior. His recent research has focused on the use of artificial intelligence and computational models in international relations; he has published a number of articles in this field and is currently completing a book on the subject.

Terrence S. Shea is Assistant Professor in Political Science at Seattle University. His current teaching and writing focuses on the inter-relationships of human rights, demilitarization, and sustainable development *vis-à-vis* the search for a new world ethic. He also serves as the President of the Institute for Global Security Studies and as a member of the Governing Council for the Intercommunity Peace and Justice Center — both working out of Seattle, Washington.

Georg Sørensen is Associate Professor of International Politics at the Institute of Political Science, University of Aarhus, Denmark. His research interests include development issues and international relations theory. His most recent book is *Democracy, Dictatorship and Development: Economic Development in Selected Regimes of the Third World*.

R.B.J. (Rob) Walker is Professor of Political Science at the University of Victoria, where he also teaches in the inter-disciplinary program in Contemporary Social and Political Thought.

Edward Weisband holds the Edward Singleton Diggs Endowed Chair in the Social Sciences, Department of Political Science, Virginia Polytechnic Institute and State University. The recipient of many major awards and commendations for teaching excellence, he was recently awarded the Philip and Sadie Sporn Award for Outstanding Teaching of Introductory Subjects as well as the 1991-1992 Virginia Tech Pi Sigma Alpha Political Science Honors Society Outstanding Teaching Professor of the Year Award. In 1987, while Distinguished Teaching Professor at SUNY-Binghamton, he was named as the State of New York Professor of the Year and Gold Medal Finalist in the National Professor of the Year competition sponsored by the Council for the Advancement and Support of Education. His publications include the widely adopted reader, *Poverty Amidst Plenty: World Political Economy and Distributive Justice*.

Introduction

Framing the Terms of Discourse

Lev S. Gonick and Edward Weisband

Teaching World Politics in the 1990s is not an altogether enviable task. The balance between the elements of continuity and the dynamics of change in world reality seems as unclear as it ever has since most of us began teaching. From within the community of World Politics scholarship, challenges to received wisdom and underlying methodological assumptions have led to a revolution of their own. The resulting contested terrain is the challenge of teaching World Politics in the 1990s. The dilemma for us as teachers, confronting these remarkable transformations, is one of presenting appropriate analytical instruments to an awe-struck student body. The disjuncture and uncertainty in the world around the student is mirrored by our discipline's most introspective moment in more than half a century. The World Politics teacher often appears adrift in a sea of theoretical confusion. Writing appropriate and timely course syllabuses has become an occupational hazard. Textbooks are outdated before they reach the shelves of university and college bookstores. Idiosyncratic selection becomes the order of the teaching day with respect to the instructional choices teachers must make in the course of any term. In short, the teaching of World Politics is thus 'up for theoretical grabs', a situation that is as unsettling as it is challenging.

This is not, however, wholly distressing. There is as much to celebrate in the teaching enterprise today as there is to decry. In raising the issues of what and how to teach World Politics, we seek to identify new and appropriate principles on which to base pedagogical judgements about what to eliminate and what to emphasize in the classroom. According to what conceptual compass do we extract direction, meaning, and significance from the dizzying world that impresses itself upon our students. Put simply, what do we wish our students to understand and how do we want them to explain the universe of World Politics. This collection of essays seeks to offer competing orientations along that contested terrain. It seeks to contribute to a dialogue among teachers of World Politics as much as it shares concerns of the wider profession in rendering intelligible the new global order-in-the-making.

Perhaps the most modest of analytical insights relating to our collective condition begins with the recognition that the old order, broadly defined (both as an ideological construct and reflecting material reality), produced both structures and institutions that sought to guard against change and agents who struggled to affect change. In a sense, the disintegration of a received tradition reflects the emergence of alternative ways of regarding world society and the workings of the international division of labor within it. The question now arises as to how best to convey both the form and substance of our research on historical transformations to our students.

When we speak in the classroom, for example, of the balance of power system as a system that regulates the decentralized international society of states, we are aware that this carries a certain set of theoretical assumptions regarding existing differentiations within civil society and the position of states within the international division of labor. As we all realize, the theoretical assumptions behind such perspectives assume the primacy of the state and the permanence of national sovereign existence. Exogenous, as well as endogenous challenges in World Politics have compelled a rethinking of these assumptions. The new discourse which we seek to generate is based upon the premise that the *power realist paradigm*, so essential to the contemporary theoretical development of world politics, no longer serves as *the* galvanizing bond among us. Balance of power, security policies and practices, strategic conventional and nuclear deterrence, retain their conceptual core-like status in teaching and research for many of us; but such interests, and the theoretical discourse generated by such concerns, no longer suffice as the only anchoring point in our various disciplinary pursuits. Alone, they are thus inadequate to define and guide our pedagogy.

It thus becomes important to establish the grounds on which a common agenda can evolve. We need to establish what we all continue to share as teachers of World Politics, even as we would address and nurture what distinguishes us intellectually and pedagogically from each other. What might these other theoretical orientations be and how might they together work to create a less than forbidding sense of conceptual overload for our students? Here, at this very juncture, we offer the following: what unifies us is the collective aim of reducing the inherited tension between justice, peace, and security. What binds us together as teachers is a commitment to our students to develop a pedagogy that retains of realism what is valid to an understanding of how the universe of World Politics functions, while grafting on to it a broader theoretical hybrid relevant to our teaching programme, a hybrid that portrays the lessons gleaned from alternative theoretical perspectives.

To what extent has the dialogue between feminism and post-structuralism on the social construction of gender, race, class, and state become central to our pedagogical portrayal of World Politics? Have the zonal conceptions of core and periphery, or patterns of differentiated modes of production, or the role of market structures, so familiar to teachers of International Political Economy, become indispensable tools in the study of World Politics.

More than this, how do we present these perspectives in ways that convey some degree of pedagogical, if not substantive, unity so that students do not leave our lecture halls needlessly bewildered by complexity. Perspectives on alternative forms of an international division of labor operate to belie the centrality of state-centric conceptions of the world political universe. These too must be introduced, but at what levels and in what ways? These include feminist perspectives on the invisibility of women in World Politics, Neo-classical perspectives on trade, functionalist perspectives on federalism, complex interdependence, anarchist as well as Marxist views on internationalism, the approach of radical geographers to zonal distributions of production and privilege, and so on.

Perhaps kernels of an answer may be generated by flushing out the underlying values that inform our collective concern with the power relations that join justice, peace, and security. Perhaps what we all share as teachers is our commitment to portray and explain power and powerlessness, justice and injustice. Arguably what differentiates us is how we cast the theoretical questions that surround the problem and give shape to our discussion in teaching. Thus, those teachers who would include in their treatment of world politics the dynamics of world capitalism, the strategic competition advanced by transnational business enterprise, and the growing universality of structural adjustment policies, must all ultimately confront issues of power relations, inequality, exploitation, and justice, despite the need to confront such value-laden issues in a broad range of contexts.

Another way to pose the task before us is to address the relationship of traditional international relations and foreign policy analysis to the theoretical units of analysis established by historical sociology, feminism, and international political economy. Indeed, if World Politics is as much concerned about the relationship of power to justice, as it is about that of power to peace and war, can it avoid the centrality of the concepts of *gender* and *class*? The challenge in this light is to apply a nonreified version of gender and/or class analysis to an understanding of class and gender as units of analysis relevant to mainstream approaches to the teaching of World Politics.

We need to confront the necessity of educating our students with regard to the structure and politics of global finance and monetary regulation. We must assess the emphasis to be granted in the teaching of World Politics to the various institutional regimes that now operate in world society, regimes established for purposes of providing coordination and authoritative decision-making in world affairs. To the degree that our collective teaching program must attempt to offer students insights into the anatomy of the evolving global order, the standing of the United Nations, specialized institutions such as the World Bank and the International Monetary Fund, and the many remaining organizations that promote institutional interdependence form a critical dimension of that new reality.

Dynamics in Europe involving the disintegration of East-West conflict, the unification of Germany, the re-establishment of historic dependencies and power relations between East and West Europe, the prospects of a European super-state, and at a minimum a super-economy all serve to expand our conceptions of world political possibility. How do we begin to replace the novelty of novelty with reasoned curriculum development? How do we systematically introduce such phenomena in terms of an instructional paradigm that make the extraordinary seem reasonably predictable and consistent with the pedagogy we choose to present to our students.

Our enterprise requires us to reflect systematically upon the changing nature of global problems and the manner in which we introduce them into the classroom. Our traditional concerns with state security can be extended to address the security of the environment and the security of human welfare. As the twentieth century pushes into the historical past, the terrain to be incorporated into courses on World Politics must reveal to our students what is fundamental to us by way of shared values. In so doing, none of us engaged in teaching world politics can avoid the shared quest to define the conceptual language we wish to employ and the set of narrative values we seek to apply. We must be careful and introspective as we evaluate, dare one say, deconstruct, the language we use in the classroom in order to resurrect the narratives we tell of how the universal world of human relation came to be what we understand it to be.

Within this context, we must entertain the fullest range possible of conceptual revisions of both language and of value orientations, revisions grounded in new and perhaps vitalized appreciations of feminism, anti-racism, liberation theology, non-Western as well as Western humanism, post-structuralism, and post-modernism. At the same time we must be careful to establish an appreciation in the classroom for the chains of intellectual heritage that inform our new questions. We must question the adequacy of our poetry as teachers in order to reconceive the relationship between the language we speak and the world of our making, to refer to Nicholas Greenwood Onuf's book of the same title.

Ultimately, therefore, our project presents us with the challenge of examining how and what we speak in class and how and what we write as texts. The contested terrain is about competing central narratives we now wish to tell in the teaching of World Politics. The essays in this collection help us to evaluate ourselves as teachers at this, the most primordial level, in order then to grapple with the significance of what we present in the classroom. Only thus can we define a pedagogy both sufficient and worthy of what we would want our students to know and to understand as they assume their mature roles in the next century.

PART ONE

Realism, Neorealism and Hyperrealism: The Changing Scripts of World Politics

1

The Production and Transmission of Knowledge About International Relations: The Disheveled Discipline

J. Martin Rochester

The Nexus Between the Production and Transmission of Knowledge

The two main objectives of academic professional pursuits are the production and the transmission of knowledge. The second of these engages other scholars and academics, policymakers, occasionally the public at large, and invariably students — academia's primary consumers — in a discourse over the nature of truth, meaning and significance of knowledge. This writing focuses on the production and transmission of knowledge as it relates to students, particularly undergraduates, within the context of the study of world politics, which today finds itself challenged to keep pace with rapidly changing developments. My observations are based primarily on American experience, although I believe they have broader relevance.

The relationship between knowledge production and knowledge transmission rarely has been the subject of serious scholarship itself, since research and teaching have tended to be treated as rather separate enterprises. Each has occupied its own particular domain and has required distinctive skills. Thus there has arisen "a tension on most campuses over their [relative] priorities."[1] The resulting fact is that, with the exception of schools of education, pedagogy tends to be viewed as an unworthy subject of scholarly inquiry by faculty at 'research universities', while faculty at 'teaching-oriented' institutions tend not to engage in research, pedagogical or otherwise. Hence, insufficient professional discussion occurs regarding the connections between the production, transmission, and, ultimately, the consumption of knowledge.

Despite this, teaching and research, in fundamental ways, are inseparable. As Kenneth Boulding once remarked, "When one prepares to walk into a classroom and asks 'what shall I teach?', one must first ask 'what do I know?'"[2] Solid teaching is premised on solid scholarship, which means that teachers must at least keep up with the latest theoretical and empirical advances reported in the scholarly literature. Solid scholarship is defined by the capacity to raise and answer important new questions in a manner that adds to the reliability of our knowledge — that is, to have something worth conveying ('teaching'). Ernest Boyer has written about 'the new American scholar', calling for a new mutuality between research and teaching and a renewed commitment to linking the two. This would help to impart a novel seriousness of purpose to both activities as elements of a common endeavor within the institutional constraints typically found at colleges and universities.[3] Indeed, as the frontiers of knowledge expand, and as the world situation changes, new approaches and perspectives would find their way expeditiously into textbooks and other educational materials.

Such observations apply to the study of world politics as much as they do to any research and teaching field. In the 1980s, World Politics as an academic field was characterized as a 'dividing discipline', with 'hegemony' competing with 'diversity'.[4] In the 1990s, the field might be characterized as 'disheveled'. In the words of George Will:

> One thing is certain: we have never seen a year like 1989. Only the Reformation is remotely comparable to today's gale-force intellectual winds and loud cracking of institutional foundations. No year, even in the 16th century, ever swept so many people or such complex societies into a vortex of change. Nineteen eighty-nine has been the most startling, interesting, promising and consequential year, ever.[5]

Even if Will is perhaps overstating or prejudging the historic significance of recent events, many scholars nonetheless are having to come to grips with this reformation in their theoretical formulations while many instructors are having to do likewise in their lesson plans; more than one manuscript and one lecture has been affected. What is one to make of these changes? What do we know today about world politics? What do we teach?

Uncertainty Over What We Know About World Politics: The Ghost of Morgenthau

Clearly, world politics historically has always entailed change. Indeed, developments throughout the postwar era have appeared to represent major transformations in the political relations among states. Writing in the 1970s, Ernst Haas referred analytically to growing "turbulence in world politics."[6] Around the same time, James Caporaso noted that "since the end of World War II there have been some profound changes in the structure of the international system."[7] Editors of a volume dedicated to the explanation of "change" published early in the 1980s declared that "the international system has undergone profound changes since World War II."[8] Change, then, has been a familiar theme and commonplace observation in the study of postwar politics. And yet, for all the attention given to the volatility of the international system in the atomic age, there were certain categories one could confidently rely on year after year to anchor one's analysis of world affairs: the 'East-West conflict', the 'nonaligned nations,' and 'Third World', and other constructs associated with a predominantly 'bipolar' order. True, some pointed to 'discontinuities' and 'subsystems' below the surface of a bipolar world; but, for the global system as a whole, the established units of analysis tended to retain their currency for decades.[9] These categories arguably have now been rendered almost useless.

Although recent developments in world politics have manifested a tumultuous, topsy-turvy quality, such convulsions can be understood in retrospect as the culmination of a longer-term pattern involving steady erosion of the postwar international order traceable back to its beginnings. The tidy bipolar imagery of an international system organized around two competing superpowers leading two relatively cohesive ideologically-grounded blocs rested on a flimsy foundation from the start. Fissures became apparent as early as the 1950s — with the beginnings of nuclear proliferation, the emergence of a third 'bloc', the loosening of the Western and Eastern alliances fractured by the twin Suez and Hungarian crises of 1956, and assorted other fault-lines. Fissures widened into cracks during the 1960s and 1970s. The North-South axis of conflict began to compete for attention with East-West issues. The Communist Chinese experienced mounting hostility with their Soviet brethren, while Greece and its NATO ally Turkey engaged in open warfare. U.S. superpower credentials were called into question in Vietnam (an American president stating he could not understand how "the greatest power in the world" was unable to defeat a "band of night-riders in black pajamas").[10] American power was also called into question in the Middle East, where a group of underdeveloped countries, many of which were tiny 'statelets' and all of which were devoid of the assets traditionally associated with power, managed momentarily to bring the Western world to its knees by quadrupling the price of oil.[11]

Cracks turned into gaping trenches during the 1980s, well before the end of the decade, with the Soviet Union's Vietnam-style failure in

Afghanistan and the U.S. becoming the chief debtor state in the world. At the same time, West Germany and Japan flirted with being the leading exporter and foreign aid donor respectively. Consequently, power structures within the international system were rendered practically unintelligible.

As I have noted, the forces of change did not go unnoticed by students of world politics in this pre-Gorbachev era. For example, Morton Kaplan distinguished between 'loose' and 'tight' bipolarity,[12] Richard Rosecrance discerned 'bimultipolarity'[13] within the system, and Stanley Hoffmann found 'polycentrism' and multiple 'game boards'[14] to be the order of the day. A general sense persisted, however, that the 'postwar system' would remain stable in many of its essential elements through the next century. That is, until the fall of the Berlin Wall toppled such illusions of stability.

As the new 'post-Cold War' order haltingly takes shape, certain elements are coming more clearly into focus. Previous trends in the direction of a more complex international system are becoming more pronounced and accelerated. First, there exists *a growing diffusion and ambiguity of power*. This is manifested by the decline of the United States as a hegemon as well as the internal and external problems of the "other" superpower, the continued rise of Japan as a financial and political power, the challenge posed by a strengthened European Community preparing itself for 'Europe 1992' while adjusting to a newly reunited German state, and the proliferation of 'mini-states' capable at times of frustrating the will of major actors. Secondly, there exists *a growing fluidity of alignments*, as suggested by the depolarization of the East-West conflict as East bloc states move ideologically toward the West while West-West economic competition threatens to become a serious axis of conflict. Additionally, the North-South conflict is losing its defining character as increasing diversity among NICs, OPEC states, Fourth World countries and other LDCs makes Southern solidarity harder to sustain.[15] All the while, greater localization and regionalization of politics related to ethnicity percolates below the global level. Thirdly, there now exists *ever more intricate patterns of interdependence*, associated with an expanding agenda of concerns (economics, ecology, technology, etc.) and a broadening conception of 'national security' beyond traditional military considerations. Finally, there exists *a growing role for nonstate actors along with increasing linkages between subnational, transnational and intergovernmental levels of activity*, despite the fact that national governmental budgets and state apparatuses resist shrinkage.

The key question remains whether we are witnessing merely the end of the postwar era and the transformation of the international system back to the more normal historical pattern of full-blown multipolarity. In this case, scholars (and teachers) can continue to rely on the state-centric paradigm with its focus on national interests, state sovereignty, power, and international anarchy. On the other hand, are we in the midst of a more fundamental and epic transformation that involves nothing less than the unraveling of the very fabric of the Westphalian state system itself? If so, there is a need for an entirely reconstituted framework for understanding and interpreting world order. The 'neorealist' school tends to seize upon the fragmentation of the postwar power and alignment structure to argue that the *déjà vu* scenario is correct, *i.e.* the international system is returning to an earlier condition, and bears particular resemblance to the early twentieth century, replete with the absence of any hegemonic stability and mounting Balkan ethnic conflict.[16] Others, notably 'neoliberals', point to the phenomena related to interdependence, transnationalism and intergovernmentalism and suggest otherwise, *i.e.* the international system is experiencing unprecedented complexity and is heading toward, as one writer puts it, a 'bifurcated global politics' torn between state-centrism and 'multi-centrism', calling for a wholly new 'post-international politics' paradigm.[17]

Both schools of thought have merit in their alternative readings of the workings of the international system. Important dramas are being played out between the forces of regionalism and globalism, nationalism and transnationalism, security and welfare, and order and change. While these represent ongoing historical dramas, the curtain appears to be rising on a new political scene. How various tensions will be resolved is hardly certain.

There are countervailing trends in the direction of both integration and disintegration. The former is evidenced by German unification, the Europe 1992 campaign, the continued proliferation of NGOs and IGOs at both the regional and global levels in addition to the spread of multinational corporations,[18] and the signing of more international agreements since 1945 than in the previous 2000 years combined (including the conclusion of a single treaty signed by virtually every state governing virtually every human activity on 70 percent of the earth's surface).[19] Disintegration, however, is manifested not only by the fragmentation of the postwar power and bloc structure, but also by the continued proliferation of 'microstates' as an extension of the postwar decolonialization process, with disintegrative tendencies expected to be accelerated further by the subnational ethnic conflicts in Eastern Europe and the former USSR.[20] Thus, we are left with the puzzling paradox of growing disintegration amidst a world that is arguably more integrated than ever. There are, of course, more than two schools of thought surrounding the current debate over the nature of change in world politics. As noted at the outset, the discipline has been characterized in many respects by growing 'diversity', represented not only by neorealism and neoliberalism, but also by different perspectives introduced by Marxism and post-modernist feminism.

Neorealism is likely to prevail in the paradigmatic struggle with neoliberalism and other challengers, however, because it provides a compelling enough framework for grappling with the facts of international life. It also meshes comfortably with the conservative bent of the 'IR establishment' — the definers of the discipline — which tends to see the world through the lenses of the larger societal establishment upon which it depends for its sustenance. While it may be true at times that "academic pens ... leave marks in the minds of statesmen with profound results for policy," the relationship is more commonly reversed.[21] That is, the scholarly community tends to take its cues from the policymaking community. It is the latter, in concert with other elites outside academia, whose worldview or 'relevant universe' generally dictates governmental and foundation funding programs, which in turn shape major research agendas at prestigious universities, whose faculty set the standards for what is publishable and take the lead in recruiting and training the next generation of the professoriate. Though at any moment we in academe may be leaving an imprint on young minds belonging in some cases perhaps to future policymakers, the images of the world they leave the classroom with are likely to owe their origins to board rooms or state rooms and other such bastions of learning. To the extent that American scholarship has dominated the development of world politics as a field of study since World War II, it has been particularly through the eyes of the U.S. establishment — through the eyes of 'a great power' — that much of what has passed for international reality has been captured.

The conservativism of the international relationist fraternity that stems from external pressures driving scholars to pursue research programs consistent with established political values is reinforced by other pressures operating within the discipline itself. In fact, conservative leanings may be more a function of the latter pressures, having to do with the sociology of the profession, than it is a function of politics and ideology. Kuhn's well-known arguments about the structure of scientific revolutions and the forces of inertia that inhibit paradigmatic change apply very clearly to the study of world politics. One can argue that the staying power of realism is attributable to 'the ghost of Morgenthau' — the strong empiricist-positivist tradition spawned by *Politics Among Nations*, with its emphasis on studying the world as it is (or at least as it is thought to be) rather than as it might be or ought to be. Since Morgenthau (through whom scholars rediscovered Thucydides and Machiavelli), the dominant professional norm has been to avoid anything that could give the appearance of idle speculation or wishful thinking overtaking serious, objective analysis. Morgenthau's work has 'colored' much of the scholarly discourse in the field throughout the postwar period, and continues to do so despite the cries of the 'post-positivist' movement.[22]

In short, the scholar-entrepreneur has, I would argue, a felt need not to be too much ahead of one's time, not to be too far out in front of trends. Yet there is also a felt need to do more than jump on the bandwagon; there is a push to be on the leading edge and at the frontiers of knowledge, since one succeeds by being new and different. The result is a 'revisionist' imperative operating within the boundaries of the established paradigm. Scholarship forever produces new wine in old bottles. Popular theses are reexamined and refuted by one set of researchers only to be reconfirmed by another. One day's prevailing orthodoxy becomes the next day's revisionist scholarship, as with the tortuous debate over the relationship between a balance or preponderance of power and the onset of war.

Consequently, reality-testing occurs against the backdrop of the latest news headlines. Again, policy seems to drive social science rather than the converse. One can see this vividly, for example, in the evolution of the international organization subfield since World War II. In successive decades, the field shifted from a focus on the United Nations and formal-legal aspects of global intergovernmental organizations (following the birth of the UN in 1945), to writings on regional integration (following the birth of the European Economic Community in 1957), to a virtual abandonment of the study of IGOs altogether in favor of 'regimes' (following the seeming failure of both regional and global approaches to international institution-building by the 1970s).[23] Major scholarly figures pronounced both regionalism and globalism dead as formal-legal experiments. Ernst Haas wrote in the mid-1970s that "theorizing about regional integration as such is no longer profitable."[24] By the mid-1980s, Robert Keohane and Joseph Nye were writing that "only rarely are universal international organizations likely to provide the world with instruments for collective action."[25] With the current revival of the EEC and UN, one senses the study of such IGOs once again may become a growth industry at least for a time. Witness to this is the new funding program on 'International Organization and Law' announced by the Ford Foundation, with "the following topics emphasized in the 1990-91 biennium: the United Nations system; international organizations and agreements generally; international peacekeeping and peacemaking; sustainable development and the management of the global commons; and institutional and legal aspects of regional integration and cooperation."[26]

The shifting intellectual currents in the international organization area over the course of the postwar era have been parallelled by similar movements in the IR field as a whole. Whatever momentum the 'cobweb' paradigm, with its focus on transnational actors and issues, had accumulated on the heels of the 1973 oil embargo was summarily arrested by the arrival of Ronald Reagan, whose return to Cold War rhetoric coincided with the rise of neorealism, which reiterated the 'billiard ball' nature of the universe.[27] It now appears that, if some international relationists exaggerated the importance of transnationalism and multinationalism during the 1970s, others may have exaggerated its insignificance during the 1980s.

It is understandable why scholars should want to keep pace with happenings in the real world. To do otherwise is to invite charges of irrelevance. However, there is always a danger of overreacting to events of the moment, thereby losing sight of deeper structures and processes. One cannot help recalling Hegel's dictum that "the owl of Minerva always rises at night."[28] Social scientists are good at predicting the past, at uncovering truths associated with the tail-end of some epiphenomenon. One would have to be blind, though, not to recognize that, in the wake of the recent upheavals in world politics, something of importance has happened, if not of millennial proportions at least of a magnitude that marks the end of a half-century of history.

We are still too close to the developments of the past few years to make informed judgments regarding just how "seismic" they may prove to be. After all, it took centuries for students of world affairs to recognize the full implications of events occurring around 1648 culminating in the rise of the "Westphalian state system." Towards the end of his life, Morgenthau suggested that our knowledge of this state system was about to become obsolete. He indicated that the Westphalian order was at odds with a new reality and, consequently, was on the brink of going the way of feudalism.[29] In most circles these were considered only the ruminations of an elder statesman of the discipline, although it was jarring for some that the apostle of realism appeared to renounce his own paradigm.

The field of world politics is now 'disheveled' as Morgenthau suspected. That the biggest events in memory largely caught the entire scholarly community off guard has been humbling. Neorealists, neoliberals and others are all trying to sort out the various trends and counter-trends in order to make sense out of a political environment that is not as familiar-looking as it used to be. Meanwhile, as we try to ascertain what we know, we also are necessarily faced with questions regarding what to teach.

Uncertainty Over What to Teach: The Ghost of Morgenthau Again

The realist tradition inherited from Morgenthau has exerted a powerful influence on pedagogy in some obvious and not-so-obvious ways.[30] Even though in reality research has overtaken teaching as the preeminent activity at many institutions of higher learning, academic departments everywhere still must normally justify their existence by demonstrating where they fit into the curriculum and why they are essential to the educational mission. The structure of the standard political science department, at least in American universities of any size, tends to be based on assumptions about the integrity and distinctiveness of specific subfields commonly labeled 'comparative politics', 'international relations', and so forth.[31] Whole curricula are built around these subfields, whose viability more or less requires acceptance of a state-centric view of the world. Although state-centrism did not originate with the realist school, realism enshrined state-centrism as the core of its paradigm. To question the latter, to adopt some sort of 'post-IR" paradigm, is to threaten the academic edifice. Such a challenge goes beyond merely revising courses. It entails wholesale changes in curricula, a rethinking and renaming of subfields, and a complete shake-up in the departmental way of life.

Yet another source of conservatism, then, is the reluctance to unleash forces that could upset departmental bureaucratic-organizational routines and culture. To those for whom even the preparation or rewriting of lectures can be a chore, macro-level changes, causing the dislocation of one's academic identity and home, promise to be all the more painful. If it is true, as Samuel Huntington says, that "command economies have no use for economists, nor authoritarian . . . [polities] for political science," a 'post-international politics' world system would have little use for international relations specialists.[32]

The path of least resistance is to keep teaching mostly the same old courses in the same old way. This is not to say that change is unheard of in the international relations and world politics curriculum. In response to shifting scholarly fashions, many colleges and universities have added an international political economy course here, dropped a United Nations course there, and made other curricular innovations. Rarely, though, is any thought given within the American social science academy to the basic premises that underlie the curriculum as a whole. Within individual courses, the typical instructor dutifully redoes his or her syllabus, updates lecture material, inserts another module, and assigns the latest editions of textbooks and other readings. But where much effort has been invested in developing a course, there is a certain aversion to undoing one's handiwork in more than a piecemeal way.

The best single barometer of the state of pedagogy in the international relations or world politics field is the manner in which the introductory course is taught. Insofar as the international relations undergraduate textbooks set the content and tone of the introductory course as well as of the upper level courses that follow, Morgenthau clearly continues to haunt the field. That *Politics Among Nations* continues to be a best seller among comprehensive textbooks is itself ample testimony to the durability of Morgenthau's approach to world politics. Other texts have come along over the years that have incorporated fresh perspectives on 'new actors' (NGOS, MNCs, and others) and 'new issues' (with notably heavier doses of economics offered), but these generally have been careful not to stray too far from the Morgenthau model. Those texts that have dared to be different have not lasted long, for example, Finlay and Hovet's *7304: International Relations on the Planet Earth*, or Sterling's *Macropolitics*. Both of these appeared in the heady 'globalist' days of the 1970s only to disappear quickly. They projected too iconoclastic an image especially as the arrival of the 1980s seemed to mark a return to yesteryear. In comparison with, say, the American politics field, where at least a few clearly 'radical' or unconventional treatments of the subject can be found such as Parenti's *Democracy for the Few*, Judd and Hellinger's *The Democratic Facade*, and Dye and Ziegler's *The Irony of Democracy*, one is struck by the virtual absence of any such texts in the world politics field.

Morgenthau's influence extends even to stylistic aspects of textbooks. One is hard pressed to think of another field in which a single work has been at once both the leading text used for beginning freshmen and sophomores as well as a preeminent scholarly tome, a treatise cited regularly in Ph.D. dissertations and professional papers for state of the art insights. Ever since *Politics Among Nations*, there has been a strong disposition to produce texts that have the air of "serious" scholarship, lest they be compared unfavorably with the standard in the field. Organski and others have followed this tradition, one that is almost unique to international relations and world politics.[33] Rather than texts reporting and summarizing the latest advances in knowledge in the field, they often have been looked to as the source of those advances. It is as if the functional relationship between research and teaching has been stood on its head. Although few text-tomes have appeared of late, there has been a tendency still to write books for the introductory world politics course aimed more at professorial peers than students.

Again, one is struck by the different educational norms that exist in the American politics field. In the latter field, even the most widely respected, 'serious' scholars who have authored beginning texts have not been above including photos, cartoons, vignettes, trivia charts, timeline chronologies, profiles of famous personages, and other ancillary materials to enliven and illuminate.[34] Something more than market factors is operating here. Should world politics texts adopt this style of presentation, as some have begun to do, they risk being dismissed as academically fluffy and pandering or talking down to students.[35] There seemingly is a different set of pedagogical assumptions informing the process of how knowledge is transmitted to the uninitiated student of American politics in contrast with the international relations novitiate. In world politics one must pass a stiffer sobriety test, it appears, although there seems to be growing tolerance for new methods of stimulating students through such devices as simulation exercises and the like.

World politics texts, as also compared to their American politics counterparts, tend to emphasize conceptual and theoretical concerns and devote relatively less space to discussion of basic descriptive information on history, geography, and institutions, or to values and policy issues. This is perhaps partly due to the 'text-tome' syndrome noted above and partly due to the sweeping nature of the subject. Professors want to teach higher-level skills than merely memorization of idiographic details relevant to current events. In any case, it is hard to fit a history and geography of the world, a discussion of cultural perspectives of over 200 ethnic groups, and a review of contemporary policy issues affecting over 150 states and 5 billion people into a single volume. While comprehension, analysis and synthesis are the noblest of educational objectives, the problem is that students too often enter, and then leave, the international relations curriculum without an adequate foundation for absorbing the sophisticated knowledge that faculty wish to impart.

Realism no less than idealism has ultimately been grounded in the pursuit of physical security among human societies. Widespread agreement on the desirability of peace exists, but disagreements arise over how peace is best achieved and how it relates to other values. Better knowledge production and knowledge transmission are needed to attain a new world order. As J. David Singer has written, in an essay found in a recent issue of *The Chronicle of Higher Education*, "the deadly connection between poor research and inadequate teaching at one end, and the devastating consequences of frequently inept foreign policy decisions at the other end, lies not in our stars . . . but in our academic community."[36]

In our teaching, we must be careful to convey to students both the cultural/value diversity that exists in the world and the complexity of international relations. For all our epistemological failings and uncertainty over what is likely to happen next in world affairs, we probably know more than we are conveying properly to students. The dominant paradigm, simplistic as it is, is still a useful guide to current reality, even if it misses a good deal of 'everyday human experience' and, together with other factors, makes us ill-equipped to recognize and point out major change when it occurs.[37] We need to impress upon students the importance of not just studying world politics but also reflecting about it and how the human condition can be improved. We should not be shy about calling attention to the values at stake and defining our field in the plainest of terms — as Deutsch puts it, "the art and science of the survival of mankind."[38]

Thinking, writing, and teaching routines no doubt have been shaken to some extent by the period of history we have just passed through since the late 1980s. Whether manuscripts and lecture notes require merely a little tinkering or much more onerous revision will depend on how events continue to unfold as the millennium approaches. One would hope at a minimum that members of the world politics profession meanwhile would use the moment to take a more self-conscious look at themselves as both scholars and educators.

Notes

1. Ernest Boyer, *College: The Undergraduate Experience in America* (New York: Harper and Row, 1987), p. 120.

2. Comment by Kenneth Boulding addressing the Consortium for International Studies Education at the annual meeting of the International Studies Association, St. Louis, March 1974.

3. See Boyer, *College*; and Boyer and R. Eugene Rice, *Scholarship Reconsidered: Priorities of the Professoriate*, report of the Carnegie Foundation for the Advancement of Teaching (Princeton NJ: Princeton University Press, 1990).

4. K. J. Holsti, *The Dividing Discipline: Hegemony and Diversity in International Theory* (London: Allen and Unwin, 1985).

5. George F. Will, "Europe's Second Reformation," column in *Newsweek*, 20 November 1989, p. 90.

6. Ernst B. Haas, "Turbulent Fields and the Theory of Regional Integration," *International Organization*, 30 (Spring 1976).

7. James Caporaso, *Functionalism and Regional Integration: A Logical and Empirical Assessment* (Beverly Hills CA: Sage, 1972), p. 5.

8. Ole R. Holsti, Randolph M. Siverson and Alexander L. George, eds., *Change in the International System* (Boulder CO: Westview Press, 1980), p. xvii.

9. On discontinuities and subsystems, see Oran R. Young, "Political Discontinuities in the International System," *World Politics*, 20 (April 1968), pp. 369-392; Leonard Binder, "The Middle East as a Subordinate International System," *World Politics*, 10 (April 1958), pp. 408-429; and Louis J. Cantori and Steven L. Spiegel, *The International Politics of Regions* (Englewood Cliffs, NJ: Prentice-Hall, 1970).

10. "I still believe he [President Lyndon Johnson] found it viscerally inconceivable that what Walt Rostow kept telling him was 'the greatest power in the world' could not dispose of a collection of night-riders in black pajamas." Quoted from Arthur Schlesinger, Jr., "The Quagmire Papers," *New York Review of Books*, 16 December 1971, p. 41.

11. The oil crisis of 1973, focusing on the role of various state and nonstate actors, is discussed in Raymond Vernon, ed., *The Oil Crisis* (New York: W.W. Norton, 1976).

12. Morton A. Kaplan, *System and Process in International Politics* (New York: John Wiley, 1957).

13. Richard N. Rosecrance, "Bipolarity, Multipolarity, and the Future," *Journal of Conflict Resolution*, 10 (September 1966), pp. 314-327.

14. Stanley Hoffmann, *Gulliver's Troubles, or the Setting of American Foreign Policy* (New York: McGraw-Hill, 1968); and "Choices," *Foreign Policy* (Fall 1973).

15. By 1989, such a wide range of differences existed among "developing countries" that the World Bank indicated it would no longer use that designation as a specific category in its data reports. See *World Development Report 1989* (New York: Oxford University Press, 1989), pp. x-xi.

16. Typical of this view is John J. Mearsheimer, "Why We Will Soon Miss the Cold War," *The Atlantic* (August 1990).

17. James N. Rosenau goes further than many neoliberals in calling for such a paradigm. See his *Turbulence in World Politics* (Princeton NJ: Princeton University Press, 1990); and "Global Changes and Theoretical Challenges: Towards a Postinternational Politics for the 1990s," in Rosenau and Ernst-Otto Czempiel, eds., *Global Changes and Theoretical Challenges* (Lexington MA: Lexington Books, 1990), pp. 1-20.

18. For trends on NGO and IGO growth, see Harold K. Jacobson, *Networks of Interdependence*, 2nd ed. (New York: Knopf, 1984), ch. 3. On the latest statistics, see *Yearbook of International Organizations*, 1988/1989, 25th ed. (Brussels: Union of International Associations, 1988), Table 1 in Appendix 7 of vol. 1. On multinational corporation growth, see David H. Blake and Robert S. Walters, *The Politics of Global Economic Relations*, 3rd ed. (Englewood Cliffs, NJ: Prentice-Hall, 1987), ch. 4, and UN Center on Transnational Corporations, *Transnational Corporations in World Development* (New York: UN, 1983).

19. For trends in treatymaking, see Richard Bilder, *Managing the Risks of International Agreement* (Madison Wis: University of Wisconsin Press, 1981); and Mark W. Janis, *An Introduction to International Law* (Boston MA: Little, Brown, 1988). The Law of the Sea treaty alluded to by the author was signed by 155 states during the 1980s. However, it has not yet received the sixty ratifications needed to come into force, primarily owing to the uncertainty created by the American objection to a relatively minor provision pertaining to deep seabed mining. See David L. Larson, "Will There Be An UNCLOS IV?" paper presented at the annual meeting of the International Studies Association, Washington D.C., April 1990.

20. The potential for added ethnic conflict and break-up of nation-states appears great, based on the fact that "data from 1986 on 166 countries show only a third to be ethnically homogenous (where one group constituted at least 90

percent of the population)." Bruce Russett and Harvey Starr, *World Politics: The Menu for Choice*, 3rd ed. (San Francisco CA: W.H. Freeman, 1989), p. 54.

21. Robert O. Keohane and Joseph S. Nye, *Power and Interdependence* (Boston MA: Little, Brown, 1977), p. 4.

22. On the dominance of the realist paradigm in shaping behavioral research in the postwar period, see John Handelman *et al.*, "Color It Morgenthau: A Data-Based Assessment of Quantitative International Relations Research" (Syracuse University International Relations Program, 1973). This paper was frequently cited in a roundtable discussion at the 1974 annual meeting of the International Studies Association entitled "International Relations and the World Society: A Trans-Atlantic Dialogue." That Morgenthau continues to shape the contours of the field was evidenced at the 1989 annual ISA meeting, where a fifteenth anniversary "Trans-Atlantic Dialogue Renewed" roundtable was held. Also see the organization of the International Relations sections at the 1991 annual meeting of the American Political Science Association. Challenges to the empiricist-positivist tradition and the rumblings of "post-positivism" are discussed in a special volume of *International Studies Quarterly*, 33 (September 1989).

23. This pattern is discussed in J. Martin Rochester, "The Rise and Fall of International Organization as a Field of Study," *International Organization*, 40 (Autumn 1986), pp. 77-813.

24. Ernst Haas, "Turbulent Fields and the Theory of Regional Integration," *International Organization*, 30 (Spring 1976), p. 174.

25. Robert O. Keohane and Joseph S. Nye, "Two Cheers for Multilateralism," *Foreign Policy*, 60 (Fall 1985), pp. 148-167.

26. *International Organizations and Law: A Program Paper of the Ford Foundation* (New York: Ford Foundation, September 1990), pp. 14-15.

27. It should be noted, though, that Robert Cox had coined the term 'neorealism' prior to Reagan's arrival on the scene in 1980, and that Kenneth Waltz's neorealist treatise *Theory of International Politics* appeared in 1979. Still, the 1980s witnessed a retreat by many who earlier had been associated with the study of 'ecopolitics', 'nonstate actors', and other new elements of world politics. Theorizing about 'hegemonic stability' tended to overshadow theorizing about 'complex interdependence'. Compare Keohane and Nye, *Power and Interdependence*, with Keohane's *After Hegemony* (Princeton NJ: Princeton University Press, 1984).

28. Georg Wilhelm Friedrich Hegel, *Philosophy of Right*, translated by T.M. Knox (Oxford: Oxford University Press, 1973).

29. Hans J. Morgenthau, "The New Diplomacy of Movement," *Encounter*, 43 (August 1974), p. 57.

30. Between 1972 and 1976, the author was director of the Consortium for International Studies Education, established by the International Studies Association to facilitate the development and dissemination of innovative educational ideas in the international studies field. As part of this effort, I directed the National Science Foundation Learning Package project which brought together well-known scholars with educational innovators in an attempt to translate the latest research into novel modular, multi-media undergraduate teaching materials.

31. The International Studies Association is unusual in its commitment to relaxing traditional disciplinary and subdisciplinary boundaries under the rubric of 'international studies', although it has had mixed success in doing so.

32. Samuel P. Huntington, "One Soul at a Time: Political Science and Political Reform," *American Political Science Review*, 82 (March 1988), p. 6.

33. Frederic S. Pearson, "The Educational Objectives of International Relations Texts," *Teaching Political Science*, 1 (April 1974), p. 169, notes how international relations seems 'unique' in the degree to which the line between a scholarly treatise and a textbook has been blurred, evidenced by A.F.K. Organski's *World Politics* and other works.

34. For example, see the latest editions of *American Government: Freedom and Power* and *American Government: Institutions and Policies*, written respectively by the American Political Science Association's current President and President-Elect. The former (New York: W.W. Norton, 1990) is written by Theodore J. Lowi (co-authored with Benjamin Ginsberg); the latter (Lexington MA: D.C. Heath, 1989) is written by James Q. Wilson.

35. I include myself among world politics textbook writers who have attempted to combine both a scholarly treatment, with hundreds of footnote citations, and a relatively lively style of presentation.

36. J. David Singer, *Chronicle of Higher Education*, 14 November 1990, p. A52.

37. Chadwick F. Alger, "The World Relations of Cities: Closing the Gap Between Social Science Paradigms and Everyday Human Experience," *International Studies Quarterly*, 34 (December 1990), pp. 493-518.

38. Karl W. Deutsch, *The Analysis of International Relations*, 3rd ed. (Englewood Cliffs NJ: Prentice-Hall, 1988), p. ix.

2

The Westphalian Paradigm: The More It Remains the Same, the More It Changes

Lynn H. Miller

The Intellectual Parameters of World Politics

In helping students to understand the intellectual parameters of world politics today, a teacher's theme may be the reverse of an old cliché: *plus c'est la même chose, plus ça change.* The same thing that endures is the nation-state; what keep changing in unprecedented ways are the nature of states themselves, the relationships among those who live within them, and the complex sets of interactions in which states are situated.

More than ever, our subject matter extends beyond the formal interactions between states to include nongovernmental interactions and, ultimately, all human exchange across nation-state lines. Teachers should focus upon the endemic problem of state reification and some effort to reveal the real — if not always the emotive — distinction between a state's government and the society it rules. They should require greater consideration of those actors (IGOs, NGOs, TNCs) that continue to compete with states for the authoritative allocation of human values.

Similarly, it is useful to stress that the very terminology of the field is out-of-date where it has not long been incorrect. "International" was always an inaccuracy for interstate or intergovernmental relations. This is not to say that international conflicts, in the strictest sense, have not recently rebounded (particularly where the Soviet Union once held sway) into the arena of world politics. But increasingly our subject includes all manner of intergroup activities that cross over state borders. Such activities frequently are influenced by the governments with which they coexist, and sometimes they are still commanded by them. Yet the actors in international politics today include governments, social groups, organizations, transnational authorities and nations in a more complex mix than we have had to contend with for several centuries.

Wherever the parameters of world politics are drawn today, reminders of how the planet has shrunk are astonishing to blasé (and ahistorical) undergraduates, especially when they are given frequent historical comparisons between the reach of their lives over geographic space to that of ordinary people in other times and places. When those comparisons can be related to the logic behind the structure of the state system, minds are stimulated to imagine comparable logical arrangements for world society in the decades just ahead. So, for example, if sovereignty emerged from the fact that, in one corner of Europe, monarchs grew sufficiently 'sovereign' over the people and territory they commanded several centuries ago to create the basis for a new theory of state interactions, then our continued collapsing of physical distance today through mass communications and instruments of mass destruction are producing ever more far-ranging and complex social interactions which continue to shape global politics in unprecedented and, in large respect, still unknown ways.

The Cold War and Its Aftermath in Historical Perspective

The end of the cold war reinforces the importance of understanding world politics in historical terms. If the term 'cold war' refers to an epoch characterized by the dominance of two mutually antagonistic superpowers in world politics, each with its approximately equivalent coterie (or empire) of compliant followers, and both camps locked in largely zero-sum perceptions of the other, then that epoch seems to have begun soon after World War II and ended before the start of the century's last decade.

Clearly, some of the characteristics of that cold war period may return — most obviously, if an authoritarian regime should succeed in imposing its control in the future in a way that the conspirators of August 1991 could not. Clearly, too, as long as U.S. and Russian nuclear arsenals remain large, even if substantially reduced from their pre-START levels, the possibilities for unprecedented destruction wait in the wings for a return to center stage. Still, what looks to be ended for the foreseeable future is the existence of a superpower where the Soviet Union recently stood. Russia has been reborn without most of the former empire, attempting democracy, facing dire economic adjustments, and in danger of fragmenting still further. Those changes alone make impossible the loose bipolarity (with its assumption of roughly equal poles) that was fundamental to the era just ended.

That brief conclusion is obviously subject to further analysis in the classroom today. At the moment, a number of relevant questions deserve exploration. They might include the following. (1) What are the implications for the structure of world politics in the democratizing revolutions that characterized events in eastern Europe in 1989? (And what are the implications if those revolutions cannot be sustained?) (2) What is the future of the former Soviet Union's foreign policy? (If, for example, the center cannot retain effective control of nuclear weapons, what are the likely consequences for a secure nuclear regime for the world?) (3) What does the collapse of central planning and consequent cold plunges into capitalism portend for the global political economy? (If the near starvation of millions is the immediate result, can a world-wide free market take root and thrive over the longer run?)

To understand possible trends and to make projections rigorous, structural-functional analysis can be helpful. What evolving functions — for governments, economic actors, and other 'mixed' groups of public and private agents — are producing what new structures in world politics? Which ongoing structures are constraining or adapting to new functions?

If our students are to consider the possibilities with both imagination and rigor, a search for historical parallels is essential. We should start with what may now seem obvious — that we are currently living in a period of rapid readjustment and realignment that marks the end of the cold war and the start of some new era, a transition comparable to that from about 1945 to 1949 that marked the era's birth. Then we can imagine a number of possibilities for the years just ahead.

The prospect of the *convergence of the superpowers* may still be one plausible way to imagine a dominant structural feature of the next period. This scenario probably assumes not only continuing reform in Russia and other formerly Soviet republics, but a society liberalizing with enough confidence, energy, and material success to carry with it, even if in loose association, most of its currently dissident republics. This assumes a continuing perception that political elites throughout the North increasingly are sharing similar values relevant to their political, social and economic goals.

The nearest historical parallels may derive from nineteenth century Europe where, after 1815, the great power concert managed peace-threatening events with considerable success for a century. Any effort to draw out comparisons to one possible future leads us, at a minimum, to consider (a) the conservative dynamic typically at work on actors that share a stake in global leadership; (b) the likely impact of a great power condominium on those it seeks to govern; (c) the probable extent of managerial agreement on the part of those who manage; and (d) the variety of ways in which those shut out of the concert can, whether intentionally or not, seize the agenda from their managers.

Obviously, too, comparisons point up differences as well as similarities. In this case, one might wonder whether today's more democratic ethos would permit a clubby elite to engage in the kind of overt carving up of the South in the way the Concert of Europe parcelled out Africa. One might note (though the Gulf War provides only an ambiguous example here) that today's instruments of warfare produce not only greater devastation, but correspondingly more far-reaching social and political upheaval than was once the case as, for example, when Disraeli's government made war against the Afghans or Tsar Alexander II conquered the khanates of central Asia in the 1870s.

But if the convergence of the superpowers implies co-equal capability for conflict management, that is far from certain. A second post-cold war scenario posits something like the *unipolar dominance* of the United States and the West in the face of political reaction and disintegration in what was the Soviet world. One conceivable historical parallel to the Soviet future might be the long decline of the Ottoman Empire. Perceived correctly as a threat to Europe until pushed back from the gates of Vienna in 1683, Ottoman Turkey was finally admitted into the Concert of Europe in 1856, presumably in recognition of its rights as a European power. Yet the latter action actually marked what by then had become the empire's real dependency on the European great powers.

To the extent comparisons are relevant, one might consider *inter alia* (a) how the Ottoman Empire's decline manifested itself internationally in its ever greater economic penetration from Europe; (b) the extent to which the national movements that gradually removed parts of the empire from Ottoman control were perceived as security threats to the European system; (c) how the leading European powers responded to the empire's problems, both diplomatically and militarily; (d) whether the empire's evident political decadence internally is a relevant key to assessing the former Soviet Union's current path.

Nor is the Ottoman case the only, or even the most obvious, parallel to the possible near future of what used to be the Soviet Union in the world. Both nearer in time, and a far more chilling example, is the failure of Weimar Germany to correct that country's manifold economic and social problems so as to forestall the rise of Nazism. Now that what is left of Soviet economic life has disintegrated frighteningly, the lessons posed to the world by Germany at the start of the 1930s seem particularly stark and compelling: if the cold war is to have a rebirth now, it presumably will come when right-wing nationalists are given another chance to corral the energies of what recently were the Soviet masses through a new round of coercion and terror.

These scenarios raise other kinds of questions and comparisons. For instance, what typically are the management and hegemonic interests of great powers? What conditions need to be sustained for the Soviet Union to share such interests more or less equally with the United States? If a genuine convergence continues, how and to what extent does it make collective security a realistic doctrine of world order? What would be required for greater divergence to support the balancing of power as a world order arrangement? What is the likelihood that, in the Soviet Union, reaction to the sudden decentralization of power following the failed coup of August, 1991, still could lead to a renewal of traditional Soviet geopolitical interests and a hard-line stance toward the West? The pedagogical *leitmotif* in exploring these and other issues should be, first, to find comparable historical examples, then determine what is unprecedented in our contemporary situation. This should help teachers to encourage students to come to reasoned judgments about possible arrangements of the evolving international system.

The Westphalian System in Historical Perspective

It has seldom occurred to our students, or to the public at large, that the nation-state system is an historical artifact, created some three-and-a-half centuries ago in western Europe to serve political actors there. Since then it has been extended across the globe as a formal system, thanks largely to the fact that it came into being at the time when Europe was beginning to dominate the world. It has also had the virtue of being readily adaptable as an organizing principle for a world where political interaction has continued to occur without strong central authority. The unthinking conclusion that such an arrangement is somehow ordained in nature tends to produce false consciousness about what is and is not a political construct.

For this reason alone it is critically important that students understand Westphalia's central premise, *i.e.*, that world politics are characterized by equal sovereigns who must engage in self-help for their survival in an anarchic system. My own preference is always to juxtapose this formal (or ideal) arrangement of equality against the real or material inequalities of states. The latter requires little explication, in my experience, since American undergraduates come to us typically with — as they suppose — tough-minded views about the way the world *really* is; it is the formal system that they often have scarcely noticed.

But the other reason for examining the nation-state system in the context of the social and political factors that gave rise to it is to demonstrate the ways in which its assumptions increasingly are challenged by the conditions of contemporary life. That challenge is, of course, only a part of the story; for, as the Westphalian logic is called into question, it also is reasserted. Neither nationalism nor statism is dead or dying even at a time when many of the social imperatives that grow out of the contemporary condition of humanity work against both.

But some trends are clearly in a direction that would transform the system. Among the phenomena that continue to work against, or at least cut across, Westphalian logic are the following: with regard to social interactions, growth in the kinds of political associations we list as NGOs and in the economic associations described as TNCs; where technology is concerned, an ability to leap across territory for purposes of our communication with or destruction of other societies; with respect to population growth, resulting pressures and developmental demands that both heighten the competition for scarce resources and render increasingly obsolete the view of the state as a semi-autonomous provider and of the planet as a limitless object of our exploitation.

Most of these have been familiar issues to students of world politics for a number of years, so that the analyses of Mitrany (1933, 1943), Herz (1959), even of Reinsch (1911) and Salter (1921) remain fresh today.[1] But as these factors intensify, they are having qualitatively new effects on our subject matter. International relations courses began to treat the impact of nuclear weapons in a serious way in the 1950s, TNCs in the 1960s, human rights in the 1970s, and environmental destruction in the 1980s. Singly and in combination, they point to increasing anachronisms within Westphalian assumptions.

Among the phenomena that reinforce the logic of the state system, many are principally in the realm of security concerns. These include, but are not limited to: first, continued or increased militarism and state terrorism, particularly in parts of the third world; second, restrictive and repressive responses by governments to the challenges of nongovernmental terrorism that is directed at the established order; third, the revival of collective security through the pre-eminent IGO of the past half-century, the United Nations. (The latter is the most ambiguous, in two respects; we cannot yet know the extent to which its revival is an important, durable phenomenon and, if it is, whether it will reinforce or — more logically — weaken state-based structures of conflict resolution.)

The resurgence of nationalism, particularly in what has been the Soviet empire, is also a strong reminder that Westphalia's effort to link national cohesion to sovereign statehood remains an extremely potent social force. The effort to make that linkage is once again the engine of some of the most volatile trends in the world today. Also included among the factors that reinforce the old order are the myriad ways in which state governments, and they alone, still are able to command us. Whether the issue is protectionism to stave off economic competition from abroad, or patriotism to arouse us to meet a common foe, governments continue as the pre-eminently authoritative and manipulative actors of world politics.

Once clarity in the classroom has been achieved as to which trends and factors are system-transforming and which tend toward system maintenance, students can be helped to evaluate the relative strength of these countervailing trends as they apply to various sectors of human experience and social development. So, for example, why has the approach of functionalism found more fertile ground in Europe than elsewhere in the world? How did the imperatives of post-industrial economics contributed to *glasnost* and *perestroika* in the Soviet Union? Why does the technique of central economic planning continue to find a place in nation-building? How are the geopolitical interests of the United States pursued through its military capability? The first two questions above relate to what may be system-transforming developments in the contemporary world, while the last two refer to trends that presumably help maintain the Westphalian system. Or so it may seem today. If definitive assessments are impossible — as of course is the case where so much is subject to projections — rigorous speculation is no oxymoron here, but a form of reasoned analysis.

The Westphalian System in Cultural Perspective

The Westphalian arrangement for some states of western Europe became universal in the twentieth century thanks to the global domination of the Western world in recent centuries. It is important to explore with students the extent to which the current era marks either the end of Western dominance of the world, or its greater victory. The collapse of the Iron Curtain in Europe in 1989 brought an orgy of self-congratulations in some quarters over the purported triumph of the West.[2] Granted, the orgy was soon interrupted by unseemly events in the Baltic republics, the Caucasus, and the Persian Gulf, which suggested strongly that history in something like its familiar guise was with us still. Nonetheless, a longer view continues to show evidence that the values of the West's high political culture are still spreading through the interactions of world politics, for example, in the activities of TNCs, the political rhetoric adopted in the arenas of IGOs, the continuing attraction of the West in eastern Europe and in important sectors within Soviet society, and much more.

It has always been a challenge in teaching world politics to American students to lead them out of their ethnocentric view of the political world. That was hard enough to do through the decades in which such students came to us knowing that their society was 'leader of the free world', the presumably benign member of a duumvirate of superpowers. It looks harder still after the collapse of the 'evil empire' and at a time when the principal free market societies of the West — still led by the United States — look more vigorous, prosperous and (*pace* Marx and Lenin) *progressive* by comparison than they have ever looked before. And if even some substantial fraction of Bush's new world order should seem to come to pass, then new levels of self-satisfaction and intolerance could well become the order of the day in America, including its college campuses. That would be unfortunate and dangerous, not least because such attitudes ill-prepare one to deal with unexpected challenges. Yet the unexpected is probably encouraged by just such postures of intolerance and complacency.

In any case, if the enlargement of the mind is one of the ends of education, then for our field, and in our time and place, that means encouraging our students to see the world as a whole, to put themselves in the position of their own contemporaries who happen to be living in very different situations elsewhere on the globe, to learn as much as possible of what other cultures can contribute to the Western overlay of what is still regarded as the high political culture of world society. Obviously, this is not easy, in particular for those of us who ourselves are products of that culture. We must work constantly to stretch our imaginations to conditions and influences beyond those that surround us if we are to help our students enlarge their minds, too.

We probably have neither the detailed knowledge nor, if we have it, the time in the classroom to inform our students so that they might imagine themselves in the place of, say, an Iraqi soldier fighting in the army of Saddam Hussein, a university student in Beijing today, or a worker on a coffee plantation in Kenya. We may be only slightly better equipped to suggest how non-western cultures and traditions can contribute to the progress of world society. But we should at least show our sensitivity to the following: (a) how hegemony stifles if it does not oppress the autonomy of those subject to it; (b) how decisions and actions originating from economic actors in the first world create dependence on those in the third; (c) how the materialism of the leading political actors is having an impact on the planet (and how the alternative value systems of others affect it); and (d) how both transnational integration and imperial disintegration in the world today can be informed by non-Westphalian and non-Western modes of organizing complex social units.

Nationalism: Transcended or Resurgent?

Nationalism represents the most evident issue arising out of any consideration of the cold war's legacy and, in larger terms, the Westphalian system in world history. It has been at or near the surface of much of the discussion of recent events above. The additional point to add here is that nationalism today has produced a variety of strains (in two senses of the word) that, in turn, may be traced to our long history of imperialism in world politics.

Looking at the North, we need to juxtapose the resurgent nationalism that helped end the Soviet Union against the progress of multinational community-building in western and central Europe. These seemingly dichotomous trends are connected in the current argument of some leaders in the Commonwealth of Independent States that their goal for a much looser federation of republics is similar to that for the European Community. As their argument goes, these long-subservient republics must first achieve a substantial measure of independence; then, their economic integration should follow the EC model. That very idea suggests a variety of questions. Must the Tatars and the Chechen-Ingush undergo their still-unachieved Westphalian revolutions before they can be expected to cooperate freely with neighboring republics? Can greater national autonomy be won at the same time a free trade area is maintained and improved within the Soviet Union as the voluntary action of sovereign republics? Will Russian domination simply replace that of the Soviets to maintain what is essentially an imperial unity over most of the region, or are qualitatively new relationships possible under more democratic government? Can a benign, cultural nationalism be achieved in today's world without a corresponding increase in the urge to trample on the rights of others that typically has made nationalism malign?

Or, for the South, one may examine contemporary nationalism in colonialism's continuing legacy, which has both laid the foundations for nation-building and impeded its progress in many parts of the non-European world. Much of the current conflict in South Africa can be understood in terms of the latter phenomenon, as can the rationale for Saddam Hussein's seizure of Kuwait, and the repeated failure of Kurdish nationalists to achieve their goals in the face of the opposition of established governments. The working out of this dialectic seems obviously related to issues of self-governance and political pluralism, and students need to explore these connections to come to a fuller sense of desirable, as well as possible, outcomes.

Changing Conceptions of Power and Security

While it probably has long been true that economic strength is one measure of influence in international politics, the economic might of Japan and Germany today has brought new salience to the notion of wealth as power. Meanwhile, the instruments of mass destruction that have largely defined the status of the superpowers for half a century are increasingly understood to have an ambiguous relationship to the state's real capability in world affairs, and to the security of those in the name of whom they are wielded. The permeability of the territorial state now extends to economic, as well as strictly military, instruments; the trading state now may be a better provider of security than is the military superpower.[3]

True, the Gulf War reminded us that the military superpower has not yet been relegated to history's dustbin. But it also showed how equivocal are the results even of a one-sided, high-tech, *Blitzkrieg* of a war today. The target of the U.S.-led operation, Saddam Hussein, remained firmly in power, and soon was slaughtering Kurds again. U.S. fire-power could neither prevent the devastation of Kuwait's environment nor improve the quality of its social and political life. Meanwhile, whatever the new-found importance of economic capability for non-superpowers, it did not translate into effective action against the aggressor. Japan and Germany refused to involve themselves militarily in the anti-Iraq coalition, and the EC was unable to muster a unified position in reacting to the crisis in the Gulf.

These developments are the obvious current tests of the hypothesis regarding the growing salience of economic power. There will be others over the next decade. Part of the instructor's obligation in the classroom is to help students achieve sufficient distance from the current waverings between military and economic applications of state influence in order to focus on the apparent long-term trends. And a grasp of the long-term trends obviously depends upon some understanding of all the factors that have been discussed throughout this paper.

Three Perspectives on Security

Three distinct levels of analysis have long been familiar to students of international politics, those of the individual, state, and global system. Assuming that security for human beings is the primordial purpose of world politics, the contemporary issues that emerge from each perspective are predominantly those of (a) individual rights, or more precisely, assuring access to enough of the world's goods to make individual empowerment possible; (b) group security, which here means allowing for defense of core values of some cohesive social unit that views itself as such (not necessarily the state as currently constituted), along with the preservation of an environment in which greater value realization is probable; and (c) preservation of the biosphere, permitting survival of the species with some prospect for its continued advance.

Each of the above perspectives amounts in a sense to a normatively oriented restatement of traditional assumptions about the nature of our subject matter. It is hard if not impossible to avoid value considerations in the teaching of international politics, even if one wanted to. I not only want, but regard it as vital, to try to help students clarify their own normative assumptions and goals through a full examination of the normative implications of the policies and outcomes of world politics. At the most general level, this amounts to providing the student with some of the tools with which to build a *Weltanschauung*. But that is probably the underlying force that drives all pedagogy. The fact is that the current period in world politics is characterized by more *chiaroscuro* in its illumination of the landscape than usual and, therefore, unusually dramatic alternatives as to what one may choose to see.

It is undeniably the case, as John Updike noted in 1991, that the immediate global result of "the melting of the cold war ... seems to be the release of fresh energies of strife and destruction...."[4] The dark vision of our condition sees the revival of nationalism, statism, geopolitics, and militarism as confirmation that the past endures. Evidence abounded in 1990-91, in the chain of events in the Middle East that produced a classic case of aggression and savage warfare there, in the tragic 'civil' conflict between Croats and Serbs, even in the near disarray of EC members over reaction to war in the Gulf, if not in the Community's inability to stop the fighting in Yugoslavia. The evidence was grim at each level of analysis: (a) innocent civilians in Baghdad and Vukovar went from suffering mere repression by governments they didn't want to brutalization and death by warfare that they also hadn't asked for; (b) those who wrestled with the question, 'security for whom?', found answers in violence that perhaps would maintain security at great cost for some communities while ruthlessly denying it to others; (c) the natural environment was abused with a more deliberate cynicism than ever before in the name of geopolitics (Kuwait), while a warped nationalism served as the excuse for destroying one of the treasures of humanity's cultural heritage (Dubrovnik).

The brighter outlook supposes that the above developments represent the understandable reactions to long-term trends that may be temporarily slowed, but are not (yet) demonstrably reversed. Here one may argue that, in the Soviet sphere, the failure of the right-wing coup in August, 1991, gives a push to the establishment of pluralistic security-communities as replacements for the repressive structures of forced amalgamation; that the EC's next major effort after 1992 will be to move toward a common foreign and security policy, including a capability to engage in effective regional peacekeeping; that among the lessons of the Gulf War are a new respect for enforcing the international law that bans aggression and an unprecedented willingness to make the peace and security system of the United Nations work effectively in the future. This outlook may imagine that (a) enough individuals under what used to be firm Soviet control have reached sufficient levels of development and awareness to know that peaceful conflict resolution serves them better than violence; (b) the outcome of the Gulf conflict may have helped initiate a peace process for the Middle East that could lead to a new order providing genuine respect and security to real communities; and (c) recent ecological catastrophes will instill at least enough reform to preclude worse ones yet to come.

One further note about the Gulf War contains hopeful implications for the near future from both state and system-level perspectives: there, for arguably the first time in history, did Security Council members try to flesh out the bare bones of the collective security concept in a way that would join something like a monopoly of power to a centralized authority possessing an organizational structure that might let force be wielded with proportionality, *i.e.*, as any police power worthy of the name requires. Without doubt, the U.S.-led action constituted a primitive application of collective security, largely because the institutional structure provided in the Charter had not been implemented throughout the cold war years. Yet, the very inadequacies of the experience as enforcement action also suggested that realistic measures for strengthening a global system of peaceful change can more plausibly be furthered at the end of the twentieth century than has ever been possible before.[5]

The change the world currently is undergoing is obvious, its outcome uncertain. Whether one's vision of where we are headed is essentially dark or bright, old structures and problems endure while new social forces evolve from the changing conditions of life on a planet that is truly a global village, if not by any means at the moment a happy or congenial one. *Plus c'est la même chose, plus ça change.*

Notes

1. David A Mitrany, *The Progress of International Government* (New Haven CT: Yale University Press, 1933) and *A Working Peace System* (Chicago IL: Quadrangle

Books, 1966, [1943]); John Herz, *International Politics in the Atomic Age* (New York: Columbia University Press, 1959); Paul S. Reinsch, *Public International Unions* (Boston MA: Ginn, 1911); J.A. Salter, *Allied Shipping Control* (Oxford: Clarendon Press, 1921).

2. The most triumphant example in the scholarly world was perhaps Francis Fukuyama's "The End of History?" *The National Interest*, (Summer 1989), pp. 3-18. Fukuyama proclaimed the "unabashed victory of economic and political liberalism" which allegedly had just occurred to constitute "the universalization of Western liberal democracy as the final form of human government."

3. The "permeability of the territorial state" was John H. Herz's description of the impact of nuclear weapons on world politics. See his *International Politics in the Atomic Age* (New York: Columbia University Press, 1959). For a provocative analysis of how some states have found greatness through trade, see Richard Rosecrance, *The Rise of the Trading State* (New York: Basic Books, 1985).

4. John Updike, "Innerlichkeit and Eigentumlichkeit," *The New York Review of Books*, XXXVIII, no 5 (7 March 1991), p. 10.

5. For one discussion of the problems with and implications for collective security as the result of the Gulf War, see Brian Urquhart, "Learning from the Gulf," *The New York Review of Books*, XXXVIII, no 5 (7 March 1991), pp. 34-37.

3

From the Flows of Power to the Power of Flows: Teaching World Politics in the Informationalizing World System

Timothy W. Luke

Teaching about the dynamics of world politics and the processes of international relations in the 1990s now must acknowledge how dramatically the structures of global political and economic power are changing. Unless and until teachers of international politics, who have been trained during the Cold War, move out into today's new post-Cold War global terrains, they will remain like those post-colonial African or Asian intellectuals that mechanically repeated meaningless colonialist lessons about old European kings and queens long ago and far away. Rather than facing up to the new politics and society of their own tumultuous post-colonial countries, they clung to familiar orthodoxies already irrelevant in their own time. Similarly, teachers of international relations today face an equally daunting array of fundamental changes, which, in turn, demand a basic reconstitution of their overall understandings of power, sovereignty, and security.

For nearly five decades, teaching about global political studies has been dedicated to interpreting the complex codes of containment at the various economic, military, political, social, and strategic fronts of the struggle between, as these confrontational rhetorics of power framed it, capitalism and communism, the West and the East, democracy and totalitarianism, the United States and the Soviet Union. From Yalta to Malta, the frozen tundra of bloc politics provided a peculiarly fixed pedagogical terrain, which the disciplinary readings of international politics could somewhat reliably survey, map, and then observe through their anti-communist, anti-totalitarian, anti-Soviet lenses. The complex national security apparatus of the United States gained full articulation from 1945-1947 as Washington recognized that America's vast economic resources, conventional military capabilities, and nuclear monopoly could be used to inscribe a new kind of transnational order upon Europe and Asia against the resistant designs of a much less capable, but equally expansionistic, Stalinist state socialism. To contain the USSR, and restrain German unification, the NATO alliance against the USSR and Warsaw Pact provided a fixed frame of international conflict and competition for over four decades. The Cold War, in large part, was an elaborate "strategy of global inscription that was both extensive and intensive in its disciplinary effects: the great scope of anti-communism as a discourse of danger was matched by its impact on the details of everyday life in the United States."[1]

During 1989-1991, however, tremendous changes, working from above and from below, upended the fields of reference and zones of difference that once anchored the disciplinary reach of such teachings to the strategic projects of Cold War-era containment. With the velvet and violent revolutions in Eastern Europe as well as the USSR, these frozen terrains of Cold War combat are melting into far more mushy expanses of confusion. The postwar division of Germany, which rested at the heart of these complex undertakings, ended in 1989-1990 as Berliners on both sides of the wall tore down this key physical and political barrier along the East-West frontier, and other Germans rapidly reunified the Democratic and Federal Republics under the guidelines of Bonn's liberal democratic constitution. Almost simultaneously, Czechoslovakia, Poland, Hungary, Romania, and Bulgaria also repudiated their involvement in Cold War bloc politics by overthrowing their ruling Communist parties in 1989-1990 and nullifying the Warsaw Pact in 1991. Finally, at the November 1990 Paris summit, Presidents Gorbachev and Bush along with other assembled chief executives of the major European states declared the Cold War, and hence its traditional containment- driven conflicts, to be dead and gone.

These changes are problematic inasmuch as the United States organized its national security, discursively and operationally for nearly fifty years, around four goals: 1) resisting a confident, expansionist, communist USSR anywhere, but especially in Germany and Western Europe, in the world; 2) keeping Germany from being unified without Washington's (and Moscow's) approval as well as with any Soviet ground forces on German soil; 3) promoting the eventual liberation of peoples and states under Soviet occupation in Central and Eastern Europe; and, 4) maintaining a nuclear deterrence structure capable of checking the USSR from initiating WWIII and/or expanding further outside of 1939 (or 1941) national borders. The strategic codes of containment policy did drive the West's resistance against the East in accord with the discursive demands of these basic goals, but now anti-communism, as a discourse of danger, largely has run out of gas. Some see this as 'the end of history'.[2] Actually, it merely appears to be the end of Cold War history.

Without these guiding principles of Cold War conflict, then, what happens to teaching about world politics in the United States as the world's political leaders now try to deal with the fragmenting Cold War blocs? This analysis attempts to address these issues in reconsidering some of the larger still unexplained tendencies exposed by the recent war over Kuwait. Cold War-style reasoning continues to dominate American strategic thought inasmuch as the premise of *containment*, directed against any threatening evil otherness now rather than simply communism, and *balance-of-power politics*, tied to the correlation of forces in particular regional competitions for primacy, underpins Washington's responses to foreign crises. Consequently, in the Kuwait conflict, one finds traces of new models of containment, new types of alliance, and new kinds of conflict to legitimate the disciplinary demands of contemporary national security as the US faces the post-Cold War era of the 1990s and beyond. Wars frequently compress social changes into brief intense bursts of rapid transformation as well as perhaps heightening the range of critical insights that might be made about the implications of these war-induced changes. Clearly, the Gulf War of 1991 is no exception to this rule.

From the Flow of Power to the Power of Flows

Beginning with the debates in the 1950s and 1960s about 'technological society' or 'postindustrial society', critical discourses of social analysis have remarked upon the many apparently new qualities of modern industrial society.[3] These transformations are still not completely understood, but they seem to be altering the basic composition of the nation-state and the essential arrangements of the contemporary world-system of nation-states, transnational corporate commerce, and supranational ideopolitical blocs. Often these transformations are discussed as aspects of postmodernism.[4] But one of the most pervasive influences driving these shifts in structure and substance appears to be the 'informationalization' of the social means of production, consumption, administration, and destruction as the global impact of mass telecommunications, electronic computerization, cybernetic automation, and rapid transportation began to be experienced on each one of the Earth continents during and after the 1950s and 1960s.[5]

What provisional observations can be made at this juncture about informationalization and its impact on the security, sovereignty, and stability of modern nation-states? The essential factors of power, time, and space appear to take much different forms in informational society than those once found in industrial social relations with their perspectival sense of location, hierarchy, and organization. The organizational logic of pre-informational society is anchored to *places* as power draws boundaries around space, erects monetary, military, and managerial borders around space, and exercises a monopolistic writ of sovereignty within these delimited expanses by exerting, guiding or directing its effects from point to point or place to place within space.[6] The stability, security, and sovereignty of state power, then, has most often been comprehended in essentially spatial terms through geopolitical discourses of the expansion, military defense or economic development.[7] Panoptic surveillance from the center and top of this space by state agencies works to normalize activities within it to suit the monetary, military, and managerial agendas of its state structures' leadership.

Security of place is ensured by guarding against intrusions from competing, and usually contiguous, state apparatuses that seek to penetrate or annex more space to enact their economic, political, and cultural/administrative agendas. Sovereignty follows from an almost mythic power of geographic authority, writing and drawing lines of identity and antagonism on the Earth. States, in turn, are those legitimate monopolies charged with inscribing, discursively and coercively, writs of difference — in money, religion, markets, ideology and militaries — from what occurs within and without the geopolitical spaces framed by international borders. Indeed, as Campbell claims, "the presence of sovereign states in an anarchic realm is a spatial conception that privileges a geopolitical reading of global politics."[8] By internalizing various disciplines of monopolistic order inside, and externalizing diverse practices of free-for-all anarchistic conflict outside, of those borders that define each nation-state's place on the planet's terrain, the fictive practices of political self-rule, or national sovereignty, define themselves spatially. Spatial terrains become etched in terms configured by landscapes as national religions, coinage, and armies set limits of their power, in terms of cloudscapes as air power renders airspace a significant concern, and, also, in terms of seascapes, as naval cannon made territorial waters more defensible. Defending borders, controlling airspace, and patrolling off-shore waters all are regarded legitimately as essential practices for drawing, defining, and then disciplining the various places of national territory that contain the social activities differentiating this nation-state from that nation-state in a conjunctive, centralizing hierarchical order. As Walker notes, "the principle of state sovereignty suggests a spatial demarcation between those places in which the attainment of universal principles might be possible and those in which they are not."[9]

What has been an essentially fictive construct of linear space in real time, nations, states, territories, or possessions are also the discursive fields inscribed by state authorship upon individuals and groups. Those subjected to the coercive gaze or normalizing hand of state power find that their attributes and behavior are continuously remanufactured. Informationalization, however, alters these power dynamics by generating new organizational logics nested in rapid and intense *flows* of ideas, goods, symbols, people, images and money on a global scale, which are disjunctive and fragmenting, anarchical and disordered. Of course, a 'transnational' flow of goods, capital, people, and ideas has existed for centuries; it certainly antedates even the rise of modern nation-states. However, this flow, at least until the late 1950s or early 1960s, tended to move more slowly, move less, and more narrowly than the rush of products, ideas, persons, and money that develops with jet transportation, electronic telecommunication, massive decolonization, and extensive computerization after 1960. Hence, it appears to be these greater intensities and densities, levels and velocities in the flow that have quantitatively transmuted it into something qualitatively new and different.

Today's global marketplace is very unlike the medieval spice trade, the Renaissance market in old manuscripts, or early modern intra-imperial trade in slaves, raw materials, and hard specie. Rather than acceding to a privileged geopolitical or geoeconomic reading of global power, therefore, global exchange generates many different grammars for a less well-understood chronopolitical or chronoeconomic reading of planetary political processes. Power today also flows placelessly beneath, behind, between, beyond boundaries set into space as one's sense of location becomes artificial defined by fluid, mobile, and shifting flows into the networks of information transporting these flows.[10] Geopolitical barriers are articulated as cartographic traces, memberships in military pacts, and diverse denominational codes in national monetary currencies.[11] Informational flows rarely are stymied for long by such barriers; indeed, cross-border transactional flows of money, influence, and knowledge are heavily eroding such notions of geopolitical borders, in favor, perhaps, of their own version of nongeographic barriers.

Tightly bounded ethnogeographic settings are augmented, if not often almost entirely supplanted, by new complex cultural activities on continuously flowing mediascapes of transnational scope and content. The flow is an ephemerally existing configuration of particular images, symbols, and meanings about power, money, and value — channelled through transnational corporations, scientific communities, banks, and telecommunication networks — in an endlessly elusive symbolic process that establishes its own terms of access, collaboration, and service through multiplex codes of sign and meaning. These informational codes create new spaces, new times, and new powers in the modes of communication.

Information communicates its effects not merely by conveying content like cargo; it also 'forms' by informing. To become informational is continually to be in-formed, in-forming, and in-formation as codings and decodings are formed-in, forming-in and formations-in communicative exchanges. With such interoperative dynamics, there is both a presence and an absence of borders, space, and process-in-time. Power, taken as coding capabilities and symbolic competence, determines access to these in-forming cyberspaces, delineates in-formed monetary, military, and managerial connections, and defines oligopolistic formations-in interoperation within these manifold streams by containing, modulating, amplifying or resisting their effects at various levels, rates or dimensions forming-in flows. Chronopolitics is grounded in the pace of exchange; how rapidly the flows can travel, expand, unfold without meeting resistant barriers or closed borders assumes unparalleled significance. Dominating the pace of process, setting the tempos of interaction, or managing the speed of exchange is the critical point of power in these informational systems of order. Here, barriers and borders are marked by user access or non-access, producer participation or non-participation, consumer linkage or non-linkage, or symbolic complementarity or non-complementarity.

This monumental transition from place to flow, spaces to streams, introduces nonperspectival, antihierarchical, and disorganizational elements into traditional spatial/industrial/national notions of sovereignty. Without conceptually making these events a simple leap from one abstract state of political economy to another newer timeless state of abstract political economy, pedagogy in world politics can begin to develop new distinctions in the classroom. The ethnogeographic settings of self-rule defined by the classical Westphalian universe of borders, shorelines, and airspaces in spatially-construed grids of or for sovereignty increasingly collide in the transnational multiverse of technoregions generated out of global monetary transactions, commodity exchanges, technical commerce, telecommunication links, and media markets. Having open and unconstrained access to the flows, not closed domination of places, becomes as crucial an attribute as sovereignty in informationalized societies. It is this that teachers should work to convey, and which students must come to understand. Likewise, stability spins through the codes by maintaining dynamic equilibria of access, linkage, turnover, connection, exchange, and service in accord with the diverse agendas of the various different encoders and decoders, while security slips alongside concerns over the integrity of codes, openness of access, extent of service, scope of linkage, and increase of turnover. Caught in the currents of these hyperreal forces moving across the mediascapes and cyberspaces of informationalization, the nation-state — with a more traditional geopolitical concerns for policing its territories, populations, and markets — often comes up short without total closure. When moving on these terrains, as Der Derian claims, one might supplement existing categories exclusively tied to geopolitics and the control of space by adopting alternative notions linked to chronopolitics and the control of pace.[12] Teachers of world politics must construct a new language and a new discourse of analysis appropriate to a world order characterized by flows, loops, and access rather than rigid mechanical closure.

The directions of such flows are intentionally guided, place-oriented, and socially sited at one, several or many places. Nonetheless, when considering the flow, "the *organizational logic is placeless*, being fundamentally dependent on the space of flows that characterizes information networks. But such flows are structured, not undetermined. They possess directionality, conferred both by the hierarchical logic of the organization as reflected in instructions given, and by the material characteristics of the information systems infrastructure."[13] Given these larger structural trends, the reality of place, expressed in terms of a sociocultural context of spatial location, gradually is being resituated within the hyperreality of flow, understood in terms of iconic/symbolic access to or process through networks of informational circulation. Hyperreal flows are not displacing nor destroying the now reconstituted realities of place. They coexist together. Indeed, flows serve as the basis for defining new core, semiperipheral, peripheral and external areas as the economic status and market niches of cities, regions and countries become redefined and thus restructured. Without adequate linkages to the electric currency of transactional flows, many once peripheral areas, particularly in Africa and Southeast Asia, seem to be slipping back into externalized zones of precapitalist existence, capturing only TV transmissions, food aid handouts or black market ties to the outside world. Actually, the shadow trade in drugs, political influence, illegal weapons, environmentally-banned contraband, or even human labor increasingly anchors many regions' tenuous cash nexus with global flows. Therefore, from these building contradictions within a dialectic of organizational centralization and informational decentralization "between places and flows" one might uncover in the workings of global change "the gradual transformation of the flows of power into the power of flows."[14] Such is the challenge before teachers of world politics.

The cycles of informationalization entail the creation of entirely new sociospatial logics that simultaneously generate the (s)pace of contemporary power, ideological, and exchange dynamics. This must thus become the new agenda for teaching. The flow is partly postspatial, partly postsovereign, and partly the beginnings of a new kind of international community. Reich contrasts the 'nominal nationality' held by many modern major corporations with their 'actual transnationality'.[15] Indeed, global parts sourcing, foreign markets, expatriate management, multinational labor recruiting, and world-wide financial operations increasingly typify corporate business operations. This observation also can be extended in teaching to many scientific communities, cultural networks, technological innovations, telecommunication links, and media markets. Nominal nationality, or geopolitical spatiality, increasingly competes with actual transnationality, or chronopolitical flowality, in the processes of many international events and trends. This tension between a decentering, despatializing, and dematerializing force as it works alongside and against the geopolitical codes of spatial sovereignty represents the primary context of teaching world politics if the study of world politics is to retain its relevance to a new world order.

Sovereignty in Cyberspace: Nation-ness as Hyperreal Estate

Flows are generating new transnational communities that are blurring the old Cold War geographics of 'them' and 'us', 'other' and 'I', or 'friend' and 'foe'. Currents can still be traced back to ethnogeographic settings or the spaces of nominal nationality, however. Their effects, taken together in the streams of the global flow, are being felt *postnationally*, or locally and globally (as 'glocal' phenomena), as actual transnationality. Many events since the 1960s have called attention changing categories of identity and belonging. The invasion of Kuwait by Iraq in 1990, provides several glimpses at the lingering logics of national security, particularly when seen closely juxtaposed to the ending of the Cold War in Eastern and Central Europe, and the incipient hold of a new aesthetics of world politics and systems.

Kuwait is a uniquely suggestive case for discussing the nature of nation-states in contemporary informational world-systems. In one sense, a good measure of its generative qualities can be linked to the Kuwaitis' feudalistic ruling family. Once the Emir and his extended family were bundled into their limousine motorcade, and rushed out of the country, the legitimate state authorities — along with their patrimonial state's essential records — were free to operate in exile. While much of Kuwait's oil wealth is tied to al-Sabah family accounts, there are also public funds established for the common good of those few hundred thousands of

Kuwaiti citizens once fortunate to be its nationals. This combination of great wealth, fixed incomes from oil resources, large remittances from foreign investments, a relatively small number of national constituents, a patrimonial ruling elite, and aristocratic state located on a tiny expanse of territory, provides evidence of how the geopolitical state and chronoeconomic flow interpenetrate.[16]

Because of its extensive oil revenues and limited abilities to absorb new investments after most 'native' Kuwaitis had been served by the welfare state, Kuwait began a diversified global investment strategy in the early 1970s in foreign real estate, industrial firms, service businesses, and cash reserves that amounted by 1990 to an estimated net worth of around $100 billion. One fund alone, the Fund for Future Generations gets about 10 percent of Kuwait's annual oil income and stood at over $40 billion when the war began.[17] Actually, even though Kuwait was the world's sixth largest oil producer, the emirate's financial earnings exceeded its oil income during the 1970s and 1980s. Having little territory, population, or industry to develop within the spaces of Kuwait, the Kuwait state acquired title to streams of wealth-production flowing abroad in larger, more populous and industrialized economies. These developments, at the same time, helped remake Kuwait into an unusual series of cyberspatial portfolios, electronically-variable capital masses, or hyperreal estates located within various streams of the transnational flow and grounded in a massive informational cross-section of commercial interoperations.

Although they are place-oriented, and initially place-generated, these financial assets, once part of the flow, also become postspatial, and even potentially postnational, as the Iraqi invasion of August 2, 1990 illustrated. Saddam Hussein, by invading and holding Kuwait's territories, also hoped to gain and keep its electronically accumulated wealth, but Kuwait's riches are, to a large extent, no more than its access codes to the flow. Saddam was foiled, on this front, as the al-Sabah family and its bureaucratic retainers retreated spatially into Saudi Arabia, while simultaneously barricading themselves and Kuwait's assets electronically inside the flow. Kuwait, as territorial real estate, was subjected to the pre-informational logics of sovereign control by its neighbor Iraq, whose conquering hordes had to content themselves with looting Kuwait City of its gold faucets, hospital equipment, Rolls Royces, 747s, and consumer electronics. Yet, even as Kuwait 'the place in space' was being annexed, or deterritorialized, Kuwait 'a stream in flow' simply changed its passwords, recoded its access protocols to open at other nodes, and respecified its service-delivery points.

Already highly postspatial, extraterritorial, and dematerialized in its pre-war activities, Kuwait as a complex of coded streams of stockholdings, bank accounts, oil business, service obligations, and ethnonational symbols only had to 'disk dump' everything to more secure nodes in flows of the computer and global media networks. Remaining free and at large in new corporate offices located in Washington, D.C. and the Sheraton Al-Hada Hotel in Taif, Saudi Arabia, Kuwait, the cyberspace, was able to keep up a minimum level of 'state services', paid for with its extensive assets, to its exiled populace in Saudi Arabia, North America, and Western Europe. It rearmed itself within the ranks of its international allied coalition and hired public relations consultants to articulate rage over Iraq's violation of its territories. During its exile, of course, the Kuwaiti state's fragility was totally exposed. As ministries were run out of double rooms with a bulletin board and a phone in the Taif Sheraton, the emirate could do very little but invalidate its old currency, try to plan for its return, and lobby on North American talk shows for its territorial liberation.

The essentially fictive nature of many contemporary nation-states, then, is fully revealed by the Kuwaiti and Iraqi experiences in the Gulf War. As a classically styled authoritarian state, using modernist myths of military conquest, supreme leadership, national mission, and chiliastic global change to create a sense of nationhood out of its various ethnic, religious, and linguistic minorities, Iraq demonstrated the bankruptcy of spatial expansion, place domination, and territorial imperialism in the informational flows of contemporary world-systems.[18] Kuwait, on the other hand, as a bizarrely postmodern fusion of premodern feudalism with informational capitalism, provides teachers with an example of a place-oriented stream within the global flow of money, ideas, goods, symbols, and power. As a point of production and consumption in the flow, then, Kuwait far outclassed Iraq in global significance, even though it has fewer people, less territory, and smaller military forces. Teachers can well draw upon the lessons of the Persian Gulf War, not to convey the traditional interpretations of balance of power and state security, but rather to portray the space, place and time warps of the new informational world order.

Petro-war as Retro-war

In many respects, political ideologies in contemporary informational society unfold "as an immense accumulation of spectacles" in the mythological discourses of the mass media.[19] Students, like all media consumers, devour these televisual spectacles like every other aesthetic commodity for sale in the media. As ideologies, various spectacular treatments of social relations can be continuously coded and recoded in streams of images, which constitute a peculiar political discourse about, but also within, the regime of transnational corporate society. One of the most fundamental and long-lasting scripts for these transnational discourses in the twentieth century is the mythology of World War II, a story repeated over and over again in the classrooms of the postwar containment system.[20] Whenever and wherever a small, weak nation is threatened by larger, stronger nation or a militaristic authoritarian dictator challenges a relatively peaceful neighboring society, the discursive work-ups of WWII can be flexibly deployed to interpret, explain, and legitimate elite and mass responses in readily accessible and virtually uncontestable rhetorical terms. This is true within the classroom as well as outside. For example, Prime Minister Thatcher's and President Bush's rapid reinterpretation of Saddam Hussein's invasion of Kuwait through these narrative tropes at their meeting in Aspen, Colorado during August, 1990, as well as the international coalition's repeated rehearsal of these themes in its war of reconquest, amply serve to underscore the irresistible power of this sort of 'good war' rhetoric, a rhetoric that framed the teaching of world politics through the 1990s.

WWII remains deeply entrenched, symbolically and rhetorically, as the Western world's vision of 'just war'. Drawing parallels in any present conflict to events, persons, or organizations in WWII can generate tremendous symbolic energies to direct against the opponent as well as to fuel domestic support. From the invasion's beginnings in August 1990, Saddam Hussein and Iraq provided a hermeneutic field day for American and global discourses to recharge these potent engines of WWII mythology. As the supreme leader of a secular one-party state, which rules in large part through terror and propaganda, Saddam Hussein immediately became Adolph Hitler. Baghdad, in turn, became Berlin, full of fascistic architecture, mindlessly loyal crowds, and imperialistic designs upon its neighbor's territories. Iraq, then, became today's expansionistic equivalent of Nazi Germany, and Kuwait assumed the role of the totalitarian empire's weak helpless victim, like Czechoslovakia, Poland, Norway, Denmark, Belgium, or the Netherlands. The Emir and his people, like the hordes of refugees of WWII, fled their homeland into exile to await the liberation of their homeland by their own Free Kuwaiti Forces and a new international coalition of anti-totalitarian nations.

To fight a 'good war', Bush rhetorically turned to one of WWII's greatest surviving international organizations: the UN. In October 1990, President Bush asked the United Nations to its assistance in his crusade against Saddam, because its resolute aid could help "bring about a new day. . . . A new world order and a long era of peace."[21] And, like WWII with its alliance of capitalism and socialism against fascism, he quickly enlisted the aid of the USSR. Seeing the changed terrain in Eastern Europe after 1989, he also signed up Poland and Czechoslovakia in the anti-Saddam coalition. When he visited Prague in November 1990, Bush announced the world had "a historic opportunity" in the Persian Gulf: "The opportunity to draw upon the great and growing strength of the commonwealth of freedom and forge for all nations a new world order far more stable and secure than any we all have known."[22] Everyone, even old Cold War enemies and quasi-feudal Islamic kingdoms, could join together with the West in this transnational commonwealth of freedom by mustering out to fight this 'good war'.

Yet, just as Bush sought to link his struggle to liberate Kuwait to the powerful WWII scripts, he also worked to differentiate it sharply from the narratives of Vietnam. As he maintained in early December 1990, "I know that there are fears of another Vietnam. . . . Let me assure you, should military action be required, this will not be another Vietnam. This will not be a protracted, drawn-out war," because in contrast to Vietnam all of the forces arrayed there "are different; the opposition is different; the resupply of Saddam's military would be very different; the countries united against him in the United Nations are different; the topography of Kuwait is different, and the motivation of our all-volunteer force is superb."[23] And, as a sympathetic reporter's sidebar essay affirmed, "a war against Iraq is winnable, and Vietnam never was," but, even more fortunately, "the United States will be going after victory with young troops free of doubts of the Vietnam era. An army trained to take on the Soviet superpower should be able to beat — and beat quickly — a Third World Force."[24] Bush sounded these themes again in his address to the Reserve Officers Association a week after the air war began: "This will not be another Vietnam. Never again will our armed forces be sent out to do a job with one hand tied behind their back. They will continue to have the support they need to get the job done — get it done quickly and with as little loss of life as possible."[25]

Having rhetorically caged the fears about 'another Vietnam', the WWII discourses kept the parallels between Nazi Germany and Baathist Iraq spinning on the screens of the global media markets, partly by rhetorical design and partly through bizarre coincidence. First, the American expeditionary forces introduced in early August, and augmented through the fall of 1990, faced an obvious enemy, 'a new Hitler', along a well-defined front with a plainly apparent objective — the recapture of Kuwait. The sharply drawn battlefront, at the same time, helped to create, again like WWII, a vital, supportive homefront in the US. In penance for Vietnam, and in continuation of the spectacular style of patriotism sparked in the Reagan era, many Americans threw themselves spiritually into the war — with yellow ribbons, letter writing campaigns to the troops or the sending of gift packages — as an opportunity to redeem the nation from its many perceived failures since

Vietnam. By finding a 'good war', to be fought, discursively and strategically, like the just war struggles of WWII, the 'bad war' of Vietnam, and its allegedly lingering syndromes of defeatism, doubt, and cynicism might be exorcised for real and for good.

Second, the war-time behavior of Saddam Hussein and the coalition also were constantly reconstituted in the still living imagery created by WWII mythologies. Like Hitler, the seemingly mad butcher of Baghdad cowered in his German-build *Fuehrerbunker* as he directed his almost *Waffen-SS*-like Republican Guards to fight to the last man. Whereas Hitler gassed millions of Jews in sealed death chambers and rocketed Allied cities with V-1s and V-2s, Saddam shot SCUDs against Israel. Now, once again, Jews sat in sealed rooms, but this time wearing gas masks against chemical warheads made possible by West German built factories in Iraq. Whereas the Nazis also blitzed the British empire as the RAF fought off Luftwaffe attacks on London, the Baathists in Baghdad sent IRBMs against Saudi Arabia, where the residents of Riyadh and Dharan toughed it out against rocket attacks as Western newsmen gave blow-by-blow accounts of Patriot anti-missile missiles rising against the SCUDs. Similarly, a multinational air force, including the emirate's own small, but frequently photographed, escadrille of A-4 Skyhawks waged in turn an intense 43 day long air war against Iraqi forces in Iraq and Kuwait, like the American and British air forces bombing Hitler's *Festung Europa*, which proved its potency to evening news viewers in gun-camera or LANTRIN-sight videos of killed MIGs and exploding buildings. Meanwhile, like the Free French forces or Yugoslav partisans, the Kuwaiti underground fought doggedly against rapacious brutal Iraqi occupiers intent upon raping, pillaging, and ruining Kuwait's people, economy, and society. Indeed, a mini-Holocaust of sorts also has been discovered after Kuwait's liberation in the Iraqi's execution, torture or abduction of thousands of Kuwaitis.

Third, the amazing 100 hour blitzkrieg of the coalition's ground forces resurrected buried emotions of global triumphalism first sparked by old newsreel film of Patton, Zhukov, Montgomery, smashing over the Rhine and Elbe into Hitler's heartland, capturing thousands of prisoners, and obliterating entire Nazi armies as fighting formations. In less time than it takes for many major TV mini-series to reach their dramatic climax, the Gulf War revitalized, refought, and reaffirmed all of the old WWII articles of faith about air-land blitzkrieg in the deserts of Araby. Even though the aircraft now were supersonic jets, the field rations freeze-dried, the rifles lightweight alloys and plastics, the helmets kevlar, the tanks turbine-driven, and the bombs smart, the coalition's script was one of triumphant WWII-style liberation as CNN 24 Hour Headline News replayed clips of quaking Iraqi prisoners begging for mercy before their coalition captors and ebullient Kuwaitis throwing kisses and flowers upon the victorious armored columns liberating Kuwait City.

This retro-war rhetoric blended contemporary images of triumph with a rebirth of WWII-historical importance for an America all to often left on the sidelines during recent years as Prague, Bonn, Moscow, Pretoria, Beijing, or Teheran made history instead of Washington. War under these conditions approached becoming its own enveloping virtual reality as American mass media audiences, including millions of university students, could sink into an almost seamless capsule of stimuli flashed from Washington, Riyadh, Dharan, Baghdad, Tel Aviv, London, and New York in real time as powerful currents of image, sound, voice, and icons. On watching the coalition forces winning such televisual victories in Kuwait, one American citizen argued, "it's taken the monkey off our back that's been there since Korea and Vietnam and Beirut and a few places in between," furthermore, while, "there's been talk of US losing our economic leadership, but this has reasserted our preeminence of a sort. VCRs may be made in Japan and Mercedes have their stamp of origin, but what's going on in the Middle East is undeniably made in the U.S.A. I think that's a source of pride we have not had since World War II."[26]

In his 1991 State of the Union address, President Bush cast the United States taking its "stand at a defining hour" doing "the hard work of freedom . . . facing down a threat to democracy and humanity."[27] The nature of the struggle, in turn, depends upon "a big idea: a new world order where diverse nations are drawn together in common cause to achieve the universal aspiration of mankinds — peace and security, freedom and the rule of law. Such is a world worthy of our struggle and worth of our children's future."[28] Just as it won the Cold War for all of humanity, and just as it led the United Nations to victory in WWII, the United States also must bear "a major share of leadership in this effort. Among the nations of the world, only the United States of America has had both the moral standing and the means to back it up. We are the only nation of this earth that could assemble the forces of peace. This is the burden of leadership."[29] In his discourse of America's new true cause, which is just, moral, and right, Bush elected America to continue doing "the hard work of freedom" by fulfilling "the long-held promise of a new world order where brutality will go unrewarded and aggression will meet collective resistance."[30] Teachers might well undertake to challenge the geopolitical lessons learned in the Persian Gulf War in light of the mere fundamental realities in which the 'victory' was embedded.

Most importantly, on the level of coding the symbolic power of global imagery flows, America has asked for, and perhaps even won, the freedom and authority to redefine itself and the world as part of the war. This, too, represents a major pedagogical issue. Kuwait is the new discursive stage for recasting American identity, purpose, and meaning. What do teachers and students want this to be and why? Like WWII, the Gulf War has brought to the US 'a victory'. And, also like WWII, it will be worked over constantly to produce particular symbolic purposes and political meanings from images of its conduct and outcomes, images especially relevant to teaching. With virtually no real military successes to underpin its political position since 1945, the US clearly needed something like the Kuwait campaign to relegitimate its own sense of its global mission. The tremendous buildup of Iraq's apparent military prowess by the Pentagon and mass media during the war only makes this triumph seem more meaningful; Iraq becomes more than a 'big' Grenada or Panama, it evolves into a small-scale, but quick and clean, WWII. From 1991 on, Saddam and Iraq can be cited, like Hitler and Nazi Germany before him, as the authoritative proof that collective action is necessary, that force effectively used in a just cause will succeed, and that aggression must not be tolerated in many other crises of containment in defense of the powers in the flow.

Such rhetorical treatments might be dismissed in the classroom as pure puffery. However, in the informationalized society, image is, or often becomes, reality. After nearly a decade of discourse about imperial overreach and inevitable decline in the US, victory in Kuwait, with only token material and grudging financial assistance from Germany and Japan, returned Washington to the master narrator's role in global discourses about dominance, authority or leadership. "For better or for worse," as one Japanese analyst concluded, "the Gulf war built a new world order, with America at its head," and, like the post-1945 arrangements of hegemony, "this will be fine as long as the rest of the world accepts its role as America's underlings."[31] Students should be asked to reflect on this state of affairs. Thus, the new discourses of post-gulf war global security also seem to be generating fresh confidence and new investments from the flow in 'American assets' in addition to shielding 'international energy supplies' from aggression. What consequences, what influences, what resolutions do students take from this? Even the most rigidly hard-line realists among our students must be made to realize that simplistic answers no longer grapple with the transnational flows that define the coming world order.

New World Order as World Order Now

At this time, we are caught between the growing antediluvianism of the existing Cold War scripts and the emerging uncertainties of the informationalizing world system. Students must understand both to comprehend the dynamics of this transition. Nonetheless, the shift from *place* to *flow* in the alliance behaviors of some nation-state interactions essentially requires the development of a pedagogical revolution. As most points of today's existing historical reference change, a new type of teaching relevant to phenomena such as the variable geometry coalition of Operation Desert Storm must replace, or at least augment, our existing understanding of the fixed geometry alliance of the Cold War era.[32] Despite Bush's inability to master 'the vision thing', it appears today that the very flexible semiurgic potentials of the WWII text are being mobilized to modify the basic philosophy of the EEC/NATO/OECD fixed geometry alliance in order to experiment with a variable geometry design in 'the international coalition' against Iraq. Still, these new variable geometries of alliance politics continue, using other means and following other goals, "a much broader postwar strategy of securing the spheres of social reproduction required for maintaining the American — and Western — way of life."[33] Such developments should become the focus of pedagogical concern as teachers introduce students to the complexities of the post-Cold War era.

The WWII script with its familiar strong leading role for the US at the head of 'the international community' can be rehearsed or continually challenged in the classroom of the future to understand how the White House can orchestrate its leadership in any one of many plausible variable geometry alliances of contemporary states against a fluid array of various offending threats. As the discursive work-ups of each moment describe them, these challenges have been ranging from Shi'ia Islam in Iran, Soviet expansion in Afghanistan, drug cartel bosses in the Andean nations, criminal strongmen in Panama to militaristic authoritarians in Iraq. But the essential teaching mission in the study of world politics is to enable students to understand that the project of containment will not necessarily disappear with the demise of the Cold War and the apparent end of the Soviet threat. Actually, containment can become more general, fluid, and comprehensive as 'the international community' becomes, in large part, the organizational ambit of the global flow, loosely anchored to American unipolarity, which needs to be defended continuously, according to the White House, at varying levels of intensity and with different amounts of formal organization against threats from 'the right, the left, and the outlaws'. To match the fluidity of the flow as well as the shifting nature of threats to its workings, it now appears that the US must contain a variety of perceived, and perhaps real, antagonists in undertaking 'the hard work of freedom'.

Teachers of world politics are presented with a rare historic opportunity to reveal how the US is transforming for good or for ill its classical discourses of anti-communism with their established codes of control, which have helped normalize the international behavior of individuals, groups, organizations, and states for decades. In addition, students must confront the events from which the US also has been producing a diverse set of new discourses about anti-terrorism, anti-radicalism, anti-Shi'iaism, anti-outlawism, and anti-narcosis to fabricate fresh series of variously flexible security agreements with their own variable geometries capable of matching all of these 'new threats'.[34] The international coalition against Iraq is only the most obvious and classically-styled of these new alliances, which are typically not like those of the Cold War and usually unlike those of WWII. But, to contain threats to the flow, the US is expanding its old fixed geometry security accords of the NATO/CENTO/SEATO era and moving toward infinitely variable geometries of collaborative containment of diverse threats, like those already made by Shi'ia radicals, Colonel Quaddafi, Columbian drug lords, PLO terrorists, the Shining Path guerrillas, Ayatollah Khomeini, Grenadean extremists, Colonel Noriega, or Saddam Hussein.

Thus, the new world order will be perhaps not one stable structure but rather a whole succession of different dynamic configurations in response to each of these different, transitory, and unrelated threats, particularly as regional conflicts are disconnected from the East-West struggle. Each adjustment in the variable geometries of alliance, therefore, will be *ad hoc*, or a transient world order *now*, to meet that particular challenge *then*. Students must confront these changes in a systematic analytical manner. Moreover, the world order of the *now* in 1991 against Saddam may not be related to the world order of the *now* against Columbian narco-warlords in 1988 or the world order of some future *now* to rescue Panama, Croatia, or Liberia from chaos. From one perspective, then, the US might be seen as a declining hegemonic power, struggling like Great Britain in the 1880s and 1890s to sustain its hegemony by enforcing a territorial security in its realm with expensive, new hi-tech weapons.[35] What Dreadnoughts and Maxim guns were for England under Victoria or Edward, Star Wars, AWACs, and Stealth are for America under Reagan, Bush or other future presidents. This reading, however, is perhaps too superficial. Like Great Britain, it is no longer the master metallurgic or key technicurgic power in the world, but this is much less critical as long as the US remains the dominant semiurgic power, creating codes of value, systems of symbols, and discourses of meaning for "the international community" contained by informational flow.

This 'informational capacity' is, to a large degree, the last reliable anchor of American hegemony in the 'new world order' of powerful flows between it and the industrial or agricultural capacity of its clients in various national places. The United States plays a significant role within the flow by discursively defining the ecological and economic form of the flow's international communities as well as the cultural and political basis of the flow's various regional enmities. It is these sources of symbolic authority, coupled with its massive consumer markets and potent nuclear capabilities, that now actually generate the tremendous unipolar powers of the United States today. Yet, even as the discourses defining 'us' and 'them', 'I' and 'other'," or 'foe' and 'friend' shift in response to these new mythologies, students must be reminded constantly of the power politics cloaked in these rhetorical artificalities. Bush's new narrative myths about 'the international community', 'a new world order', or 'the commonwealth of freedom', only serve to mask unequal exchange in the global flow and American space throughout the rhetorical realm of unipolarity.

From Geopolitical Realism to Chronopolitical Hyperrealism

Given all of these speculations, what can teachers of world politics learn from Kuwait? The Westphalian system of autonomous nation-states, organized around spatial logics of domination and development on the basis of geopolitical agendas, is not yet dead, although it does seem to be dying. Yet, a post-Westphalian system of global networks, transnational flows, and informational communities, tied into a fluid logic of influence and interaction set into the code of chronopolitical programs, is also not yet fully formed, even though it does appear to be rapidly developing. These distinctions, of course, are crude. The notions of geopolitics undoubtedly are themselves the products of increased technological velocities in the nineteenth century as steamship travel, telegraphy, telephony, and railroad-building immensely increased a nation-state's capabilities for inscribing its power on the globe by rapidly responding to each new opportunity to define and defend territorial space. Likewise, the frameworks of chronopolitics have their own geopolitical gloss inasmuch as extremely rapid telecommunications, jet travel and missile velocities, or computerized transactions project their own hyperreal spaces, which states must continuously manufacture and maintain as sources of authority, unity or prosperity. In some sense, then, geopolitics might be chronopolitics at nineteenth century paces, and chronopolitics could be geopolitics in twenty-first century spaces.

Where might these interlaced, but still contradictory tendencies end up? This analysis does not provide all of the answers to questions of ecological limits or challenges of economic growth in an informationalizing international political economy. However, it does provide a set of categories to interpret some of the emerging conflicts in this transition. Prior to the consolidation of modern nation-states during and after the Thirty Years War, sovereignty, security, and stability were also deeply conflicted as power was exercised legitimately by extra-statal institutions, like the church, feudal manors, and urban guilds. On one level, the international politics today against the backdrop of the flow might presage an 'info-medievalism' or 'cyber-feudalism' in which quasi-statal, non-statal, post-statal, or semi-statal forces engage in violent political struggles over land, resources, and population as the modern nation-state system collapses. Here, religious, ideological, economic, technological and even lifestyle identities and interests might appear to be warring over the control of markets, territory, and minds with low-intensity conflict and high-intensity persuasion. Yet, on another level, the politics of the flow also might preview a global order of 'hyper-realism', where many of the old signs and symbols of realist *realpolitik* are retained as a simulation of autonomous nation-states with their own territories, militaries, and currencies. In practice, however, the flow reduces their differences to basic equivalents, corrodes their borders as meaningful barriers, and eliminates older geopolitical divisions of 'them' and 'us', 'inside' and 'outside', 'foreign' and 'domestic'. While the shapes and sounds of inter-national relations as geopolitics remain as nominal nationality, the stuff and substance of actual transnationality may now dominate intra-glocal interoperations as chronopolitics.

For teachers of world politics today, it must be recognized how the rhetorical simulations of reality, like President Bush's New World Order as a spectacular resurrection of World War II's Grand Alliance, become can become 'real', but real only within the imagery known to be readily accessible and comprehensible to the flow's mass clienteles in the ever-flexible symbolic scripts. Recognizing the dynamics of this process can provide teachers with a project of constant demystification that should become one of their essential normative engagements in the teaching of international politics today. One 'nation-state', or the US (that now actually behaves like a truly transnational economic, military, technological, and financial empire of immense informational capacity) organized an international alliance of other 'nation-states' (mainly strong informationalized core economies or weak post-WWI and WWII neocolonial constructs in Eastern Europe and the Third World) to aid another 'nation-state', namely Kuwait, the cyberspatial amalgam of transnational oil dealing, televisualized Iraqi atrocities, and unstable hyperreal estate held by a few hundred thousand access-holding Arabs. And, where the symbols of nominal nationality means something, like the White House or the Sheraton Al-Hada, they can be played upon to revitalize national will or repossess national territories.

Yet, it is the actual transnationality of the flow, and the variable geometry alliances of diverse sets of nation-states within its streams, that allows nominal nationality to serve these purposes. The nominal nationality of America clearly is critical, as it remains the semiurgic core of this new unipolar New World Order, but the Latin Americanization of its society, the Beirutification of its major cities, and the Japanization of its economy in the interactive workings of the flow suggest that *Pax Americana* does not mean what it did in 1945-1946. Instead, fifty years later, as teachers of world politics must learn from Kuwait, the actual transnationality of America perhaps is becoming much more significant. The codes of containment and discourse of security, once pounded out in a metallurgic/technicurgic era of geopolitical realism, are being thoroughly recoded to boot into the semiurgic hegemony of informational power, responding to the political possibilities intrinsic to chronopolitical hyperrealism.

References

This chapter originally was presented at the annual meeting of the Midwest Political Science Association, April 18-20, 1991. Another version of it also appeared in *Alternatives*, 16 (1991), 315-344.

Notes

1. David Campbell, "Global Inscription: How Foreign Policy Constitutes the United States," *Alternatives*, XV (Summer 1990), p.280.
2. Francis Fukuyama, "The End of History?," *The National Interest*, 16 (Summer 1989), pp.3-18.
3. Peter Drucker, *The New Society: The Anatomy of the Industrial Order* (New York: Harper, 1950); Ralf Dahrendorf, *Class and Class Conflict in Industrial Society* (Stanford CA: Stanford University Press, 1959); Zbigniew Brzezinski, *Between Two Ages: America's Role in the Technetronic Era* (New York: Viking, 1970); Marshal McLuhan, *Understanding Media: The Extensions of Man* (New York: McGraw-Hill, 1964); Alain Touraine, *The Post-Industrial Society* (New York: Random House, 1971); and Daniel Bell, *The Coming of Post-Industrial Society: A Venture in Social Forecasting* (New York: Basic, 1973).
4. David Harvey, *The Condition of Postmodernity* (Oxford: Blackwell, 1989); Frederic Jameson, *Postmodernism, or, The Cultural Logic of Late Capitalism* (Durham NC: Duke University Press, 1991); and Jean Francois Lyotard, *The Post-Modern Condition* (Minneapolis: University of Minnesota Press, 1984).
5. Timothy W. Luke, *Screens of Power: Ideology, Domination and Resistance in Informational Society* (Urbana IL: University of Illinois Press, 1989), pp. 3-14.
6. Luke, *Screens of Power*, pp. 46-54.
7. Richard K. Ashley, "Untying the Sovereign State: A Double Reading of the Anarchy Problematique," *Millennium: Journal of International Studies*, 17 (1988) pp.

227-262; R.B.J. Walker, "Security, Sovereignty, and the Challenge of World Politics," *Alternatives*, XV (Winter 1990), pp. 3-27.

8. David Campbell, "Global Inscription: How Foreign Policy Constitutes the United States," *Alternatives*, XV (Summer 1990), p.279.

9. R.B.J. Walker, "Security, Sovereignty, and the Challenge of World Politics," *Alternatives*, XV (Winter 1990), p. 11.

10. Luke, *Screens of Power*, pp. 46-54.

11. Timothy W. Luke, "On Post-War: The Significance of Symbolic Action in War and Deterrence," *Alternatives*, XIV (July 1989), pp. 343-362.

12. James Der Derian, "The (S)pace of International Relations: Simulation, Surveillance, and Speed," *International Studies Quarterly*, 34 (September 1990), pp. 295-310.

13. Manuel Castells, *The Informational City: Information Technology, Economic Restructuring, and the Urban-Regional Process* (Oxford: Blackwell, 1989), pp. 170-171.

14. Castells, *The Informational City*, p. 171.

15. Robert B. Reich, *The Work of Nations: Preparing Ourselves for 21st-Century Capitalism* (New York: Knopf, 1991) p. 131.

16. See John Blair, *The Control of Oil* (New York: Random House, 1976); and Steven Schneider, *The Oil Price Revolution* (Baltimore MD: Johns Hopkins University Press, 1979).

17. Judith Miller and Laurie Mylroie, *Saddam Hussein and the Crisis in the Gulf* (New York: Times Books, 1990), p. 202.

18. See Adel Darwich and Gregory Alexander, *Unholy Alliance: The Secret History of Saddam's War* (New York: St. Martin's, 1991); and Judith Miller and Laurie Mylroie, *Saddam Hussein and the Crisis in the Gulf* (New York: Times Books, 1990).

19. Guy Debord, *Society of the Spectacle* (Detroit: Red and Black, 1967), p. 2.

20. Timothy W. Luke, "History as an Ideo-Political Commodity: The 1984 D-Day Spectacle," *New Political Science*, 13 (Winter 1984), pp. 49-68.

21. Fred Barnes, "Brave New Gimmick," *New Republic*, 204 (25 February 1991), p. 15.

22. Barnes, "Brave New Gimmick," p. 15.

23. *Newsweek*, 10 December 1990, pp. 24-25.

24. *Newsweek*, 10 December 1990, p. 30.

25. *Washington Post*, 24 January 1991, p. A24.

26. *New York Times*, 24 February 1991, pp. 4-3.

27. *Washington Post*, 30 January 1991, p. A14.

28. *Washington Post*, 30 January 1991, p. A14.

29. *Washington Post*, 30 January 1991, p. A14.

30. *Washington Post*, 30 January 1991, p. A14.

31. *Washington Post*, 13 March 1991, p. A26.

32. Simon Dalby, "American Security Discourse: The Persistence of Geopolitics," *Political Geography Quarterly*, 9 (April 1990), pp. 171-188; and Bradley S. Klein, "How the West Was One: Representational Politics of NATO," *International Studies Quarterly*, 34 (September 1990), pp. 311-325.

33. Bradley S. Klein, "Hegemony and Strategic Culture: American Power Projection and Alliance Defense Politics," *Review of International Studies*, 14 (1988), p. 141.

34. James Der Derian, "The Terrorist Discourse: Signs, States, and Systems of Global Political Violence," in Michael T. Klare and Daniel C. Thomas, eds., *World Security: Trends & Challenges at Century's End* (New York: St. Martin's, 1991); and Simon Dalby, "American Security Discourse: The Persistence of Geopolitics," *Political Geography Quarterly*, 9 (April 1990), pp. 171-188.

35. Paul Kennedy, *The Rise and Fall of the Great Powers: Economic Change and Military Conflict From 1500 to 2000* (New York: Vintage, 1987).

PART TWO

Reality Without Realism: Pedagogical Constructions with a Human Face

4

History and Culture in the Teaching of World Politics

Deborah J. Gerner and Philip A. Schrodt

Both the international political system and international politics as a field of study have changed dramatically in the past fifty years. Since the end of World War II, the number of states in the United Nations has increased by a factor of three, the volume of world trade has increased by a factor of forty, and the cost of a trans-Atlantic phone call has fallen by a factor of 100.[1] These alterations in the size, extent of interdependence, and ease of communication in the international system have had a profound impact on how that system affects our lives. Its continuing evolution is reflected in the titles of many introductory international relations textbooks that emphasize change and continuity. New topics, such as the environment or international political economy, have forced themselves onto the agenda while the traditional foci of international relations — war, peace, power, international law, diplomacy — continue to have tremendous importance for the survival of the human species. As a theory for interpreting global politics, realism is criticized from all directions, but no single alternative paradigm has arisen to take its place.[2]

In this context, how do educators attempt to create some coherence in the study of international relations? This essay addresses four components of the pedagogy of international politics: culture, history, theory, and method. We begin by discussing the role of international politics, and political science more generally, in the liberal arts curriculum, then examine the individual components of that instruction.

International Relations in the Liberal Arts Context

At the undergraduate level, political science is primarily concerned with developing a general set of skills and fostering overall intellectual development rather than teaching a specific set of facts and techniques to be used in later life.³ Most students of political science do not become political scientists, nor do they become actively engaged within subfields relevant to it except as citizens. Among the liberal arts skills that the study of political science facilitates are verbal and written analytical discourse and a range of research techniques relevant to the study of historical and contemporary social interactions. The international relations field is especially useful for examining competing cultural and historical points of view, as well as for conveying how the modern political, economic, and cultural system came into being.

The basic pedagogical problem in undergraduate political science is the typical student's limited experience with political behavior. Their first-hand awareness of politics — international or domestic — generally dates back no more than half a decade. Furthermore, they tend to have had little familiarity with important determinants of political behavior such as large-scale organizations (the college or university often providing the first such experience), the challenges of leadership, and the constraints of adult responsibilities such as sustenance and concern for children, partners, and parents. This lack of political experience is compounded by a widespread lack of knowledge of global history or even current international events. At the same time, students have experienced a wide range of basic human emotions and motivations and are firmly enmeshed in a set of cultural assumptions and biases. Most students have a fairly coherent personal political ideology, although one that often goes unarticulated. The personal opinions and life experience of students provide a basis on which teachers can build, but these opinions can also be a restricting factor if students do not quickly learn the limits of universalizing from their own experiences.

International relations introduces students to new concepts over time (history), across cultures (throughout the global system), and within a variety of theoretical and methodological perspectives. Furthermore, all these aspects of international relations need to be addressed in such a fashion that students learn to examine ideas and evidence in a disciplined way, while still feeling free to think creatively and critically develop normative positions. This ability to think broadly and with confidence is essential to the intellectual development of students. Yet, as Munir Fasheh points out in discussing his role as a professor in the West Bank, this is a threatening notion for some people as it has the potential to undermine existing structures of society:

> I realized that encouraging youngsters to think freely and critically and to question things honestly is very dangerous to any authority. For the first time, I faced . . . the fact that teaching is basically a political activity:

it helps "unveil reality," as Freire puts it, and creates new attitudes, values, and intellectual models that will help students understand and be critical about what is going on around them and confident that they can go beyond existing structures; or it produces students who are passive, rigid, timid, alienated, and lacking in self-esteem.[4]

To us the choice in favor of the first approach seems obvious.

Culture and Interdependence

In order to comprehend international politics, students must learn to think globally, to view themselves as actors on a larger stage than just their country, and to understand that the world may look very different from the perspective of a Kenyan than it does from the perspective of a Venezuelan or a Thai or a Swede.[5] There are two mistakes that students tend to make about other cultures and other societies: one is to assume that other cultures are completely alien to their own; the other is to assume that other cultures are all the same.

It is a common cliché that teenagers everywhere wear blue jeans and listen to rock-and-roll, that the Coca-colonization of the world is complete, and that — by inference — if you understand the United States you understand the world. This attitude is both inaccurate and arrogant, despite superficial evidence in its support. The medium is *not* the message, nor are the faddish tastes of a rebellious youth culture necessarily indicative of a fundamental homogenization of world culture. The success of U.S. popular culture has no more changed the cultural bases of other societies than the success of Bob Marley in the United States has made that country Rastafarian.

Essential differences remain in cultures: The lesson of *The Odyssey* — taught to virtually every educated person in Europe and North America — is rugged individualism. Ulysses returns home to triumph, although all of his companions perish. In contrast, the lesson of the great South Asian epic, *The Ramayana*, is one of the loyalty of a leader to his wife, his family and his followers. The messages are not the same, and *The Odyssey* and *The Ramayana* are likely to outlive the videos of Madonna and Michael Jackson.

Learning that there is a vast, fascinating diversity in other cultures is the first step in recognizing that one's ideas, values, practices, and worldview are not always universally shared. From this point it is possible to encourage a student to step back and examine how individuals in other societies look at one's own culture. With this broader awareness, one begins to recognize that attitudes toward global politics that emphasize dominance, power, and control are not necessarily useful for solving contemporary problems. Edward Said's comment during the 1991 Gulf War reflects the type of new thinking that is required:

> George Bush's idea that a new world order has to flow from an American baton is as unacceptable as the idea that Arabs can muster a big army led by a big tough hero and at least win a few wars. This is disastrous nonsense. Americans, Arabs, Europeans, Africans — everyone — need to reorient education so that central to common awareness is not a paranoid sense of who is on top or best but a map of this now tiny planet, its resources and environment nearly worn out, its inhabitants' demands for better lives nearly out of control. The competitive, coercive guidelines that have prevailed are simply no good any more. To argue and persuade rather than to boast, preach, and destroy, *that* is the change to be made.[6]

This did not sit easily with many of today's U.S. students even before the war against Iraq; now, with the echoes of victory and resulting U.S. boosterism, it is difficult to convey that not all the world's people were as enthusiastic about U.S. military actions as U.S. citizens might like to believe.

Juxtaposition of inconsistent U.S. policies is one means of drawing attention to differing points of view. The United States mobilized a half-million troops to expel Iraq from Kuwait, yet has tolerated, with only muted diplomatic protest, Turkey's occupation of much of Cyprus, Morocco's takeover of the Western Saraha, and Israel's occupation of Palestinian, Syrian, and Lebanese lands. In 1989, the United States invaded a sovereign state and killed hundreds of its residents in order to capture one man accused of drug dealing; yet when the Islamic Republic of Iran claimed the right to impose religious law beyond its borders, the U.S. systematically condemned Iran's position. In November 1991, the United States expressed displeasure with Britain's forced repatriation of Vietnamese refugees from Hong Kong while simultaneously intercepting and forcibly repatriating individuals fleeing Haiti's military government (a regime the U.S. condemned and against which the U.S. imposed an economic embargo).

Students are sometimes uncomfortable with this approach — contradictions in policy provide evidence that the emperor, however powerful, may not be fully clothed — but it does force them to *think*. In some cases, this approach also provides students the opportunity to contribute information, gained from travel or from friends from other countries, that runs against the common wisdom. For example, when discussing Panama, students who have travelled in Latin America may bring up that individuals from that region tend to view the U.S. invasion of Panama as the bullying action of a superpower rather than the glorious apprehension of a drug lord.

At the same time, this recognition of alternative points of view and profound cultural differences can be taken too far. The most insidious version is the argument often heard that culture X "places little value on human life." Not coincidentally, X tends to be whatever culture the United States happens to be attempting to subvert militarily at the time: Vietnam in the 1960s and 1970s, Nicaragua in the 1980s, or Iraq in 1991. A white South African once attempted to explain to us that the intrinsic immorality of the Zulu culture could be seen by how their warriors were forced to attack, even in the face of bullets, and any who resisted such orders were executed. When asked how this was any different than the Europeans at Verdun, where a half-million good civilized Christian youths were killed in six months for no discernible political or military end, the woman quickly changed the topic.

Students grow up in an environment filled with these types of myths and stereotypes. In all likelihood they have rarely considered alternative interpretations to the ones they have been taught since childhood. Not surprisingly, when students are introduced to other versions of reality and different facts, they often resist. This tendency is reinforced by the large and influential segment of the academic population who, ethnocentrically, still consider it more important that U.S. students know the names and mode of demise of each of the wives of Henry VIII than anything about the political career of his Japanese counterpart, Ieyasu Tokugawa.

One approach that we have taken to present a multicultural context is to show ways in which the United States — the reference point for most of our students — is culturally and economically interlinked with other states and cultures. For example, the version of history taught in most United States high schools presents virtually all important scientific discoveries as occurring in the United States, or before the United States, in Europe (usually England or Germany). It is helpful to point out that three critical innovations marking the transition between the medieval and modern periods in Europe came from outside that region:

- Widespread literacy and improved communications were a direct result of the invention of moveable type — making possible the mass production and standardization of documents — and paper, making documents affordable. The first was introduced to Europe from China, the second from China via the Arabs.

- The revolution in warfare between 1450 and 1650 that culminated in the 'New Model Armies', making possible the centralized

Westphalian nation-state, began with the introduction of gunpowder into European warfare, another innovation from China.[7]

- European financial accounting was unable to handle elaborate transactions until an Italian who had grown up in North Africa introduced Arab and Indian accounting and calculation methods to southern Europe in the 1300s, paving the way for the establishment of a modern banking system.[8]

This cultural interplay extends to the present: for example, the 'stealth' technology that enabled the United States to design aircraft dramatically less visible to radar ironically derives from key theoretical work contributed by a Soviet physicist.[9] United States automakers responded to a decline in their competitiveness in the 1970s by experimenting with both northern European and Japanese production techniques before finally adopting, almost completely, the latter model.

In addition, our classes explore aspects of the international system that do not involve the United States at all, or only in a peripheral role, such as the Omani trading empire in East Africa in the 18th and 19th centuries, or the challenges that democratization placed on the conservative European international system during the 19th century. More generally, we try to convey a sense of the interrelationship among various global issues such as population growth, economic development, human rights, health, environmental problems, political evolution, human migration, domestic strikes, and interstate violence. This leads directly to a discussion of the role of the nation-state in promoting or preventing peace, justice, and security; and the ways contemporary global challenges reinforce, undercut, or transcend that form of political organization. It also provides a framework for examining issues of gender, race, and class that are typically ignored in international relations courses but that take on greater relevance once one moves away from a strictly state-centric view of the global system.

Stability, Change, and Prediction

History is an empirical guide to what is possible in international politics. Ours is not a solely deductive science and a solid grounding in history will in part vicariously compensate for a student's lack of experiential political knowledge. But this use of history is tricky. While history tells us what has been, it does not, and cannot, fully tell us what will occur in the future. We cannot assume that because there always have been wars, there always will be wars, or that because an approach to managing global affairs did not work in the past it will never succeed in the future. A European social theorist in the eighteenth century would have been on firm historical grounds in assuming that dueling and slavery were inevitable social institutions. Yet by the end of the nineteenth century both had been abolished.

To help students make sense of this situation, one must provide a generous dose of history, not necessarily for its own sake, but to set the context for understanding the present and the future. The 'momentum' of history is not some vague metaphysical concept, but is firmly linked to the cognitive processes of national leaders. Rulers of Third World countries in Africa and Asia do not need to read about colonialism, for example, they *lived* colonialism. In analyzing contemporary international politics, one needs to know how the existing structural arrangements, particularly those of the post-WWII period, were established to have any sort of chance of ascertaining how they will develop in the future. Teachers should also seek to provide students with intellectual tools that will be relevant fifty years into the future. Thus, the brief exposure to politics of most students must be expanded twenty-fold to encompass a century.

When teaching international relations in the United States, the instructor is often confounded by the existence of an international political leadership whose vision and political world was shaped by the early days of the Cold War: individuals such as George Bush, Mikhail Gorbachev, Yasir Arafat, Deng Xiaoping, Fidel Castro, and Kenneth Kaunda. Whether conservative or revolutionary, the outlook of these leaders cannot help but be influenced by the historical period during which they grew to political maturity. That 50-year-old vision is passed on to the current generation, and leads to a certain amount of cognitive dissonance in the face of recent events.

In a recent survey of the role that the 1950s and 1960s play in the United States' perception of itself, *The Economist* noted:

> [The civil rights campaign of the 1950s and 1960s] was the finest accomplishment of an America that was heroic in all sorts of ways — even to the extent of having an unambiguous antihero, headquartered in Moscow, for an enemy. Men and women now aged 40 to 60 — in other words, most of those who run America's politics and its business — were either children or newly married during the post-war years. It is not surprising that they are nostalgic about them. . . . In the 20 years after the war, according to conventional wisdom, America's political elite was able to demonstrate something called "leadership". Post-war America never met a problem it could not solve.[10]

This political self-confidence was combined with economic isolation. Prior to WWI, the United States had received millions of immigrants from Europe and Asia, and in the early 1920s imports and exports accounted for over 15% of GNP. But by the 1950s:

> There is no evidence that the Cleaver family of "Leave it to Beaver" had a Japanese car; or, for that matter, anything Korean, German, British or French in their house. In no year of the 1950s did imports of goods account for more than 1959's 3.2% of America's GNP. In 1954 the figure was as low as 2.8%. Moreover, in no year did exports of goods account for more than 1957's 4.7% of America's GNP, and in 1959 the figure was just 3.6%. Nor is there any reason to think that any of the Cleaver's neighbours could not speak English. America in the post-war years really was a self-contained economy that could provide its unquestionably American people with virtually everything they wanted.[11]

U.S. students today face a somewhat schizophrenic situation where the expectations expressed by the media and the political leadership are still those of the 1940s and 1950s, but students know a different reality. Their parents experienced the U.S. military involvement in Vietnam, the devaluation of the dollar, the OPEC energy price increases, and the inflation and economic uncertainties of the 1970s. Ironically, however, the 1970s are often portrayed as anomalous, and political leaders promise to restore the United States to its earlier glory. Against that backdrop, educating students that the world is a little more complicated and that we are no longer in the world of 1950s situation comedies is problematic.

The world is subject to rapid change. In April 1989, German reunification was widely assumed to be a problem to be resolved in the next century; by October 1990, the flag of a reunited Germany was raised in Berlin. In addition, Communist governments throughout Eastern Europe had been replaced by democratically elected regimes with a range of political and economic policy approaches. In the spring of 1990, discussions of U.S. defense policy focused on the 'peace dividend'. Six months later, a half-million U.S. troops had been deployed in the Persian Gulf to defend a small, conservative monarchy, and talk of a lower-profile military had disappeared, only to arise again in the 1992 presidential campaign.

Prediction

While it is important for students to understand the past and the present, they will spend most of their adult lives in what is, at this moment, the future. We must deal not only with what is and was, but with what will be. As anyone who worked with the media during the Iraq War can testify, predicting the future is one of the tasks political scientists are called upon to do. Historians are questioned on what happened in the past and journalists attempt to tell us what is happening in the present; it is political scientists who are asked what will happen next.

A key role for history in political science, and for the liberal arts in general, is to provide lessons or patterns. History does not, strictly speaking, repeat itself, but it provides ample examples of how political activity can go right or go wrong. Gilpin has stated that "Thucydides is as meaningful a guide to the behavior of states today as when it was written in the fifth century B.C."[12] Recent works such as Neustadt and Mays' *Thinking in Time: The Uses of History for Decision Makers* and the penultimate chapter on decision-makers as "practical-intuitive historians" in Vertzberger's *The World in their Minds* provide systematic discussions of how history can and should influence both the planning and the interpretation of current events.[13]

In teaching, we often convey the importance of history implicitly through the use of examples. The best way to convey a concept is to tell a story to show that a seemingly abstract case occurred at least once in the real world. In some instances, the historical example becomes the concept: 'Munich', 'Pearl Harbor', and 'Vietnam' are synonymous in US foreign policy debates with the hazards of appeasement, lack of military preparedness, and the risks of involvement in wars in the Third World, respectively.

As important as knowing how to predict is knowing when not to predict: knowing when you do not have sufficient information to make an intelligent judgment. The media do not like this reticence. The more popular political commentators on television tend to be those who never fail to make predictions. This is probably also part of the reason such commentators are so frequently wrong, which in turn leads to the impression that political scientists have no more idea of what will occur in politics than does the person on the street.

In fact, given the difficulty of the task — the number of unknowables — political scientists often do a surprisingly good job. For example, the speed and effectiveness of the technical military victory in the 1991 Gulf War came as a surprise: most political scientists failed to anticipate it, but then so did the U.S. military, the U.S. intelligence communities, and virtually everyone else. Political scientists did considerably better in predicting the problems in the aftermath of the conflict: the Kurdish uprising and its brutal suppression, the inability of the Kuwaiti government to reestablish its political legitimacy and its unwillingness to extend suffrage beyond males whose families had been in Kuwait before 1920, and the durability of Saddam Hussein.

The average political science student is unlikely to show up as a commentator on the evening news. However, as consumers of political knowledge, students need to be able to make some predictions in their own right in order to ascertain the likely effects of policies. They should also be able to evaluate the legitimacy of the predictions of others and to distinguish reasoned judgment from mere wishful or pessimistic thinking. In particular, they should be able to differentiate between a careful assessment that takes into account the idiosyncratic circumstances surrounding a political situation and an analysis that is largely ideological (in the sense of looking only at the most basic aspects and then filling in the remaining information based on prior assumptions unrelated to the circumstances at hand). For United States students, decisions involving Vietnam present a textbook case of the latter situation. Once it was known that Diem was 'our guy' and Ho was 'their guy', most of the remaining details were filled in ideologically: Ho's a communist, Mao's a communist, communists help other communists, therefore the Vietnamese and Chinese are natural allies against us. This approach ignores both a thousand years of Chinese and Vietnamese history and basic percepts of international relations theory.

One of the best ways to learn about the strengths and weaknesses of the predictions of others is to make predictions oneself. An exercise one of us undertook in an international conflict class during the fall of 1990 was to have students make an explicit prediction about the state of the Iraq crisis as of the final day of class in mid-December. This was done at the end of September after students had read Blainey's *The Causes of War* which discusses a number of ways that wars start.[14] Interestingly, the vast majority of the students (and the instructor) got the prediction wrong, expecting the outbreak of armed hostilities in late October or early November. However, three or four students predicted the situation almost exactly, including the use of the United Nations, the continued allied buildup, and the coalition-building activities of the Bush administration. Even more striking was that the correct predictions did not emerge in class discussion. That discussion quickly zeroed in on a 'groupthink' consensus predicting early military actions.

This type of exercise might be used more broadly by international relations instructors. It forces students to confront the fact that (a) their assumptions about the future may be wrong; (b) international politics is not necessarily dramatic but instead may be quite mundane; and (c) the common wisdom is not necessarily very wise.

Theories

The role of theory in political science is one of the more difficult aspects of the discipline to communicate to students. In the United States, part of this problem is self-inflicted by the separate development of political theory as a distinct subdiscipline.[15] In a course that is not explicitly theoretical, such as 'Introduction to International Relations', students will often impatiently implore: "we don't want to hear about theory; we want to learn about the real world." One must therefore communicate that what is understood as 'real' depends, in large part, on theory.

Just as geometry begins with certain assumptions — axioms — and makes deductions based on axiomatic principles, theories in political science are grounded in differing assessments of human nature, the inevitability of war, the legitimacy of the distribution of wealth that is generated by a capitalist, market-based system, and the immutability of the modern nation-state system. Unlike geometry, however, there is no consensus on these fundamental building blocks; nor, in many cases, can alternative starting points be proven to be true or false. Instead, our judgements are — or ought to be — made on the basis of a combination of scholarly research and our basic belief systems.

An international relations course should survey the existing theories about how the system works from both a pragmatic and intellectual standpoint. As political scientists, we are obviously concerned about conveying our current understanding of contemporary policies and practices, the alternatives to those policies, the motivations behind them, and the connections between intentions and outcomes. As suggested earlier, students also need to become aware of the role of theory in perceptions of reality. Theories are the way we organize a world that is complex, in the sense that it always contains more information than we can analyze. Theories serve as a filter that sorts out from the incomprehensively large number of daily political activities of six-billion people in 150 nation-states the tiny set of events that we regard as deserving of attention. Theories tell us what variables are important. There is an old saying in geology that is equally true for the study of political behavior: "if I hadn't believed it, I wouldn't have seen it."

One way to illustrate this point is to present a simplified version of how different theories would interpret U.S. involvement in Vietnam. An idealist or legalist would look at U.S. treaty obligations under SEATO and the Geneva accords. A realist would examine U.S. national interest and perhaps, finding that none were at stake, would oppose the involvement, as Hans Morgenthau concluded. A Marxist would focus on U.S. economic interests such as trade and colonial linkages in Southeast Asia, control of the agricultural resources of the Mekong delta, or the possibility of offshore oil. A bureaucratic politics theorist would investigate U.S. decision-making, much as the Gelb and Betts or Berman studies have done.[16] Each approach highlights different aspects of the involvement. On some aspects they reach contradictory conclusions, while on others they agree.

There is currently a severe case of 'paradigm proliferation' in international relations. Students need to have some exposure to these approaches, particularly in courses designed for political science majors, if they are to understand much of the contemporary literature and debates. The old realism-idealism division — in its simplest form a debate as to whether international stability is best insured by anarchic self-help or an international legal order — is still relevant, but in addition it must be supplemented by other classes of theories that define additional research dimensions.

One such new dimension is demarcated by the neorealist theories versus economic theories. For the neorealists, political structures determine or help shape economic interactions; for economic theorists, the fundamental aspects of international behavior are molded by economic forces and political activity occurs within these boundaries.[17] Economic approaches include interdependence theories, neo-Marxian structuralism, dependency theory, and much of the long-cycle and world-systems literature.

The other new dimension is defined by decision-making approaches versus the aggregate formal theories of the mathematical modelling and statistical literature.[18] The decision-making approaches assume that international behavior is best explained atomistically as the consequence of the behavior of sub-national units such as individuals and bureaucracies rather than at any global level, and incorporate cognitive theories, bureaucratic approaches, and the rational choice literature.[19] The aggregate formal models include systems theorists, the statistical behavioralists, and the two branches of dynamic modelling: the Richardson arms race model tradition and the 'global models' approach.[20] This dimension also reflects some of the older arguments about the levels of analysis problem with comparative foreign policy occupying the middle ground.

Much of the material we teach is controversial, for that is the nature of politics. Instructors face a choice: to attempt to present information in a completely neutral, value-free context or to confront head-on the role that values and theories play in framing the issues that are considered important, the questions that are asked about these issues, and the answers that are identified as either plausible or implausible. For those trained in a behavioralist tradition, the first approach is often more comfortable. Its main advantage is that it avoids the problem of students feeling they must reach the same value judgments as the faculty person since students don't actually know what their instructor thinks. This approach also conveys a critical point: personal values should not be allowed to distort research findings. An individual commitment to nonviolence should not blind us to historical cases when nonviolent action proved unsuccessful, for example; nor should a belief in the necessity of the use of military force prevent us from recognizing instances when other, nonmilitary, alternatives might bring about a desired outcome.

This approach, however, has a major liability. While protecting the instructor from a potentially uncomfortable vulnerability and intimacy in having his or her views known, it also allows students and instructors to disregard the clear value-laden nature of the study of international relations. It promotes a *status quo* orientation without serious consideration of other alternatives and it ignores the role of theories and paradigms as legitimating techniques for particular ideologies. Furthermore, instructors *do* have opinions and to refuse to provide this information to students is to deprive them of the years of research and experience that we bring to our subject, just as surely as if a geologist, after giving the evidence for two competing theories on the extinction of the dinosaurs, refused to indicate the one he or she found more compelling.

At the same time, it is essential to encourage students to make up their own minds based on legitimate scholarly evidence, rather than pushing them through eloquence or subtle pressures to conform, into a mold that fits our values. Students must be taught to be intellectually independent, to come to their own carefully reasoned conclusions based upon evidence provided from a variety of sources, rather than being spoon-fed an ideology.

Is it possible to give opinions while encouraging independent thought? If the instructor is prepared to be honest with his or her students and is willing to facilitate consideration of epistemological and normative questions, in addition to presenting 'factual' material, the answer is clearly yes. One pedagogical method in this regard is to summarize as fairly as possible various theories and interpretations with respect to, for example, the causes of war, and then indicate to students how various conclusions based upon different approaches were reached.

This provides students with an ability to make their own decisions while illustrating ways of logically assessing and interpreting information. An additional benefit of this teaching method is that it communicates several important messages. First, it says that the field of political science is complex and multifaceted and that, although there are certainly historical facts that need to be learned, interpretations of these facts will vary. In addition, it illustrates that scholarship is an ongoing process of evidence-gathering, assessment, and evaluation, rather than the transmission of a fixed canon of knowledge.

Finally, it is essential to indicate that ethical issues play a role in international relations theory itself. For some topics — such as parts of international law or most structuralist theories of international political economy — a normative component is explicitly part of the material. In other areas, particularly the study of international conflict and foreign policy, it is often hidden or implicit. For example, students tend to equate realism with an amoral, 'might makes right' approach. They assume that realism's contention that different ethical standards apply to individual and international affairs means that *no* ethical standards apply in international affairs. They also conclude that since realism is the dominant paradigm — at least in the United States — it must truly represent 'reality'. In looking at international conflict, then, the 'war is hell and you gotta do what you gotta do' approach of John Wayne and Rambo movies is usually as close as students have come to an ethical model of war.

For a number of years, we have included a section on classical 'just war' theory in our introductory international relations courses, despite the fact that this topic is rarely covered in depth in the standard textbooks. This starts with a survey of early Jewish, Christian, and Graeco-Roman approaches, as well as Islamic, Buddhist, Confucian, and Hindu views of war and peace. We then look at the merger of the Judeo-Christian and Graeco-Roman approaches with Augustine and Aquinas, and the resulting last resort/just cause/just means/just authority/proportionality framework. The transition of the religious to legalist framework in the 17th century is covered next. The section ends with a few contemporary issues such as personal responsibility (Nurenberg, My Lai) and the strategic bombing of civilian targets (Dresden, Hiroshima, Vietnam, and Afghanistan).[21]

Teaching just war theory in an introductory international relations class has proven to have three advantages. First, it helps to illustrate how some issues respond to changes in time, technology, and culture. The basic premises of European just war theory have changed little since Augustine, almost 1 500 years ago, providing an example of extraordinary continuity. New issues generated by technological changes such as submarines and nuclear weapons continually impose themselves on just war theory, however, leading to modifications in historical circumstances.

The Islamic concept of *jihad* is also useful for illustrating cultural changes however, in its original form, *jihad* was remarkably similar in function to just war doctrines of pre-Reformation Europe; but in the 19th and 20th centuries it acquired a strong anti-colonial focus. Finally, just war theory is alive and well in the present day: the nuclear freeze movement in the early 1980s resulted in just war statements by several Christian denominations. More recently, George Bush attempted to justify the U.S. intervention in Kuwait with explicit, if flawed, reference to classical theories.

In our experience, students enjoy reading and discussing materials on just war. Our sense is that while they are usually not pacifists, they are uncomfortable with a completely amoral approach to international affairs and are seeking some way of thinking about issues of peace and security that contains an ethical component. Just war theories and controversies expose them to ideas they have not encountered or analyzed systematically in the past but with which they want to deal.

Methodology

New methodologies of political science expand the ways that political science theory may be applied and extended. This represents an additional challenge for teachers. Nineteenth-century realists and twentieth century idealists disagreed on theoretical grounds, but their techniques, based largely upon historical and legal research with an emphasis on diplomacy and military affairs, were similar. *Limits to Growth*, the Correlates of War project, or Axelrod's research on the evolution of cooperation in the iterated Prisoners' Dilemma game present different ways of studying political phenomena.[22]

While students rarely have the background to be able to understand advanced statistical studies or mathematical models fully, it is important that they know such research exists and that there is more to political science than reading history. Nor is there any reason that undergraduates cannot be actively engaged in meaningful research in international relations. New computer technologies such as CD-ROM and on-line data bases have made as much current information available to students, even in small liberal arts colleges, as was once accessible only to graduate students and faculty at major research universities. In addition, increasingly powerful microcomputers make statistical analysis inexpensive and practical. Thus, there is every basis for expecting that a motivated student with adequate faculty assistance could produce original (and quite possibly publishable) research. This has been done in the physical and biological sciences for a number years; the same model could be used in political science.

Probably the best way to teach political science research methodology is by adopting explicitly the model of the natural sciences: one learns research by doing it, not by reading about it. Hands-on experience with data and computer techniques is very important, as are term-length research projects that can be carried through from beginning to end. Bibliographies and research designs, while important first steps, are never a substitute for actually doing research.

This participatory approach can be quite demanding in terms of time for both the student and instructor and in the past required such a substantial institutional investment in computers and data sets that it was only possible in small classes. This may change in the future: personal computers with the power of a 1970s mainframe are now readily available to most students — whether as personal possessions or in accessible computer labs — and a computer disk costing less than a dollar holds the equivalent of about eight boxes of punch cards. Data on international affairs are readily available in the public domain — for example, from the Inter-University Consortium for Political and Social Research, the U.S. government, or various international sources — but at the present time reasonably-priced, high-quality, software is not. If that problem could be overcome, we would be able to make simple data analysis a standard part of our courses. Students could then demonstrate for themselves that higher military expenditures lead neither to fewer wars nor to fewer casualties of war, or could study the relative levels of economic development and quality of life indicators in Sri Lanka and Peru, and so on.

Conclusion

A century ago, the study of international politics was primarily the examination of the military, diplomatic, and colonial competition among European powers. A half-century ago, some non-European upstarts — notably the United States and Japan — complicated matters. In addition, a global depression fostered economic interdependence, and modern ideology had hindered diplomacy. But it was still possible to view the world through an aging lens and to make sense of it. Today international politics has become universal rather than European. Economics is at least as important as military conflict. The slow formal diplomacy of the nineteenth century has been augmented by personal phone calls between heads of states who may or may not be able to influence their national parliaments to ratify whatever agreements they have personally negotiated. The world has become a much more complicated place.

To the teacher of international relations, this presents both challenges and frustrations: the skilfully crafted lecture on the Warsaw Treaty Organization is relegated to back of the file drawer; one struggles to get students to understand both nuclear deterrence theory and floating exchange rates in a single introductory course. But one also sees changes in student population: an increasing number of students have travelled abroad, often outside of Europe as well as outside of North America, and first year students more often express an interest in 'exotic' languages such as Japanese, Arabic, and Hausa, rather than staying with the familiar Spanish, French, and German. New technologies make it possible for campuses to receive Soviet news broadcasts and Hindi soap operas and students can watch the most concentrated air bombardment of an urban area since World War II live on CNN. Students know that international politics is important. Few instructors of this subject have difficulty filling their courses. Our challenge is to identify those lessons of history, patterns of culture, and indicators from theory that our students will find useful in interpreting the world for the next half-century.

Notes

1. "Prices Down the Years," *The Economist*, 22 December 1990, p. 116.

2. For a useful discussion of one alternative approach, peace studies, as well as nearly one hundred sample syllabuses, see Daniel C. Thomas and Michael T. Klare, eds., *Peace and World Order Studies*, 5th ed. (Boulder CO: Westview Press, 1989).

3. Our experience has been confined to teaching international politics in the context of a general political science major. Many schools provide a separate major in 'international studies'. We believe most of our suggestions will be relevant to that context as well as to political science, although international studies curricula tend more naturally to integrate a multicultural approach and intensive exposure to world history.

4. Munir Fasheh, "Impact on Education," in Naseer Aruri, ed., *Occupation: Israel Over Palestine*, 2d ed., (Belmont MA: Association of Arab-American University Graduates, 1989), pp. 522-23.

5. Edward T. Hall's discussion of monochronic and polychronic time and his distinction between high-context and low-context cultures are only two of numerous comparisons that can be drawn between various societies. See Hall, *Beyond Culture* (Garden City NY: Doubleday, 1976; reprint, New York: Anchor Books Division, 1981).

6. Edward W. Said, "Ignorant Armies Clash by Night," *The Nation*, 11 February 1991, p. 163.

7. See Charles Tilly, *Coercion, Capital and the European State* (Cambridge MA: Basil Blackwell, 1990).

8. A wonderful book that illustrates the global interconnectedness of political, cultural, and technological shifts is James Burke, *The Day the Universe Changed* (Boston MA: Little, Brown, 1985). See Chapter 3 for the story of the man who introduced the new accounting system.

9. Malcolm W. Browne, "2 Rival Designers Led the Way to Stealthy Warplanes," *New York Times*, 14 May 1991, p. C1.

10. "Survey: America," *The Economist*, 26 October 1991, p. 5.

11. "Survey: America," *The Economist*, 26 October 1991, p. 7.

12. Robert Gilpin, *War and Change in World Politics* (New York: Cambridge University Press, 1981), p. 7.

13. Richard Neustadt and Ernest Mays, *Thinking in Time: The Uses of History for Decision Makers* (New York: The Free Press, 1986); and Yaacov Vertzberger, *The World in their Minds: Information Processing, Cognition and Perception in Foreign Policy Decisionmaking* (Stanford CA: Stanford University Press, 1990).

14. Geoffrey Blainey, *The Causes of War*, 3d ed. (New York: Free Press, 1988).

15. One does not, for example, see separate courses in 'Biological Theory' or 'Psychological Theory' in the curriculum; in these fields, as well as the physical sciences, theory is integrated with substance. Ironically, the compartmentalization of theory as a distinct, separate and, by implication, avoidable aspect of the study of politics was partly a result of the behavioralist rejection of traditional approaches. Yet this change resulted in theory taking a very different role in political science than it has in the natural sciences model that the behavioralists were attempting to emulate.

16. Leslie H. Gelb with Richard K. Betts, *The Irony of Vietnam: The System Worked* (Washington DC: Brookings, 1979); Larry Berman, *Planning a Tragedy: The Americanization of the War in Vietnam* (New York: W.W. Norton, 1982).

17. Key neo-realists include Kenneth Waltz, *Theory of International Politics* (Reading MA: Addison-Wesley, 1979); Stephen Krasner, ed., *International Regimes* (Ithaca NY: Cornell University Press, 1983); Robert Gilpin, *War and Change in World Politics* (New York: Cambridge University Press, 1981).

18. For a general review of these different bodies of literature, see Deborah J. Gerner, "Foreign Policy Analysis: Renaissance, Routine, or Rubbish?", in William Crotty, ed., *Political Science: Looking to the Future, Vol. 2: Comparative Politics, Policy, and International Relations* (Evanston IL: Northwestern University Press, 1991), pp. 123-185; and Paul E. Johnson and Philip A. Schrodt, "Analytic Theory and Methodology," in William Crotty, ed., *Political Science: Looking to the Future, Vol. 1: The Theory and Practice of Political Science*, pp. 99-163.

19. Irving Janis, *Groupthink* (Boston MA: Houghton-Mifflin, 1982); Robert Jervis, *Perception and Misperception in International Politics* (Princeton NJ: Princeton University Press, 1976); Graham T. Allison, *The Essence of Decision* (Boston MA: Little, Brown, 1971); Bruce Bueno de Mesquita, *The War Trap* (New Haven CT: Yale University Press, 1981).

20. Harold Guetzkow and Joseph J. Valdez, eds., *Simulated International Processes: Theories and Research in Global Modeling* (Beverly Hills: Sage, 1981); Stuart A. Bremer, ed., *The GLOBUS Model* (Frankfurt: Campus/Westview Press, 1987); Morton A. Kaplan, *System and Process in International Politics* (New York: Wiley, 1957); Lewis F. Richardson, *Arms and Insecurity* (Chicago IL: Quadrangle Books, 1960); J. David Singer and Melvin Small, *The Wages of War* (New York: Wiley, 1972); J. David Singer, ed., *The Correlates of War* (New York: Free Press, 1979).

21. This material is covered in about two lectures in introductory IR. It takes a week in a U.S. defense policy course and is a full one-third of the international conflict course, using Michael Walzer's *Just and Unjust Wars* (New York: Basic Books, 1977).

22. Robert Axelrod, *The Evolution of Cooperation* (New York: Basic Books, 1984); Donella Meadows, Dennis L. Meadows, Jørgen Randers, and William W. Behrens, III, *The Limits to Growth* (New York: University Books, 1972).

5

The Pedagogical Is Political: The "Why," the "What" and the "How" in the Teaching of World Politics

Mark Neufeld

Introduction

For educators, the growing interest among university and college students in the study of world politics presents itself as both an opportunity and a challenge. It provides, on the one hand, an opportunity to foster an awareness of the global dimension of contemporary social relations — of the way in which the local is linked inextricably to the global. At the same time, the growing interest also presents a clear challenge to those of us who are active in the teaching of world politics. It challenges us to rethink — on an ongoing basis — how we teach, what we teach, and why we teach.

In this contribution, my purpose is twofold. First, I will address the three questions just noted: how do we teach? what do we teach? and why do we teach? However, in focusing on these questions, I will go beyond merely suggesting possible answers. In each case, I will also draw attention to the inherently and inextricably *political* dimension of the activity of teaching world politics. To that end, I will address the questions in reverse order, beginning with the one that is, arguably, most important and yet often overlooked: 'why teach world politics?'.

Question One: Why Teach World Politics?

In the study of world politics — as in most academic disciplines — more attention has been paid to the question of analysis than to that of teaching. Furthermore, in those instances in which teaching has been addressed, the focus, more often than not, has been on content and methodology — the 'what' and the 'how' — rather than on the impetus: the 'why'. For that reason, I have chosen to begin with the question of 'why'. I shall argue that the best answer to this question is to be found in the orientation of classical political theory — an orientation, moreover, that is increasingly reflected in the work of leading scholars in the field of world politics.

"The leading of a good and just life in the *polis*" was the "Aristotelian telos" of all political inquiry.[1] Exploring and cultivating public awareness of the basis upon which the citizens of the *polis* might lead such a life — the 'Aristotelian project' — was the task of all responsible students of human society. No other justification for their activity as scholars and teachers was necessary, or, indeed, acceptable.

The nature of the *polis* was of central concern for those working within the Aristotelian project. It is important to stress that the *polis* was not so much a 'place' as a 'way of living'. As Hannah Arendt has argued, the Aristotelian conception of the *polis* was that of a very special and freely chosen form of political organization.[2] In short, the *polis* was more than just the locality in which citizens were to live — the *polis* was the "moral-political order that rendered its citizens capable of leading a good and just life."[3]

Central to this form of political organization was the understanding that to live in a *polis* meant that everything was decided through words and persuasion, and not through force and violence.[4] But the idea of the *polis* involved more than the simple absence of overt violence. It was also coterminous with the values of liberty and equality. The *polis* "knew only equals" whose shared objective was "neither to rule nor to be ruled". And it was on this basis of equality that the realm of the *polis* was to be the "sphere of freedom."[5]

It should be noted, however, that equality between the members of the *polis* was not understood in terms of some objective quality of human beings located outside of history. It was viewed neither as a natural condition of human beings, nor as an attribute or right with which human beings have been endowed by their creator. Rather, this freedom-guaranteeing equality was seen as a function of the *polis* itself. In Arendt's words,

> Isonomy guaranteed . . . equality, but not because all men were born or created equal, but, on the contrary, because men were by nature . . . not equal, and needed an artificial institution, the *polis*, which . . . would make them equal.[6]

It is clear then, that the *polis* was not a naturally-existing locality. Nor should it be understood as a locality defined by fixed geographical boundaries. Rather, the *polis* was a socially-created 'political space' whose dimensions were determined by the people participating in its creation. Notes Arendt, "not Athens but the Athenians were the *polis*":[7]

> The *polis*, properly speaking, is not the city-state in its physical location; it is the organization of the people as it arises out of acting and speaking together, and its true space lies between people living together for this purpose, no matter where they happen to be. "Wherever you go, you will be a *polis*": these famous words . . . expressed the conviction that action and speech create a space between the participants which can find its proper location almost any time and anywhere.[8]

Arendt's point that the *polis* can be created by willing participants 'almost any time and anywhere' is an important one. It is also important to note that different times and historical contexts may require different conceptions of the spatial dimensions of the *polis*.

As was observed above, the function of the political arrangement known as the *polis* was to ensure the conditions necessary for the leading of a good and just life, a life encompassing the values of equality and freedom. It follows that to be capable of this, the *polis* "must be coterminous with the minimum self-sufficient human reality . . . ."[9]

During the time period of classical Greece, the small city-state was viewed as adequate to this task. In modern history, however, it has been considered that a *polis* of those dimensions can no longer suffice. For Hegel, writing at the beginning of the 19th century, the political institution that best conformed to the requirement of being "coterminous with the minimum self-sufficient human reality" was that of the modern nation-state.[10] In contrast to the focus of the classical Greeks on their fellow-citizens in the city-state, for thinkers such as Hegel - and especially for his followers, the Young Hegelians - it was the fellow-citizens of one's nation-state who were to be of central concern to those committed to working within the Aristotelian project.

Even before Hegel's time, however, there were those who openly questioned whether the modern nation-state was an adequate geopolitical container for the ideal of just human relationships. Perhaps one of the best representatives of this group was Immanuel Kant. What was innovative about Kant's approach to international politics was the substitution of 'human beings' for 'citizens' as the proper subjects of moral concern.[11] This substitution can be seen as an important step in the modern effort to redefine the Aristotelian project in more universal terms through the "extension of the area of the common good."[12]

This effort has taken on new impetus in the twentieth century. The threats to human well-being and autonomy posed by nuclear weapons, the ecological crisis, the systematic violation of human rights around the globe, and the growing disparity between rich and poor within an increasingly interdependent world economy, have been interpreted as requiring a supercession of the present world order, and as demanding a transformation of our most basic political categories.[13]

In a context in which the factors that will determine whether the human species will survive or perish, suffer or prosper, operate on a global scale, a good case can be made that the *polis* that is 'coterminous with the minimum self-sufficient human reality' is the planet itself. In short, the problems presently faced by the human species call out for the identification of the idea of the *polis* with the planet as a whole: a truly *global polis*.

As was noted at the beginning of this essay, the 'Aristotelian project' involved theoretical reflection on — as well as cultivation of public awareness of — the conditions necessary for the leading of a "good and just life in the *polis*," where the *polis* is defined as a "sphere of freedom."[14] It follows that if we are now to speak of a global *polis*, distinguished by the presence of global-level threats to human well-being, then we shall require a discipline capable of conceptualizing the 'Aristotelian project' on a global scale and in terms of contemporary challenges. In short, what we require is nothing less than a body of knowledge and pedagogy that can provide us with a "new, encompassing language for political discourse on a planetary scale."[15]

It could be argued that the most logical candidate for such a task is the discipline of "international relations." In the words of Stanley Hoffmann:

> . . . the architectonic role Aristotle attributed to the science of politics might well belong today to international relations, for these have become in the twentieth century the very condition of our daily life. To philosophise about the ideal state in isolation, or to theorise about political systems in the abstract, has become almost meaningless.[16]

Indeed, a number of prominent international relations scholars would seem to share classical theory's concern with contributing to the quality of human life. "An introduction to the study of international relations in our time," writes Karl Deutsch, "is an introduction to the art and science of the survival of mankind."[17] "We study world politics," affirms Robert Keohane, "because we think it will determine the fate of the earth."[18] And "specialists in world affairs," argues J. David Singer, "have a special responsibility . . . to address the major problems confronting the global village."[19]

To conclude this first section then, the acceptance by an increasing number of scholars of the centrality of the 'Aristotelian project' provides a clear answer to the question of 'why' in the teaching of world politics. At the same time, this acceptance also underscores the inherently political dimension of a pedagogy that places the question of human survival and welfare at its center.

It can be argued, however, that the political dimension of the teaching of world politics extends well beyond an answer to the question of 'why teach?'. To see its full extent, one must pass to the second and third questions: those of 'what' and 'how'.

Question Two: "What To Teach?"

> Maybe there are periods when one can get along without theory, but at present its deficiency denigrates people and renders them helpless against force. — Max Horkheimer[20]

The first point to be made in a discussion of the content of teaching world politics is that theory has been and remains a core emphasis. But this has never been merely 'theory for theory's sake'. Rather, with a few exceptions, theory has been seen as the only route to an effective understanding of empirical reality. In short, it has been the discipline's starting premise that 'there is nothing so practical as a good theory'.

This explicitly theoretical orientation in the study of world politics is, indeed, vital and propitious. For it is only by means of theory that links between facts can be made. It is only through the abstraction which theory allows that the raw data of world politics can be given meaning. It is only by means of theory that the study of world politics can overcome the limitations inherent in 'interdisciplinary' study (*i.e.*, where knowledge from a number of disciplines is added together in the hopes of arriving at the 'big picture'), to become truly 'supradisciplinary' in nature, where the isolated claims of a variety of disciplines are sublated in a critical, integrated synthesis.[21]

Of course, it must be noted that the treatment of theory in the teaching of world politics has not been without its problems. One of the most serious is the high degree of parochialism in the kind of theory to which students are typically exposed.[22] Happily, one of the more beneficial effects of the 'inter-paradigm debate'[23] in IR theory at the end of the 1980s has been the creation of a number of textbooks that present a plurality of (meta)theories (or paradigms) for the analysis of world politics.[24] Increasing attention is being paid to the range of competing conceptions of the relevant actors (states, groups, classes), modes of interaction (conflict, cooperation, class struggle) and structuring principles of the global order (anarchy, interdependence, inequalities in wealth and power).

Of course, certain perspectives continue to be overlooked in these textbooks — perhaps most notably that of feminism.[25] At the same time, it seems clear that the move away from an approach that restricts the notion of theory to that derived from political realism to include traditions such as liberal-pluralism and Marxism is a step in the right direction.

There remains, however, a serious problem associated with the majority of treatments of theoretical diversity in the teaching of world politics. It is this problem I wish to address in the process of underscoring the political dimension of the 'what' in the teaching of world politics. The problem derives from an outmoded and indefensible view of theory as a 'neutral instrument' for describing and analyzing the world in which we live. The problem with such an understanding of theory is that if social and political theory in general — and post-positivist philosophy of science, in particular — have been telling us anything over the past two decades, it is that theory is not a 'mirror' which reflects the world, it is a 'lens' through which one sees the world.[26] Theory does more than establish links between neutral bodies of facts, and it even does more than tell us which facts are important and which are not: a theory, by means of the oft hidden assumptions which serve as its base, tells us what counts as a fact and what does not.

This understanding of theory has important implications for the study of world politics. What it makes clear is that contending meta-theoretical traditions for interpreting world politics are not only often incompatible but are, in fact, *incommensurable*.[27] That is to say, because it is the function of theory not only to interpret evidence, but to define what will count as valid evidence, not only to explain but to define what will count as valid explanation, the quest for direct access to a neutral, theory-independent realm of evidence for the purpose of adjudicating between competing explanations must be abandoned; the faith in analytical salvation through the doctrine of 'immaculate perception' must be relinquished.

In concrete terms, what this understanding of theory means is that we, as educators, cannot advise our students to choose that meta-theoretical tradition (realism, liberal-pluralism, Marxism, feminism, etc.) that provides the most 'accurate' description of the realities of world politics. At the same time, having been exposed to a smorgasbord of contrasting meta-theories, each based on incompatible sets of assumptions about world politics, students often and justifiably desire to know which meta-theoretical tradition is best. If it is not possible to adjudicate between contending meta-theories on the basis of objective evidence, how is one to choose?

The answer to this question is not a simple one, and it is for this reason understandable that so many scholars choose to close their eyes to post-positivist philosophy of science and re-affirm (neo-)positivist orthodoxy. As problematic as it appears, the positivist tenet of 'truth as correspondence' between theory and reality does, at least, provide a regulative ideal for judging between competing theoretical accounts. There is an alternative, however, to radical relativism's affirmation that given incommensurability, one meta-theory is as good as another.[28] This alternative requires us to re-orient our understanding of theory by giving up the view of theory as a neutral tool for the analysis of objective reality for an understanding of theory as

> evolving descriptions and ever-changing versions of objects, things, and the world [which] issue forth from various communities as responses to certain problems, as attempts to overcome specific situations, and as means to satisfy particular needs and interests.[29]

In short, it involves recognizing that "ideas, words, and language are not mirrors which copy the 'real' or 'objective' world" — as positivist conceptions of theory and knowledge would have it — "but rather tools with which we cope with 'our' world."[30]

Re-orienting our thinking in this way has important implications for the way we, as educators, represent contending meta-theories in the study of world politics. To illustrate, let us take the example of the tradition of political realism. In concrete terms, the acceptance of the post-positivist understanding of theory means that we no longer present political realism as a neutral description of the objective realities of world politics, but rather as the 'coping' vocabulary of a specific community (*e.g.*, U.S. state-managers) designed to address certain problems, to satisfy particular needs and interests (*e.g.*, the maintenance of US hegemony). Moreover, we explain the success of realism not in terms of an alleged superiority in grasping the 'realities' of international politics, but in terms of a demonstrated utility for guiding state managers in their activities of "state- and nation-building"[31] in the face of "a specific set of foreign policy problems."[32]

At the same time, we stress to students that if the success of the realist paradigm cannot be understood apart from its utility for particular social actors and their political projects, then a similar relationship must hold for other paradigms.[33] If true, then the answer to the question of which paradigm is 'best' can be formulated as follows: that paradigm is best that most closely conforms to one's political commitments, that seems best suited to the realization of one's understanding of what constitutes the 'good life' in the 'global *polis*'. As such, the reasoned examination of political judgements about what is desirable and possible must form a central element of the teaching of world politics.

The implications of this understanding of contending meta-theories in world politics are two-fold. The first is that students come to see the existing world order as the product of the achievement of hegemony by specific social actors working in terms of specific 'coping vocabularies'. They come to understand that the global order — like the dominant coping vocabularies that produce and sustain it — is an historically-emergent human creation. In this way, a revised understanding of theory helps to transform the traditional 'banking model' of education, where students gain no more than knowledge about how things work, and where existing social arrangements are 'givens' to which people must adapt, into truly 'critical' education, where students come to see existing social arrangements as 'limit-situations' that can be transcended.[34]

The second implication relates to the political dimension of the content of our teaching of world politics. Following this revised view of theory, it becomes clear that to work — and to teach others to work — in the 'normal science' tradition of any paradigm (including realism and pluralism as much as Marxism or feminism) is to lend support to particular social forces in pursuit of a specific social and political agenda. To engage — and to teach others to engage — in 'puzzle-solving' activity in terms of any meta-theoretical tradition is, consciously or not, intentionally or not, to lend support to a particular global order. Similarly, to make the link — and to teach others to make the link — between theory and practice, analysis and political project, is to promote the possibility of creating a counter-hegemony to that underlying the global order as it is presently constituted.

In conclusion, we see that there is an inescapable political dimension not only to the 'why' of the teaching of world politics, but to the 'what' as well. Yet it can be argued that the political dimension of the teaching of world politics extends even further. It is to a consideration of the third aspect — the 'how' of teaching world politics — that we now turn.

Question Three: How To Teach?

We have seen that there is an undeniable political dimension to both the impetus for (*i.e.*, the 'Aristotelian project') and the content of (*i.e.*, theoretically-informed analysis of the global order) the teaching of world politics. I wish to complete this thematic trajectory by examining the question of 'how' one teaches, and by noting once again that one cannot escape politics even in what is seemingly the most technical of domains.

Part of the answer to the 'how' question is already provided by the answer to 'what'. If theory is to be a central emphasis of teaching, it is clear that assignments must involve a theory component designed to foster theoretical self-awareness on the part of students.[35] Similarly, if reasoned examination of political judgements about what is desirable and possible in terms of the global order is to form a central element of the teaching of world politics, it is clear a course must include seminar-based discussions as well as lectures.

Here I wish to focus on one of the central challenges of teaching world politics: that of making global structures and processes, which almost inevitably appear distant and abstract, real and meaningful to students. Furthermore, in terms of the response to this challenge, one can distinguish at least two distinct strategies.

The first strategy designed to meet this challenge is that of 'making the local global'. By this I mean efforts within a course to make the localized experiences of students in the classroom conform as much as possible to the global-level experiences of international actors. Perhaps the most common operationalization of this strategy is that of the in-class 'simulation exercise'. Here, typically, students are asked to take on the identities of 'international actors' — *e.g.*, diplomats, government officials, officers of international organizations — and to engage in mock international-type activities (*e.g.*, inter-state negotiations to resolve a 'crisis'). Such simulation may be played out over a period of days or even weeks, with written assignments designed to provide a knowledge-base for effective participation.

Simulations have much to offer. They provide a useful window into the world of diplomats and policy-makers that, realistically speaking, few of our students will ever experience first-hand. Of at least equal importance is the fact that students generally find simulation exercises extremely enjoyable and interesting — on its own a good reason to consider building simulation exercises into one's course.

At the same time, there are reasons to be cautious about relying too heavily on simulation exercises. The principal reason relates once again to the too-often unrecognized hidden political content of such exercises. The strategy of 'making the local global' which such exercises represent does more than just open a window onto the world of diplomats and policy-makers. It also and simultaneously reinforces the notion that it is the experience of diplomats and elite policy-makers which is the real essence of world politics — that in studying world politics, the optimal approach is one in which we:

put ourselves in the position of a statesman who must meet a certain problem of foreign policy under certain circumstances. . . . [in which we] retrace and anticipate . . . the steps a statesman — past, present, or future — has taken or will take on the political scene . . . [in which we] look over his shoulder when he writes his dispatches; we listen in on his conversations with other statesmen; we read and anticipate his very thoughts."[36]

In short, it can be argued that in the strategy of 'making the local global' — as represented by simulation exercises — there is a built-in prejudice in favor of seeing world politics through realist eyes. And as was already noted, a realist vision, like any other, is an inherently political vision. As a consequence, to privilege the strategy of 'making the local global' in the classroom is to privilege one form of politics — one political project — over others.[37]

Thus, in the interest of combatting the kind of theoretical parochialism and political closure to which the study of world politics has too often been prey, it would seem prudent to complement the strategy of 'making the local global' with its opposite: that of 'making the global local'. This second strategy entails identifying within the already existing experiences of students — both inside and outside of the classroom — the manifestation of the global structures and processes which, at first encounter, seem so distant and abstract.

By way of example, the strategy of 'making the global local' can be implemented i) by drawing links between male domination of class-room discussion time (on average, men interrupt women twice as much as the inverse)[38] with global structures of patriarchy (*e.g.*, 'women do 60% of the world's work, make 10% of the world's income, own 1% of the world's property'); ii) by drawing links between global economic processes such as IMF austerity programmes and the Third World's export of poorer women to serve as domestic servants in wealthy families in the north;[39] iii) by drawing links between racist comments in the northern press and racist colonialist and neo-colonialist foreign policies; iv) by drawing links between the working conditions of Third World workers engaged by TNCs in Export Processing Zones and the high-priced, fashionable running shoes that are *de rigueur* on so many campuses.

Like its counterpart, the strategy of 'making the global local' is an effective means of making world politics real and meaningful. Furthermore, it has the added benefit of counterposing to the traditional view of world politics — *i.e.*, a political realm constituted by and consisting of the activities of state elites — a vision which makes the activities and experiences of 'ordinary' non-elites as important in the production and reproduction of the global order as any other. It is a strategy which challenges the realist orientation which informs that of 'making the local global', and thereby opens a space for contributions from less orthodox approaches such as Marxism and feminism. As such, it is a strategy deserving of at least the same amount of attention from educators of world politics as its alternative.

Conclusion

It has become rather commonplace of late to encounter expressions of disapproval regarding the alleged 'politicization' of pedagogy and curriculum in institutions of higher education.[40] Yet if the arguments advanced here have merit, then it must be conceded that the practice of teaching — certainly, the practice of teaching world politics — is already and inherently political in nature.

In short, politics is not just something 'out there' which we study and about which we teach — politics is something we do both as we study and as we teach. Consequently, the question for us as educators is not whether or not to be political in our teaching. The real question is, upon what kind of politics do we wish to base our pedagogy, and how honest do we intend to be about our politics — both with our students as well as with ourselves.

Notes

I wish to thank Tracy Heffernan, Stephen McDowell, and Thom Workman for their help in developing the ideas in this paper, as well as the Social Sciences and Humanities Research Council of Canada for financial assistance.

1. Richard J. Bernstein, *The Restructuring of Social and Political Theory* (New York: Harcout Brace Jovanovich, 1976), p. xxii; Leonard Harris, "Review of *The Restructuring of Social and Political Theory*," *International Philosophical Quarterly*, 19 (1979), p. 485.
2. Hannah Arendt, *The Human Condition* (Chicago IL: University of Chicago Press, 1958), pp. 13-14.
3. Thomas McCarthy, *The Critical Theory of Jürgen Habermas* (Cambridge MA: MIT Press, 1978), p. 2.
4. Arendt, *The Human Condition*, p. 26.
5. Arendt, *The Human Condition*, p. 32.
6. *On Revolution* (New York: Viking Press, 1963), p. 23. See also Richard Bernstein, *Beyond Objectivism and Relativism* (Philadelphia: University of Pennsylvania Press, 1983), p. 208.

7. Arendt, *The Human Condition*, p. 195.

8. Arendt, *The Human Condition*, p. 198. Of course, it can be argued that in historical terms the 'golden age' of the Greek city-state deviated in many respects from the ideal contained in classical political theory: *i.e.*, that those made 'free and equal' by the *polis* tended to be a narrow strata of men, with a sizable female and slave underclass excluded from the noble interaction of unconstrained speech and action. Nonetheless, it is the powerful image of the *polis* as a 'realm of freedom' for all with which I am concerned here.

For a recent challenge to this unflattering appraisal of the Greek city-state, see Ellen Meiksins Wood, *Peasant-Citizen and Slave: The Foundations of Athenian Democracy* (London: Verso, 1988).

9. Charles Taylor, *Hegel and Modern Society* (Cambridge: Cambridge University Press, 1979), p. 93.

10. *Hegel and Modern Society*, p. 93. See also, Andrew Linklater, *Men and Citizens in the Theory of International Relations* (London: Macmillan, 1982), pp. 146-149. As Linklater notes, Hegel opposed any doctrine of "cosmopolitanism which took issue with the roles and responsibilities integral to the state" (p. 147). At the same time, however, Linklater also underscores the fact that there does appear to be a contradiction between Hegel's "principle of human freedom, which demands the rational organization of political life, and the actual operations of the international states-system, the coercive or uncontrolled relations which pertain to the life of states" (p. 148). Avineri's argument that for Hegel, history involved the creation of a community of states within a world "united by culture and reason" may be one way of resolving this contradiction. See Shlomo Avineri, *Hegel's Theory of the Modern State* (London: Cambridge University Press, 1972), p. 207. It may also serve to temper the Hegelian claim that "the European state represented the highest form of political association" (Linklater, p. 149).

11. Linklater, *Men and Citizens*, It can be argued that Kant was preceded in theorizing the conceptual shift from the rights and freedoms of 'citizens' to 'persons' by Rousseau. See Linklater, *Men and Citizens, passim*. See also Michael C. Williams, "Rousseau, Realism and Realpolitik," *Millennium*, 18, No. 2 (1989), pp. 188-204. It is also Linklater's contention that Kant's "desire for a universal community of free individuals" stands at the centre of the theorizing of Karl Marx (p. 159). For a good overview of Linklater's discussion of Kant, see the review essay "Philosophers crossing borders: recent literature on ethics and international relations," Raino Malnes, *Journal of Peace Research*, 20, No. 2 (1983), pp. 193-200.

12. The words are T. H. Green's from his *Prolegomena to Ethics* (Oxford, 1906), p. 283, and are quoted in Linklater, *Men and Citizens*, p. 208, note #20.

13. Including the nation-state system. See, for example, Richard Falk, *The End of World Order* (New York: Holmes & Meier, 1983). See also, Linklater, *Men and Citizens*, p. 6. For a similar conclusion, this time from a realist perspective, see John Herz, *The Nation-State and the Crisis of World Politics* (New York: David McKay, 1976), pp. 15-19. Notes Herz, "only a radical change in attitudes [in the direction of universalism] and policies could, in the long run, save the world from disaster", pp. 15-16.

14. A way of life, it will be remembered, designed to promote equality between those participating in it.

15. Falk, *The End of World Order*, p. 15.

It should be noted that Arendt herself, and despite her assertion that the *polis* could be created almost anywhere and anytime, would most probably have had great difficulty in conceptualizing the *polis* in global terms. This is because Arendt held that only small groups of people allowed for the creative actions which distinguished the *polis*. In larger collectivities of people, argued Arendt, creative action was invariably supplanted by conformist behaviour. See Arendt, pp. 42-43. See also Terence Ball, "Ontological Presuppositions and Political Consequences," in Daniel R. Sabia, Jr., and Jerald T. Wallulis, eds., *Changing Social Science* (Albany NY: State University of New York Press, 1983), pp. 40-42.

In response, one could argue that there is no reason why a world order created in conformity with the idea of the *polis* could not be based on loose federation of communities small enough to allow for the kind of creative, non-conformist behaviour Arendt fears is lost in larger groups. For an effort to theorize a global order in terms of the notion of a 'global *polis*' while attempting to accommodate the kind of concerns raised by Arendt, see Richard Falk, "Anarchism and World Order," *Nomos*, 19 (1978).

16. Stanley Hoffmann, *Contemporary Theory in International Relations* (Englewood Cliffs NJ: Prentice-Hall, 1960), p. 4. Also quoted in Linklater, *Men and Citizens*, p. 5.

17. See Karl Deutsch, *The Analysis of International Relations*, 3rd ed. (Englewood Cliffs NJ: Prentice-Hall, 1988), p. ix.

18. Robert Keohane, "Theory of World Politics: Structural Realism and Beyond," in Keohane, ed., *Neorealism and Its Critics* (New York: Columbia University Press, 1986), p. 199. Keohane is clearly making reference to the work of Jonathan Schell. See J. Schell, *The Fate of the Earth* (New York: Alfred A. Knopf, 1982).

19. J. David Singer, "The Responsibilities of Competence in the Global Village," *International Studies Quarterly*, 29 (1985), p. 245.

20. "Die gesellschaftliche Funktion der Philosophie," in M. Horkheimer, *Kritische Theorie: Eine Dokumentation*, ed. Alfred Schmidt (Frankfurt: S. Fischer Verlag, 1968), II, 308, my translation.

21. On the distinction between 'interdisciplinary' and 'supradisciplinary', see Douglas Kellner, *Critical Theory, Marxism and Modernity* (Baltimore MD: Johns Hopkins University Press, 1989), p. 7.

22. Perhaps the best documentation of theoretical parochialism in the teaching of world politics is to be found in Hayward Alker and Thomas Biersteker, "The Dialectics of World Order: Notes for a Future Archeologist of International Savoir Faire," *International Studies Quarterly* 28 (1984), which concluded that a 'parochial behaviouralism' - perhaps best represented by neorealism - dominated the instruction offered at 'leading' universities.

23. Also known as the "Third Debate". See Michael Banks, "The Inter-Paradigm Debate," in M. Lights and A. J. R. Groom, eds., *International Relations: A Handbook of Current Theory* (London: Pinter, 1985); and Yosef Lapid, "The Third Debate: On

the Prospects of International Theory in a Post-Positivist Era," *International Studies Quarterly*, 33, no 3 (1989), pp. 235-54.

24. Examples of works suitable for use as textbooks that employ such an approach are Paul R. Viotti and Mark V. Kauppi, *International Relations Theory: Realism, Pluralism, Globalism* (London: Collier Macmillan, 1987); R. D. McKinlay, and R. Little *Global Problems and World Order* (Madison Wis: University of Wisconsin Press, 1986); and most recently, Barry B. Hughes, *Continuity and Change in World Politics: The Clash of Perspectives* (Englewood Cliffs NJ: Prentice Hall, 1991). In the sub-field of international political economy, both Stephen Gill and David Law, *The Global Political Economy: Perspectives, Problems and Policies* (Baltimore MD: Johns Hopkins University Press, 1988) and R. Gilpin, *The Political Economy of International Relations* (Princeton NJ: Princeton University Press, 1987), have adopted this approach as well.

25. For a textbook written from a feminist perspective which can be used to complement - and undermine - the others listed above, see Cynthia Enloe, *Bananas, Beaches & Bases: Making Feminist Sense of International Politics* (London: Pandora, 1989).

26. It is, of course, Richard Rorty from whom the idea of theory as a 'mirror' of external reality is borrowed. See his *Philosophy and the Mirror of Nature* (Princeton NJ: Princeton University Press, 1979).

27. The contribution of the historian of science, Thomas Kuhn, is, of course, germinal. See his *The Structure of Scientific Revolutions*, Second Edition (Chicago IL: University of Chicago Press, 1970).

28. The best treatment of the implications of incommensurability remains Richard Bernstein's *Beyond Objectivism and Relativism*.

29. Cornel West, *The American Evasion of Philosophy: A Genealogy of Pragmatism* (Madison Wis: University of Wisconsin Press, 1989), p. 201.

30. West, *The American Evasion of Philosophy*, p. 201.

31. E. Keenes, "Paradigms of International Relations: Bringing Politics Back In," *International Journal*, 44 (1989) p. 65.

32. S. Smith, "Paradigm Dominance in International Relations: The Development of International Relations as a Social Science," *Millennium* (1987) 16, no 2, p. 197.

33. As Alker and Biersteker note:
> Two global superpowers both able to destroy each other, but likely to self-destruct in the same process, are likely to have scholars especially interested in "global interdependence" or "peaceful coexistence" ... Anti-colonial revolutionaries in relatively underdeveloped countries are driven by other practical imperatives. (p. 139).

34. The notion of the 'banking model' of education is Paulo Freire's. See his *Pedagogy of the Oppressed* (New York: Herder and Herder, 1972). For a discussion of Freire's work in the context of 'critical social science', see Brian Fay, *Critical Social Science: Liberation and Its Limits* (Oxford: Polity Press, 1987), esp. Chapter Five.

35. For example, a recent assignment in a course on international organization(s) was to employ one of the major paradigms examined in the course to analyze a formal international organization.

36. The words are, of course, Hans Morgenthau's. See his *Politics Among Nations*, fifth edition, (New York: Alfred A. Knopf, 1973), p. 5.

37. It could be argued that there is nothing inherent in the concept of simulation exercises that requires them to be structured in conformity with a realist world-view. Theoretically, simulation exercises could involve a wide number of scenarios and roles in international relations: *e.g.*, organizing a union in an export processing zone in South-East Asia; women picketing Greenham Common in the United Kingdom; social activists committing civil disobedience to stop an 'arms bazaar' from being held in Ottawa; a peace group making a submission before the Canadian House of Commons Committee on Defence and External Affairs. Indeed, the very fact that these possibilities for alternative simulations of world politics exist, and yet are ignored by mainstream simulators, serves to show even more clearly the political project behind simulation exercises. (I am indebted to Stephen McDowell for drawing my attention to this point.)

38. A particularly useful reading on this point is Bernice R. Sandler, "The Classroom Climate: Chilly for Women?", in , A. Deneef, C. Goodwin, & E. McCrate, eds., *The Academic's Handbook* (Durham NC: Duke University Press, 1988).

39. On this, see Enloe, *Bananas, Beaches & Bases*, Chapter Eight. In a recent course, one of my students informed me that her family had employed over one dozen women from the Third World as domestic servants in her lifetime, and that in studying the global structures and processes that systematically underdeveloped Third world peoples, she had come to understand the position of those women in a radically new way.

40. See R. Kimball, *Tenured Radicals: How Politics Has Corrupted Our Higher Education* (New York: Harper & Row, 1990); and Dinesh D'Souza, "Illiberal Education," *The Atlantic Monthly* (March, 1991).

6

Undisciplining World Politics: The Personal Is Political

Anne Sisson Runyan

Trends in Knowledge Transformation

The changing nature of the field of world politics is due not only to external events in the "real" world of international politics and the internal debates within the discipline of international relations, but also to the more generalized epistemological and methodological revolutions sweeping across the humanities, social sciences, and natural sciences. Three of these interconnected challenges to post-World War II academic orthodoxy are summarized by Robert Keesey as:

> (1) the rise of 'contextualism' and the rehistoricizing of the humanities and social science disciplines after a period of their being dominated by ahistorical, synchronic, critical theories; (2) the historicizing of the natural sciences, challenging beliefs about the relationship between 'method' and 'science,' circumscribing notions of 'certainty,' and restoring the process of discovery to social and institutional contexts; (3) revisions of the presumed relationships among language, mind, and reality offered by the various linguistics-based movements like structuralism, deconstruction, hermeneutics, semiotics, generative grammar, and those attempting to model 'mind.'[1]

A fourth challenge, which both underlies and facilitates these contemporary intellectual movements, is the reconstruction of knowledge as embedded in and arising from the social constructions of gender, race, and class. These constructions enable us to historicize and contextualize knowledge claims, leading to an illumination of heretofore hidden processes with respect to the structural organization of knowledge and the production of meaning. Thus, at a time when the very foundations of discrete disciplines are being questioned, it is not surprising that what constitutes the field of world politics is in a state of flux.

Undisciplining World Politics

Ironically, the field of world politics and its 'father' discipline, International Relations (IR), have often been presented as the products of interdisciplinary approaches. However, the utility of the contributions of political science, economics, history, philosophy, anthropology, sociology, and psychology have been judged primarily on the basis of their explanatory power with respect to the presumed anarchical relations of self-interested states and the 'security dilemma' this poses for them, which is assumed to lie at the 'core' of international relations inquiry. If, however, we were to adopt Sarah Brown's definition of International Relations as the study of "the identification and explanation of social stratification and of inequality as structured at the level of global relations," we could resituate world politics.[2] This would enable us to reveal the linkages in the narratives of these supposedly discrete disciplines as well as other fields of inquiry that have been neglected by being deemed 'outside' the purview of the 'core' of IR orthodoxy. Such neglected fields include literature, art, and the 'natural' sciences as well as such more deservedly-named 'interdisciplinary' projects as women's studies, minority studies, and ecology.

For example, rather than organizing interdisciplinary contributions to world politics on the basis of which level of analysis — 'man' or 'the state' or 'war' — they 'fit', it seems far more productive, in terms of interconnected (and, thus, more meaningful) learning, for teachers to draw the attention of students to the intersection among the disciplines as revealed by their rather similar narratives regarding the forces of modernity and Westernization. It is no accident that the historical construction of almost all disciplines coincides with early European state formation and "expansionism that linked together separate peoples of the earth into a modern world system."[3] Indeed, any analysis of dominant approaches to science, technology, literature, history, anthropology, economics, and world politics, without reference to Western conquest, colonization, and modernization from the 15th through the 20th century distorts understanding of how disciplines 'produce' bodies of knowledge. Moreover, inattention to the related historical process involving the rise of elite, white, male, power at all levels and in all areas incorporated within Western hegemony and modernity also obscures in whose interests these academic disciplines have been constructed and divided.

When we recognize the similar genealogy of disciplines in contemporary academe, we begin to think about other ways to organize knowledge for ourselves and our students. In world politics, we need to explore central IR concepts, such as 'progress', 'security', 'power', and 'violence', 'autonomy', 'sovereignty', and 'objectivity', in the context of the construction of disciplinary preoccupations and practices in the Western, masculinist historical frame. Our task would also be to demonstrate how the centrality and dominant definitions of these concepts are being challenged by contemporary interdisciplinary thought and social movements. By assuming such an approach, we can provide more systematic historical and interconnected accounts of the interrelationship between political, economic, social, cultural, scientific, and technological forces that have shaped social stratification and the relations of inequality which characterize so much of world politics.

A similar pedagogy can be effected through an issue-oriented approach which would emphasize examination of global issues and their relationships to the processes that take place at personal, local, national, and regional levels. For example, by organizing our thinking around such subjects as ecological degradation, poverty, human and cultural alienation, and militarization, we may employ the contributions of other disciplines far more effectively and cohesively. There is little question that these problems may be approached under the rubric of security, as evidenced by recent international relations scholarship that has investigated the non-military aspects of security as well as questioned the viability of military security. However, applying such a 'singular logic' as 'security studies' for the sake of parsimony and disciplinary coherence often leads to the sacrifice of other, equally valid ways of organizing knowledge about world politics, such as the post-structuralist focus on universalistic vs. particularistic ideologies, practices, and tensions as well as gender, race, and class analysis.

The data base for world politics can be enlarged by individual scholars and teachers committed to interdisciplinary investigations. However, if we are to move towards making IR "more international and more about relations," we need to think about how we can best integrate different schools of thought, not only intellectually, but practically.[4] If we are to help our students make the connections between disciplinary narratives and a more complex and critical understanding of not merely world politics, but, more importantly, how the world is constructed, deconstructed, and reconstructed through experiences, perspectives, and narratives, we need to make the enterprise of teaching less individual and more collective. Team teaching, course clusters, and interdisciplinary programs within the academy, although sadly underutilized, offer the kind of practical and structural alternatives necessary for making connections among disciplines for both teachers and students.[5]

Increasingly, some type of course in 'international awareness' is becoming a part of general education requirements, with introductory courses in world politics sometimes serving that function. However, it is not enough to expose students to one such experience and then send them off to disciplinary enclaves, possibly never to discuss the 'world-as-connected' again. It may be that nothing short of the reorganization of the academy along interdisciplinary lines is necessary to avoid the all-too-disparate learning process that the majority of our students experience. This does not mean the abandonment of the disciplines as places for specialized knowledge production. Even if disciplinary programs remain the principal way of organizing the academy, it is still possible to mitigate the worst features of disciplinary separation through interdisciplinary 'core' curricula.

The construction of such "core" curricula would have connection as their premise. This would function in opposition to the premise of separation that pervades disciplinary concerns about their 'hard cores' as well as the all too typical skills-based 'core' of general education programs.[6] What form the connections take would depend upon which courses constitute what 'core', which instructors offer them, and how they engage in a collective discussion about how to connect their courses. For instance, a cluster of courses or an interdisciplinary program focused on the theme of 'progress' could make and reinforce connections among historicized narratives in world politics, economics, anthropology, and science about the rise of the nation-state, capitalism, science, modernization, and Westernization in general. Similarly, a cluster of courses or an interdisciplinary program organized around the subject of ecology could connect the social, cultural, economic, scientific, technological, and political forces, intertwined at and intertwining local, national, and world levels, that facilitate or ameliorate ecological degradation. Central to such endeavors would be the perspectives of gender studies, minority studies, and area studies which would serve to illuminate suppressed knowledge within and across the disciplines.

Undisciplining the World Politics Classroom

For anyone who has had the very common experience of discovering that students do not 'get it' even after carefully reading assigned texts and listening to carefully constructed lectures designed to make a specific argument, the postmodern claim that 'texts', whether as books, lectures, events, or structures, do not necessarily have *a priori* meanings that can be 'discovered' begins to make sense. Students, like all 'readers', come to 'texts' with their own experiences and perspectives, and it is the intersection of reader and text or the dynamic relationship of observer and observed that produces meaning.[7]

Thus, given that the 'text' of world politics can have multiple 'readings', it makes sense to devise pedagogical techniques that privilege the political nature of knowledge about world politics. By revealing that we never operate as value-free, disembodied observers, that we carry prior assumptions that determine what puzzles are worth solving and what evidence is worth heeding, we render explicit those values, perspectives, and, thus, facts, that are excluded from traditional accounts of world politics.

One of the most obvious ways to bring attention to these exclusions in IR orthodoxy is in the use of texts and materials by and/or about those 'subjects' commonly hidden within and by international relations. As Fred Halliday has observed in his introduction to the 1988 special issue of *Millennium* on Women and International Relations, among the reasons for the 'invisibilisation' of women and gender in IR is the 'selective insulation' of IR from women's or gender studies at a time when other fields in the humanities, social sciences, and even sciences have experienced significant feminist incursions.[8] Despite numerous critiques of Western political thought by feminist political theorists, these feminist challenges to such 'fathers' of IR as Machiavelli, Hobbes, and Morgenthau are rarely visible in mainstream IR journals and generally absent from traditional world politics texts. Similarly, gender research and theorizing within the areas of development studies, peace studies, international political economy, and state-society relations are conspicuously absent from conventional treatments of the North-South and transnational dimensions of world politics. Finally, feminist perspectives on such 'core' concepts in IR as power, security, sovereignty, and strategic thinking are never or rarely acknowledged in general discussions of these subjects.

It seems obvious, then, that the only way to fill these lacunae is in the use of at least some of this germinal literature by women/feminists and/or about women/feminism in the classroom as required and/or supplemental reading. This is a particularly urgent project, not only because feminist literature and incursions in IR are steadily increasing and representative of the generalized, post-positivist trend currently transforming the social science in general and IR discourse in particular, but also because the inclusion of women and feminist perspectives is vital to attracting women to the field. The increasing enrolment of women in higher education is, not surprisingly, leading to demands by women students for greater sensitivity and attention to their experiences and perspectives which have been devalued and dismissed in a gendered, and, more specifically, masculinist world. As Halliday argues, IR has been constituted in an especially gendered way. This privileges the masculinist and male-dominated constructs of states, economies, and realist politics as 'high politics' and mystifying the reality that international processes are far from gender neutral — that is, they, in fact, have significant "effects on the position and role of women in society, and on the relative placings of women and men."[9] When this is denied by both traditional IR discourse and conventional world politics texts, women students, who are potential theorists, researchers, and practitioners, get the message that IR or world politics generally has nothing to do with them and, thus, cannot be influenced by them.

A similar argument can be made with respect to minority students who are disempowered and alienated by the relative paucity of attention given to racism in international relations. That international relations is fundamentally about 'interracial relations' according to Paul Gordon Lauren, seems to escape the notice of many authors of introductory and advanced world politics texts.[10] Racism is not so inconspicuous, however, to those struggling against it, whether they be minorities, anti-colonialist and anti-imperialist nationalists, or Third World states. To discuss the state system, war, colonization and imperialism, nationalism and revolution, processes of development (or 'modernization'), and the international division of labor without reference to racial consciousness, racial stereotypes, and racism is odd, indeed. Yet, it has happened with much frequency in the absence of a what is now a growing literature by and about minorities and non-Western people of color. There is no good reason not to engage at least some of this literature in the undergraduate world politics curriculum, particularly in the face of the diversification and internationalization of North American student culture, the increase of racism on North American college campuses, and the obvious 'orientalism' that has accompanied the Gulf War.

Perhaps one of the best ways to illuminate the contestability of world politics paradigms and perspectives is by means of in-class simulations. While these have taken, traditionally, the form of some kind of mock United Nations where students take the roles of conventional state actors to debate a current issue, this approach tends to privilege the perspectives of elite state actors, such as governmental representatives, who have little in common with the poor, women, and people of color they purport to represent. Moreover, this approach implies that only states are actors in international relations and suggests that foreign policies are and should be separable from domestic politics. A preferable method for introducing multiple perspectives is the creation and assignment of very different roles for students to play. For example, one might take the cue from Cynthia Enloe in her recent book, *Bananas, Beaches and Bases: Making*

Feminist Sense of International Politics, wherein she depicts some very unlikely actors (under present IR orthodoxy, that is) in world politics who might serve as alternative role models.[11] These include domestic servants who are sent abroad by Third World states to ease their foreign debts; diplomatic and military wives who must sacrifice their careers for those of their husbands; prostitutes who service military bases and peace camp women who protest nuclear installations; and light assembly workers in offshore industries and free trade zones who both profit and resist the world's multi-national corporations and their host or parent states. These non-state, anti-state, and trans-state actors would likely have very different perspectives on world events from state leaders, diplomats, multinational corporation executives, representatives from the IMF and the World Bank, military officials, and United Nations bureaucrats.

A particular application of this approach could be generated from Enloe's article, "Womenandchildren: Making Sense of the Persian Gulf Crisis."[12] In it, she uncovers those actors in the Gulf whose presence and conditions were 'covered up' in and by Gulf War coverage partially because their presence and conditions would disrupt the triumphant Gulf War narrative. In particular, she points to the thousands of Filipina 'guest workers' (read domestic servants) in Kuwait who constitute a large number of 'Kuwaiti' refugees as well as those who were reportedly raped by invading Iraqi soldiers. She notes that the Philippine women's movement has pressed their government to provide greater protections for these domestic servants working abroad, particularly in the Middle East, who sometimes face brutalization by their employers. However, these efforts have largely failed because the Philippine government (and the IMF to which it is beholden) places greater priority on access to oil and foreign exchange. Tellingly also, *New York Times* columnist Leslie Gelb shares the following anecdote:

> A senior Kuwaiti cabinet minister acknowledged to "60 Minutes," the CBS news program, that the war "has made us know that what we used to do was wrong." For example, he offered, "I had four maids, or three maids in my house; you can have two maids. Why should you have four maids in the house? Why doesn't your wife do some of the work?"[13]

Enloe also speaks to the Saudi women's movement that has been effectively neutralized by the ever-watchful Islamic police who abused women (in the name of keeping them uncontaminated by Western troops) for the slightest show of skin or demand for rights. Beyond this, Judith Miller, in "Saudi Arabia: The Struggle Within," argues that the increased repression of Saudi women was not tangential, but critical to the 'success' of the war effort.[14] Through interviews with Saudi analysts, she finds that Islamic extremists within Saudi Arabia objected to the presence of foreign troops on Saudi soil. In order to quell these objections, King Fahd offered up 'uppity' women as the real threat to Saudi society. As one commentator put it, "The religious opposition opposed both the foreign troops and women driving. He gave them one, and demanded acquiescence, if not outright support on the other. And he got it."[15]

As for the women who made up the U.S. troop complement in the Gulf, Enloe argues that it is mistaken to assume that these women represent 'liberation' in contrast to the veiled Arab woman. She cites, in particular, the amount of sexual harassment that women in the U.S. military have endured to suggest that their status in the military, in the economy, and the polity is far from equal. Finally, Ali Mazrui, in "Contradictions in the Gulf," points out that Iraqi women were among the most 'liberated' in the Middle East, at least to the degree that they were integrated into the industrial workforce of that more secular country.[16]

Thus, if students were to assume these roles in the context of the Gulf War, in addition to the more conventional actors in such conflicts, a very different set of conflicts and possible coalitions might emerge. Moreover, students might be less likely to engage in facile assumptions about the utility and justness of the war than they are when the war is cast in undifferentiated terms, thus, denying the presence and perspectives of not only non-Western actors, but also non-elite, non-male, and non-white persons. Certainly, such an exercise would call into question the implicit and explicit claims that this war has been in the interests of liberation, democracy, the civilizing influence of the West, and the protection of 'womenandchildren'. Simulations of this type encourage students to look below and beyond the level of the state. This unorthodox approach to role-playing engages students in the kind of research and gaming that demands interdisciplinary knowledge, an analysis of the construction and effects of gender, race, and class in the international system, an empathy for and a privileging of the lives of and relationships of ordinary people in world politics, and a sense of personal connection with world political events. Some of these objectives can also be achieved through the use of testimonial and life story literature in world politics courses. Often times more accessible than academic discourse, and certainly written far more often by women and people of color than are academic texts, such narratives offer the everyday struggles of people living under neo/colonialism, political repression, and/or war. Such materials not only permit a more visceral understanding of the human stakes involved in world politics, but also allow us to hear voices that speak 'from' rather than 'for' various communities in the world. According to Chandra Mohanty, the major purposes of testimonials are to:

> a) document and record the history of popular struggles, b) foreground experiential and historical "truth" which has been erased or rewritten in hegemonic, elite, or imperialist history, and c) bear witness in order to change oppressive state rule. . . . their strategy is to speak "from within" a collective, as participants in revolutionary struggles, and to speak with the express purpose of bringing about social and political change.[17]

Such is also the case of testimonial films which invite viewers to move from the status of passive audience to active participants in social and political change projects.

Just as students should become more familiar with testimonial and life story literature in the context of world politics, they should also learn to become more critical observers of hegemonic cultural products because these images are not only reflective of significant aspects of world politics, but also productive of world politics. In a world dominated by the marketing and consumption of such cultural commodities as 'Rambo', blow-up-the-world, video games, and Super Bowls, it is little accident that war gets constituted like a football game which cannot be won with 'one hand tied behind your back' or without sophisticated surgical strike weapons. Thus, in order for students to be sophisticated observers of world politics, they must be critical analysts of those cultural artifacts which produce, mediate, and dominate perceptions about world politics. This means not just 'the news', but also such hegemonic discourses as "Rambo" and "Top Gun." In addition to developing this critical literacy among students with respect to popular culture, it is also necessary to introduce them to the counter-hegemonic genres of testimonial literature and film that portray the underside of and struggles against 'Ramboism'.

Teaching Transformation in World Politics

The epistemological, methodological, and pedagogical revolutions in the academy relevant to world politics here are certainly not without their critics. Those who would argue that subjects and approaches presented are not 'International Relations', at least as they have learned, taught, or practised it, might find allies among those who have made it their business to protect 'the canon' and the primacy, and, indeed, superiority of Western thought. Similarly, those who would still argue that facts are separable from values, and that the variables of gender, race, and class have little to do with, and indeed, obfuscate the classic IR security dilemma of an anarchical world of self-interested states, might also find allies among those who view post-positivist, feminist, anti-racist, and generally critical theories, methodologies, and pedagogies as leading to a dangerous 'politicization' of the academy. This, of course, assumes there was nothing political about the academy or the curriculum before, that there were no power relations in the academy, and no privileging of white, Western, male, perspectives and constructs in the curriculum. It also assumes that those deemed 'politically correct' are somehow engaging in a hegemonic discourse that has already and thoroughly marginalized the Western tradition. Interestingly, this supposed hegemony of the 'politically correct' is far from evident, one could hazard, in the majority of journals, texts, and syllabuses in world politics and international relations generally. While it is 'correct' to say the current transformations in academe are politically oriented, it is also the case that past and lingering canonical orthodoxies in IR and U.S. higher education generally were and are themselves ideologically grounded. As a particularly American creation that has strongly represented a U.S. worldview, conventional IR has been very much implicated in American higher education preoccupations over the last century. These preoccupations, according to William Spanos in his genealogy of higher education reforms in the twentieth century, coincide with major wars in which the U.S. has been involved.[18] After World War I, when the first federally mandated war issues courses were offered, the canons of higher education began to reflect U.S. elite fears of the Bolshevik revolution and working-class movements organized by European immigrants. After World War II, much of American higher education was geared to produce a national consensus against the Communist threat, an ideology that, one could argue, realist IR served well during the Cold War. It was only during and after the Vietnam War that there was sufficient political dissent and space for the current challenges to these state-sponsored orthodoxies.

It is within this post-Vietnam War context that things have been changing in world politics curriculum and pedagogy. Greater attention to the North-South dimension of world politics has brought such issues of Third World women in development to the fore. Greater discussion of the new international political economy has opened the way for exploring the conditions of the poor and, particularly women, in the international division of labor. Greater concern about ecological security has led to the discussion of social movement struggles to protect fragile ecosystems from the ravages of state violence and corporate exploitation. Even treatments of Cold War, East-West politics have, to some degree, utilized peace research and focused on peace movements, particularly in the context of the rise of peace studies programs on many campuses. Moreover, the end of the Cold War has revived interest in nationalism and ethnicity in world politics, leading to a greater sensitivity to cultural forces.

While these developments have broadened the purview of world politics considerably and led to a greater acknowledgement of what James Rosenau, in his recent text, *Turbulence in World Politics*, defines as the 'multi-centric' world which co-exists with, resists, and assists the state-centric world, they have not yet displaced the hegemony of state-centric perspectives in the undergraduate curriculum.[19] They, too, often may be presented as 'add on' topics as opposed to transformational discourses.

The transformational potential of these discourses is also undermined by such traditional pedagogical techniques as the 'expert' lecturing to the passive masses, with little classroom discussion, group projects, or participatory exercises. Such discouragement of active, non-individualized, and non-cognitive, learning is not only pedagogically unsound, but also biased against 'non-traditional' learners such as women, minorities, and older students who may be disempowered not only by content that does not address their perspectives and experiences, but also by pedagogical styles that particularly silence them. To the degree that only the most aggressive student is the one afforded the time and space to speak, others more routinized to being silenced in society (and in world politics) will also have their silence perpetuated in the classroom. Thus, small group discussions, more inclusive simulations and exercises, in-class writing time and the like are critical components for teaching critical discourses in world politics.

If 'the personal is political' and, indeed, 'international' as Enloe has argued, then so too is the classroom.[20] It is not separate from, but rather a microcosm of, world politics. One need only think of the images in American classrooms during the Gulf War: yellow ribbons and black armbands on the sleeves of students; Arab students fearful of reprisals and surveillance; reservist students who were called up, leaving empty chairs; African American students who are more absent in our classrooms, but more present in the armed forces, as their college enrolment continues to decline; women students who can make no sense of the images of American women soldiers defending a regime that denies women the right to vote and drive; and students who may not be able to complete their degrees because of tuition hikes in the wake of state fiscal crises and in the face of massive federal spending on the war.

This world politics classroom can be, and often is, a place where we teach and learn when, how, and why states wage war. Since the Gulf War, the generalized lesson being taught and learned in American society and elsewhere is that the United States wages war particularly well. As *New York Times* columnist Anna Quindlen observes:

We have learned that we do this superlatively. And that frightens me.
Oh, if it makes each nation in the world think thrice about aggression

because it fears the biggest kid in the class, I say hooray. But if it makes us cocky — and a cocky American is the cockiest creature on earth — that will be a disaster. The failure of Vietnam made us gun-shy for almost two decades. It is a much greater failure to be trigger-happy. If the Iraqi rout becomes our model of conflict resolution, we will have suffered a great defeat.[21]

Let us hope that the Gulf War, which (not surprisingly) has coincided with conservative attacks on 'multicultural' or 'politically correct' curriculum and pedagogy, does not usher in another closure of the American mind in the interest of creating yet another national consensus against 'our enemies' — the poor, the disenfranchised, those who struggle for peace and social justice. If World Politics students, particularly in the U.S., do not get messages other than the chronicling of 'successful' violence by 'the biggest kid in the class' and the presumed necessity for (even if not the justness of) it, then this failure of imagination will be perpetuated not just in the classroom, but also in the world.

Notes

1. Robert Keesey, "Transformations in Disciplinary Knowledge Assumptions and Their Implications for Reforming the Undergraduate Curriculum," *Issues in Integrated Studies* (1988), pp. 83-84. I am indebted to Robert Keesey, Professor of English at SUNY Potsdam, for a number of insights that appear in this piece about creating a more interdisciplinary undergraduate curriculum.

2. Sarah Brown, "Feminism, International Theory, and International Relations of Gender Inequality," *Millennium* 17 (Winter 1988), p. 461.

3. Keesey, "Transformations," p. 112.

4. Peggy McIntosh, Director of the Center for Research on Women at Wellesley College, argued for this in her remarks at the Gender and International Relations Conference, Wellesley College, 12-13 October 1990.

5. See Keesey, "Transformations," pp. 112-113, for a discussion of the necessity of team teaching for knowledge integration. Alternatives to team teaching, which may not be possible where faculty are spread thin, are course clusters, for which faculty coordinate the syllabuses of several separate courses, and coordinated interdisciplinary studies programs in which disciplinary courses are organized around a central theme.

6. See Keesey, pp. 114-117, for an extended discussion of the false dichotomy between skills and content in educational reform debates.

7. Keesey, p. 96.

8. Fred Halliday, "Hidden From International Relations: Women and the International Arena," *Millennium* 17 (Winter 1988), p. 419.

9. Halliday, p. 420.

10. See Paul Gordon Lauren, *Power and Prejudice: The Politics and Diplomacy of Racial Discrimination* (Boulder CO: Westview Press, 1988).

11. Cynthia Enloe, *Bananas, Beaches and Bases: Making Feminist Sense of International Politics* (Berkeley CA: University of California Press, 1989).

12. Cynthia Enloe, "Womanandchildren: Making Feminist Sense of the Persian Gulf Crisis," *Village Voice*, 25 September 1990, pp. 29+.

13. Leslie H. Gelb, "Dear Mr. President . . .," *New York Times*, 3 March 1991, p. E17.

14. See Judith Miller, "Saudi Arabia: The Struggle Within," *The New York Times Magazine*, (March 1991), pp. 27+.

15. Miller, "Saudi Arabia," p. 46.

16. Ali A. Mazrui, "Contradictions in the Gulf," *Peace Review* 2 (Fall 1990), p. 306.

17. Chandra Talpade Mohanty, "Cartographies of Struggle: Third World Women and the Politics of Feminism," in Chandra Talpade Mohanty, Ann Russo, and Lourdes Torres, eds., *Third World Women and the Politics of Feminism* (Bloomington: Indiana University Press, 1991), p. 37.

18. William Spanos, Professor of English at SUNY Binghamton, presented the broad outlines of this genealogy in his talk on "Academic Freedom and the Politically Correct" for a panel on diversifying the curriculum at SUNY Potsdam, 11 October 1991.

19. See James B. Rosenau, *Turbulence in World Politics: A Theory of Change and Continuity* (Princeton NJ: Princeton University Press, 1990).

20. See Enloe, *Bananas, Beaches and Bases*, p. 196.

21. Anna Quindlen, "The Microwave War," *New York Times*, 3 March 1991, p. E17.

7

Teaching Concepts and Theory: A View from Denmark

Georg Sørensen

For the last ten years or so, I have asked my undergraduate students of world politics the same question during our first class: 'what are the three most important problems in the world today?'. They are given all of five minutes to write down their answers. There is a very high degree of consensus in the answers, not only among the students in a specific class, but also over the years. Even if the exact formulations may differ, they point to the same three sets of problems: (a) the arms race and the risk of nuclear war; (b) poverty and underdevelopment in the Third World; (c) environmental problems.

Having experienced the consistency of their answers, it is difficult for me not to show off by declaring beforehand that I know what the students are going to answer, write it down on a piece of paper, and proudly show it to them afterwards. But some of the students are always less impressed, and perhaps rightly so: would not most of us point to the same three, or very similar, sets of problems when asked the question in this general, abstract manner?

In any case, the important part of the exercise involves two elements. The first is an attempt to make students think about institutions and actors that shape their view of the world and to consider what it is that has moulded their conception of world or global issues.

The other element is to connect world issues and international institutions to the theoretical tools that our discipline has to offer. The theories and concepts of International Relations (IR) may not have ready-made *solutions*, but at least they offer the possibility of *understanding* and *explaining* the basic problems.

Thus, I tie the problems of war and arms race to the realist understanding of world politics, the problems of poverty and underdevelopment to globalist or dependency theories; and the environmental problems are related to pluralist and world society perspectives. This is merely an appetizer, of course. It demonstrates that the discipline does possess an arsenal of approaches, paradigms and theories that can lead to a more profound understanding of 'the most important problems in the world today'. Before expanding on this, let me briefly introduce the institutional context of IR studies in Aarhus.

IR at the Institute of Political Science in Aarhus

The Institute of Political Science in Aarhus is, with its enrolment of some 1,400 students and faculty of 55, among the largest political science institutes in Western Europe. It accepts students out of upper secondary school (gymnasium) and offers a full B.A., M.A., Ph.D. program.

There are two semesters per academic year; no classes are offered in July and August. The undergraduate course in IR occupies four weekly lecture-hours (over fifteen weeks) in the fourth semester. At graduate level, students will take at least two, often more, seminars specializing in chosen areas of IR. It can be anything from the Gulf crisis to Danish security policies or the debate over United States hegemony or EC-integration or the political economy of the Asian tigers or Japanese foreign policy or religion and international politics, etc. The graduate seminars are two hours per week in one semester, with a reading requirement of approx. 2,000 pages.

But the focus here is on the undergraduate course. It should be stressed that we are not free to organize this course in any way we want; there are serious resource limitations. What this means, for example, is that we cannot provide small-group teaching. There is a two-hour lecture per week given to all participants; approximately 240 students take the course each year. In addition, there is another two-hour weekly lecture offered to groups of 60 students. The course is concluded by a six hour written examination; the reading requirement for the course is about 1,000 pages.

The Undergraduate Course in IR: How and What

Two different analytical cuts are made in the lectures presented in the course. In the two-hour lecture offered to all participants the structure is according to levels: the level of actors, focusing on the identification of different actors and the formulation of foreign policy; the level of interaction, with a focus on international conflict, security, cooperation and international negotiations; and finally the system level, which concentrates on balance of power, interdependence, international organisation, and issues of global concern.

In the other two-hour lecture, the structure revolves around different main approaches or paradigms: realism, in classical and newer formulations, including the analysis of security complexes; globalism, basically covering world system perspectives, as well as dependency theory and theories of imperialism; and pluralism, which also covers international political economy, plus theories of integration with an emphasis on the current dynamics in Western Europe.

The ultimate objective is to integrate these two analytical cuts as we go along with a view to the overall aim: a comprehensive presentation of the analytical tools which the discipline provides students of world politics. And even if confusion can sometimes turn out to be our most important product, I do think that the students come out with a reasonably clear understanding, at least of the most significant theories and concepts of IR.

Several different textbooks have of course been tried over the years; the one currently in use is by Viotti and Kauppi.[1] It should be stressed that parts of the book are set for extensive voluntary reading. This is in order to make room for a broad selection of different articles, supplementing the presentation of core elements of the paradigms given by the textbook. Some of these supplementary texts come from Kegley and Wittkopf.[2] It will appear both from the structure of our course and the readings use that most of the inspiration for our teaching comes from Anglo-American sources. The students do read German, but with much more difficulty than English; French texts are only very rarely used at undergraduate level.

Having used Viotti and Kauppi for three years, we are currently considering newer textbooks; however, the students have been rather fond of the Viotti and Kauppi volume and so have we. Its great merit is the instructive presentation of three basic images or paradigms; it reveals very clearly how different approaches focus on different aspects of reality or come out with different interpretations of the same set of events.

But the strength of this approach is also a weakness; the danger is that too many theoretical undercurrents are lumped together in paradigmatic categories which then tend to become more confusing than illuminating. Take for example the image of pluralism; its core is the notion of complex interdependence as developed by Keohane and Nye. But in order to make the there-are-three-basic-paradigms-idea stick it is stretched to cover the world society approach of John Burton, international political economy in the vein of Gilpin, and the theories of integration. In the process, the intellectual roots of pluralism are presented as an amalgamation of liberalism, interest group liberalism, decision making, and transnationalism — a collection of parents who would have a hard time recognising their pluralist offspring as summarised by Viotti and Kauppi. I would have preferred a much more substantive and reasoned presentation of the core elements of each paradigm — the textbook spends only two or three pages on each outline of "major actors and assumptions" — together with a more discriminating approach towards the identification of intellectual precursors.

A good part of the problems that I here conveniently blame on the textbook are repeated in the classroom. I try to use three corrective measures. One of these is to demonstrate how different paradigms develop from their cores to cover issues and problem areas which are at the heart of other paradigms. It is clear, for example, that both pluralism and globalism or world systems analysis recognize the existence of anarchy as a basic condition of the system of states, even if they assign different roles and significance to it in their respective theoretical constructions. The second corrective measure involves emphasizing the degree to which theoretical sidecurrents can develop into main rivers of their own right — as in the case of pluralism in relation to interdependence, and world systems analysis in relation to dependency theory. The final measure consists of plainly admitting that some new approaches and theories fit in badly with existing main paradigms and will have to be in categories of their own. Post-modernism/structuralism and feminist approaches to IR are examples of this.

New Challenges I: Theories

As long as one keeps it open-ended, the competing-paradigm-perspective is well-suited for introducing new theories and approaches in the field. In many cases the problem of incorporating new thinking is where to stop. At one point IR merges into development theory; it is difficult to give a comprehensive introduction to dependency thinking without introducing the modernization paradigm, the ECLA school of Raul Prebisch and his colleagues, and even orthodox Communist thinking about Latin America. This is, of course, an entire exercise in itself. At another point IR merges into peace studies. The comprehensive concepts of peace and security are mandatory, but how much should one go into thinking on non-violence, Galtung's thinking on cosmologies, non-offensive defense thinking, conversion studies and the like?

I have no definite answer. Many other examples of relevant theoretical fields could be added to the few mentioned here. In the final analysis, we have limitations of time and space within which we give priority to those theories and approaches in the discipline which we find most significant.

This makes it crucially important to be aware of the underlying forces guiding our own choice of "significant" theories. There are three relevant elements involved here. The first is our own set of *theoretical assumptions*. They structure our perception and make us more or less sensitive to new theoretical proposals. It is not that a die-hard neo-realist, to give an example, will be blind to anything else; but, I venture that he or she will be more interested in, or open to, fresh theory which accepts basic realist assumptions than to that which does not.

The second important element is *events*. Current events, or concrete dynamics of world politics if you will, make us look in specific directions for new theories and approaches. Integration thinking is coming into vogue again because of the renewed dynamics in Western Europe; increasingly dangerous environment problems make us look for theories which takes these issues seriously; the peace movement and the women's movement have helped push IR-theorizing in new directions.

The third and perhaps most crucial element guiding our choice of theories is *values*: i.e. beliefs and convictions, political and others. For many years, the dominant value system gave only limited access for other ways of thinking. When I was an undergraduate student of IR twenty years ago, Marxist theories of imperialism and unequal development were kept hidden. Marxist inspired theorizing has recently gained more distinction both in international political economy and as part of globalist concerns. Perhaps the shutting out of Marxist thinking was always strongest in North America. In Western Europe, a more prominent role for Marxist ways of thinking was, already in the 1960s and 1970s, part of the reaction among European IR-researchers to the wisdom delivered to them from across the Atlantic.[3]

It is, incidentally, another feature of the West European scene that currently popular post-modern/structuralist endeavors of critically examining theoretical constructs and methodological underpinnings were also started in the 1960s and 1970s, as a part of the European reaction mentioned above.[4] Some contributions drew on the work of Jürgen Habermas and it was perhaps only to be expected that German scholars could have a 'postmodernist' debate about IR-theory based on the philosophical work of a fellow German some twenty years before that debate reached American shores.[5]

At the same time, I must confess, however, that post-modern/structuralist work plays a rather limited role in our undergraduate IR-course. I find many of the contributions destructive rather than constructive, strong in the critique of other approaches and theories, weaker in the formulation of alternative theoretical tools that could provide viable alternatives. Yet it is also clear that the majority of post-modern/structuralist contributions do not replace but, rather, supplement existing paradigms. Thus, postmodernist debates are hardly kept away from our undergraduates. Take for example this year's written exams in comparative politics which required the students to analyze an article by a Norwegian sociologist, Marit Wærness, "The New Germany — Modern or Postmodern," by reflecting on the distinction between modern and postmodern society in terms of its relevance to the former DDR and the Soviet Union.[6] Finally, we have also offered graduate seminars, specifically aimed at discussing post-modernist/structuralist approaches in terms of international relations.

Yet even if the 'post-modern' climate of today allows considerably larger space for theoretical innovation of all kinds, we should not be blind to the dominant value system — in our discipline I would call it Liberal-Realist — and the ways in which it influences our theoretical priorities.

I would like to mention two other types of contributions that I believe hold promise of inspiring our theoretical endeavors, in the classroom and elsewhere. The first group consists of the theories that focus on the environment and ecological concerns. This can have repercussions in many areas and stimulate rethinking of many of our traditional, almost sacred concepts. Take, for example, the argument by Patricia Mische[7] favoring an emphasis on ecological security, even to the point where ecological concerns make inroads on the sovereignty of states; or, the recent contribution by Matthias Finger which points to the fact that "the military has become a key polluter over the years,"[8] and further traces the relationship between the military and the environment. It is also interesting to see how at least one of the most recent IR-textbooks[9] gives very substantial space to approaches concerned with environmental issues.

The second group of contributions are of a more synthesizing nature, attempting to draw together our knowledge of international system dynamics with due respect for concrete historical development.[10] It is not that such contributions will eventually present us with any 'final' solutions to our theoretical problems; but, the mere attempt to draw our knowledge together in constructions that are sufficiently rich and dynamic to avoid leaving out most of the issues that we find important is a laudable enterprise.

I would also like to mention the theoretical legacy of Gramsci as a fruitful place to start when looking for rich and flexible paradigmatic constructs. I find it a pity that Gramsci's work is frequently reduced to a footnote (especially his concept of hegemony) because he attempted to formulate an approach combining economics, politics and ideology, domestic and international concerns, conflict and cooperation in a coherent, non-reductionist manner. But perhaps he is in for a well-deserved come-back.[11]

New Challenges II: Dynamics of World Politics

It is often current events in the world that constitute the most dynamic input to the teaching of IR. The changes in Europe since 1989 are, from a Danish perspective, of paramount importance and it is clear that some of the most heated debates in the classroom have concerned the consequences of these changes. In relation to an undergraduate course in IR, the most valuable text-basis for such debates are those scholarly contributions that formulate an argument on the basis of an application of a certain theoretical perspective. This has the advantage of seeing a theoretical perspective in concrete action, trying to grasp important current events, which in turn opens a clear view of the promise and limitations of the perspective in question. In these discussions, I normally play the role of the devil's advocate (until we get to the concluding stage, of course), defending the viewpoint of the text in question in opposition to the students' critique.

A good example is a contribution by John J. Mearsheimer on European security after the cold war.[12] Here we have a stern application of rigorous structural realism to current security problems in Europe. The students were flabbergasted by the recommendation that we hold on to the Cold War in order to save security and stability in Europe, or, even if this were not feasible, allow Germany to have nuclear weapons. It must be remembered that Germany has historically been the most important threat to the security of small-state Denmark. Even the early news of German reunification was met with some hesitance, both in the Danish population and in political circles, including the government. Yet the students rejected the more outrageous suggestions in Mearsheimer's analysis for two more solid reasons than historical fear of Germany. One was their knowledge of developments inside Germany, before and after reunification. It is not first and foremost that Germany has formally renounced nuclear weapons; rather, since the world war developments in Germany have gone from '*Machtbesessenheit*' ('obsession with power') towards '*Machtvergessenheit*' ('obliviousness to power'). This means a development from one extreme, where Germany was obsessed with securing its status as a strong military power, towards the opposite extreme, where Germany gives highest priority to European and international cooperation. In other words, Mearsheimer's analysis is too focused on structures and disregards the changes that have taken place in the actors, and thus is incomplete.

The other main reason for the students being sceptical towards Mearsheimer's analysis is their knowledge of other contributions which, while not rejecting realist insights, combine them with other theoretical perspectives that point in different directions. One interesting attempt is the scenarios for Europe outlined in Buzan, based on different combinations of 'power', 'fear', and 'interdependence' among the main actors, Europe, the Soviet Union and the United States.[13] Another is the analysis by Jack Snyder.[14]

It is clear that the Gulf war has also played a prominent role in discussions with the students. In fact, our last written exams required the students to apply realism and globalism respectively to the Gulf crisis and evaluate the explanatory and analytic power of the two perspectives. Most students gave priority to realism with globalism in a more humble role of grasping the North-South dimension of the crisis.[15] Current events in Europe and in the Gulf merge into the debate about a new world order that is taking place on both sides of the Atlantic. The debate provides another opportunity to examine the arguments set forth by different analytical perspectives and challenges students to formulate their own view.

A different aspect of European politics that generates discussion is the dynamics of the European Community integration process. Although ambivalence clearly remains, Danes have become more receptive to the idea of political and economic union. The end of the Cold War, German reunification, and the decision by Austria and Sweden (with Finland, Norway and others to follow) to apply for EC-membership has played an important role in this.

On the other hand, the precise content of both the economic and the political union remains undefined, in spite of much discussion and negotiation. The situation is a great challenge to students of integration. It is clearly inadequate simply to claim that the dynamic of European integration has picked up again from where it stopped in the seventies and early eighties. Therefore, it is also theoretically insufficient to recycle conventional, neo-functionalist, theories of integration. The current situation in Europe is characterized by two different, grand 'projects'. One is the construction of a new European peace and security order, the other European integration led by the European Community. They affect each other profoundly, but the precise ways in which this happens are not very clear. A fresh theory of integration must be able to analyze such processes. At a minimum, this means a higher awareness of domestic processes in single countries as determinants of national attitudes and policies towards integration, and also a higher awareness of the general international political and economic context in which attempts at integration take place.[16] Furthermore, a general theoretical framework for the study of integration must be able to allow both for periods of rapidly advancing integration and for periods of stagnation and setbacks. In the context of such a general framework it will then be possible to conceive middle-range theories directed at more specific problems. Previous theories of integration, functionalism, federalism, transaction analysis and neo-functionalism all have relevant insights to contribute to this endeavor, but it is also necessary to go beyond these earlier attempts.

The escalation of ethnic conflict, both in Europe and elsewhere is another important current issue. These events challenge the whole notion of the nation-state as well as the conventional distinction between domestic and international conflict. They are also tied in with the attempts to formulate a broader concept of security.[17] I believe all this will lead to a stronger emphasis on the notion of the region, and regional conflict and cooperation. In Europe there is a tendency towards increasing importance of events both 'below' (sub-national) and 'above' (supra-national or regional) the level of the nation-state. One way of emphasising the notion of region is through the study of regional security complexes, but this is only the beginning.[18] The regional perspective is well-suited for overcoming many of the problems posed by the traditional nation-state analytical straitjacket.

From a more general perspective, the process of integration in Europe holds new challenges for understanding and teaching world politics.[19] Between the nation state and the European Community, Europe is characterised by a situation of 'divided sovereignty': in some areas, the Community has taken over political functions that were earlier the prerogative of the nation state.[20] First, this is a challenge to the logic of anarchy, which is premised upon the notion of states' refusal to acknowledge any political authority higher than themselves. If integration proceeded swiftly, there would be no problem: a united Europe would be a new state, a unitary international actor. But the situation of divided sovereignty is likely to last for quite some time. In the area of foreign policy, moreover, the situation is particularly confusing, because leading Community members agree on common policies and formulate their own postures simultaneously.[21] Second, this adds to the complexities in understanding the relationships between economics and politics. I have argued elsewhere that we are far away from a comprehensive understanding of this relationship in international relations.[22] The European Community adds a new dimension to the puzzle, because forces of economic cooperation and liberalization interact with the security issues of high politics in the process of integration.[23] Finally, there is increasing debate about the effects on democracy and democratization. On the one hand, increasing cooperation helps spread democracy to parts of Europe with weak democratic traditions. On the other hand, members of the Community experience the transfer of an increasing number of decisions from national, democratic bodies, to organs at the Community level that are either not democratically elected (the Commission) or where debates take place without public scrutiny (the Council of Ministers). Consequently there is, for good reasons, talk about an increasing 'democratic deficit' in the Community.

The Danish Angle

When looking at the way our IR course is structured and the reading materials we use, it might appear that we have forgotten the Danish angle; could such a course not be taught in many other places in world? To some extent that is indeed the case. The general introduction of significant paradigms, theories and concepts is a common baggage. It is true that some theories and approaches are designed much more with great-power United States in mind than small-state Denmark, but this does not render them irrelevant for Danes. We are as painfully aware as everybody else of the decisive role played by the United States in the international system.

At the same time, there are a number of differences that indicate that the students are sitting in Denmark and not in Wisconsin or elsewhere. In their undergraduate work, the students receive a comprehensive introduction to all important aspects of the Danish political (and economic) system, including the areas of international political and economic relations, and Danish foreign policy. Moreover, there is always a selection of graduate seminars on offer that emphasize various aspects of Danish international relations. In more general terms, the Danish IR scholars are very much part of the Anglo-American mainstream of the discipline. But I do not think there is much cultural dominance in this. I rather see the Danish position as situated at a productive intellectual intersection, capable of picking up ideas and inspiration, not only from the Anglo-American scene, but also from German and French milieux. Yet it should also be said that both German and French scholars increasingly declare that they have to write in English in order to get a voice in the international scholarly debate. For Danish scholars, this has been the case all along.

There is one aspect tied in with the small-state status that is worth mentioning in this context. It concerns the fact that it is never difficult to get students interested in international relations. They speak several foreign languages and many of them have travelled extensively both in

Europe and other parts of the world. Most importantly, they are critically conscious of the importance of events outside Denmark for their own future and the situation for Danish society. To this should be added a keen interest among many students, both in international developments in general, and in the problems facing countries in the Third World.

This does not mean that the students are always entirely happy with the menu we serve. They would like more time for discussion, preferably in classes much smaller than 60 or 240 people, instead of sitting much of the time at the receiving end of a lecture. Students also sometimes complain about conceptual overload and it is hard to disagree completely with that. Finally, they would like to have more chances of trying out their abilities in the form of shorter term papers before they have to go to the final exam. Given scarce resources, some of these problems are difficult to avoid entirely. At the same time, the vast majority of students agree - and so do I - that the crucial factor in a good course has less to do with these elements; the crucial factor remains the enthusiasm and commitment of the teacher.

Notes

I am grateful to colleagues at the IR-department of my Institute and especially to Lev S. Gonick for a number of comments to an earlier version of this article.

1. Paul R. Viotti and Mark V. Kauppi, *International Relations Theory: Realism, Pluralism, Globalism* (London & New York: Macmillan, 1987).

2. Charles W. Kegley Jr. and Eugene R. Wittkopf, *The Global Agenda. Issues and Perspectives* (Englewood Cliffs NJ: Prentice Hall, 1988).

3. See for example the books by Ekkehart Krippendorff, *Internationales System als Geschichte: Einführung in die internationalen Beziehungen 1* (Frankfurt: Campus Verlag, 1975) and *Internationale Beziehungen als Wissenschaft: Einführung 2* (Frankfurt: Campus Verlag, 1977).

4. See, for example, Wolfgang Hein und Georg Simonis, "Theoretische und Metodische Probleme einer kritischen Theorie in internationaler Politik," *Politische Vierteljahresschrift*, 14 (1973), pp. 85-106; Georg Simonis, *Aussenpolitik und Abschreckung: Ansätze zu einer kritischen Theorie des internationalen Systems* (Frankfurt: Campus Verlag, 1977); Kurt Tudyka, *Wandel des Erkenntnisinteresses an den Internationalen Beziehungen* (Nijmegen, 1972).

5. Jürgen Habermas, *Technik und Wissenschaft als "Ideologie"* (Frankfurt, 1968).

6. Marit Wærness, "Det nye Tyskland - moderne eller postmoderne?," *Samtiden*, 1 (1991), pp. 23-29.

7. Patricia M. Mische, "Ecological Security and the Need to Reconceptualize Sovereignty," *Alternatives*, XIV (October, 1989), pp. 389-429.

8. Matthias Finger, "The Global Environmental Crisis and the Social Implications of Delaying Action: The Example of the Military," Paper for the 23rd Annual Convention of ISA, Vancouver, March 20-23, 1991, Panel B-3, p. 2.

9. Barry Hughes, *Continuity and Change in World Politics: The Clash of Perspectives* (Englewood Cliffs NJ: Prentice Hall, 1991).

10. A prominent example is the "Dialectics of World Order" project by Hayward Alker, Tahir Amin, Tom Biersteker and Takashi Inoguchi, which explicitly looks for "*convergent* interpretations, or feasible syntheses, among empirically observable, normatively articulated, *divergent* world ordering theories and practices"; see: Hayward Alker, "World Ordering Alternatives," paper for the 23rd Annual Convention of ISA, Vancouver, March 20-23, 1991, p. 9. Some of my own undertaking works in a similar direction, even if my emphasis is more directly on theoretical synthesis; see: Georg Sørensen, "A Revised Paradigm for International Relations: The 'Old' Images and the Post-modernist Challenge," *Cooperation and Conflict* XXVI (1991) pp. 85-116.

11. See the recent volume edited by Stephen Gill, *Gramsci and International Relations* (New York: Colombia University Press, 1991).

12. John J. Mearsheimer, "Back to the Future: Instability in Europe after the Cold War," *International Security*, 15 (Summer, 1990), pp. 5-56.

13. Barry Buzan et al., *The European Security Order Recast: Scenarios for the Post-Cold War Era* (London and New York: Pinter Publishers, 1990).

14. Jack Snyder, "Averting Anarchy in the New Europe," *International Security*, 14, (Spring, 1990), pp. 5-41.

15. A recent contribution by Wallerstein has many of the same qualities that were emphasised about Mearsheimer's article: a 'clean' application of a defined theoretical perspective, this time Wallerstein's world system perspective applied to the Gulf crisis, setting it in the larger perspective of the end of the cold war and the prospects for the Third World. I have not yet had the opportunity to use it in the classroom, but it definitely provides the basis for a fruitful discussion. Again, one may agree or not with the arguments set forth; the important thing is the demonstration of the potential and limitations of the perspective in concrete application. See Immanuel Wallerstein, "The Cold War and the Third World. The Good Old Days?," *Economic and Political Weekly*, 27 April 1991, pp. 1103-7.

16. See: Morten Kelstrup, "Politologisk integrationsteogi og den ny dynamik i Vest-og Østeuropa," in Morten Kelstrup, red., *Tendenser i politologien III. Bidrag til studiet af international politik og den ny europæiske udvikling* (København: Forlaget Politiske Studier, 1990). See also Jens Henrik Haarh, "Regional Integration Theory: Contents and Current Relevance," (Mimeo, Aarhus: Institute of Political Science, 1991).

17. Barry Buzan, *People, States and Fear. The National Security Problem in International Relations* (Brighton: Wheatsheaf, 1983).

18. See: Buzan et al., *The European Security Order Recast*.

19. What follows is inspired by Morten Kelstrup, "Studiet af vesteuropæisk integration. Tilgange og resultater," (mimeo, Aarhus: Institute of Political Science, 1991).

20. That is, functions concerning the authoritative allocation of values for the member states.

21. As has been demonstrated both during the Gulf war and in the Yugoslav crisis.

22. Georg Sørensen, "Economics and Politics in International Relations," (mimeo, Aarhus: Institute of Political Science, 1991).

23. See: Jens Henrik Haahr, "Looking to Europe. European Integration and Social Democracy: The Case of Britain and Denmark. Outline of a Research Project," (mimeo, Aarhus: Institute of Political Science, 1991).

8

Peace as Pedagogy: The Challenge of Sorting Fundamental from Transitory Aspects of International Politics

Frederic S. Pearson and Simon Payaslian

Contrary to conventional accusations that Peace Studies is mere flirtation with dogmatic pacifism removed from the realities of global power struggles, the pedagogical foundations of peace encompass a whole range of issues requiring more systematic investigations in classrooms as well as in government. The primary difference between the traditional school of *Realpolitik* and Peace Studies is that the latter believes war is conquerable through education for peace.[1] Traditional and more recent approaches to peace, as taught in World Politics courses and actually practised in world politics, have included such strategies as collective security, diplomacy, disarmament, arms control, confidence building, conflict resolution, adjudication, and mediation. Concomitantly, since its inception at Manchester College in 1948,[2] the field of Peace Studies has evolved from analyses of specific conflicts such as the Korean and Vietnam Wars in the 1960s and 1970s, to treatment of more general phenomena, including not only deterrence, arms races, arms transfers and variants of conflict resolution at the global level, and interpersonal relations, dispute resolution, and mediation at the local or micro level.[3]

Peace Studies and Social Sciences

During the 'behavioral revolution' in the social sciences, critical thinking to question myths, clarify values, define measure concepts, and specify alternative explanations and theories for political phenomena became central to the role of teachers of World Politics, Security, and

Peace Studies. The behavioral revolution and the subsequent proliferation and predominance of social science methods elevated our modes and criteria of analyses, although admittedly it did not consistently generate the broad theoretical generalizations promised. Nevertheless we are now in a position to employ the insights gained from our research and findings for pedagogical purposes in education for peace. The study of World Politics in general and Peace Studies in particular thus fits into a larger academic framework of teaching students to answer questions for themselves by considering rival perspectives, contrary hypotheses, opposing historical interpretations, and alternative policy choices.

The need to focus on such objectives is even more pronounced today when various 'lessons' suggest that traditional approaches to teaching World Politics are too confined to certain concepts and assumptions about the 'game of nations'. Most realists and behavioralists, for example, assume that the game was about the struggle for power or influence among national actors, and that the basic political struggle is over the 'authoritative allocation of values' in a context of semi-anarchism. More recently, new debates have emerged involving movements to modify or abandon traditional perspectives. The neo-realists have incorporated concepts such as political economy and global structural hegemonies into their analyses of the pursuit of state power.[4] Others, such as feminists, environmentalists, and Marxists, have argued that the game itself is not a natural order of competition or social organization, but an artifact of a white-male dominated Western political tradition.[5] Implications of the latter view are that priority should be given to the transformation of such artifacts to less competitive and destructive values rather than mere understanding of how these processes work.

There are, of course, elements of continuity in all this, and Peace Studies, developed as a particular academic discipline in reaction to the experience of both World Wars, is both an amalgamation of and a point of convergence for these movements. Concerned with the proliferation of technologies of mass destruction, human savagery, sufferings, and injustices as well as the numerous international wars and militarized conflicts throughout the twentieth century,[6] it focuses on teaching approaches to conflict resolution at different levels of human interaction (for example, mediation) from the international level to the familial.[7]

By its very interdisciplinary nature, Peace Studies in the 1990s contributes to teaching on a variety of subjects, including: the traditional subjects of Political Science proper, such as the periodic reemergence of ambitious and ruthless leaders; continued tension between law and force; the legacy of imperialism and colonialism, with the consequent troubling status of ethnic minorities and nationalities (for example, Amer-Indians, Armenians, Irish, Kashmiris, Kurds, Palestinians, Quebecois, Tamils, and so forth); as well as such 'alternative security policy' issues as ecological and economic conditions involving reliable daily sustenance, shelter, pollution, climatic changes, ozone depletion, and the psychological, religious, interpersonal and intercultural dimensions of peace.[8] Above all, then, Peace Studies is premised upon the assumption that there is also the possibility of learning the habits and expectations of peaceful resolution of these issues and disputes.

Peace Studies in a Changing Global System

It could be argued that potentially none of the shifts in political relationships, experienced during the late 1980s and early 1990s (for example, the collapse of the Soviet Union and the end of the Cold War) has invalidated the fundamental forces inherent in the nation-state system — forces of competition for power and influence. In world politics as in interpersonal relations, people as well as countries tend to gravitate toward the politically and economically more powerful (for example, southeast Asia toward Japan and China, Eastern Europe toward Germany and Russia). Yet, in the twentieth century, especially since the Second World War, we have also witnessed the emergence of regional and universal functionally integrative structures, "international regimes," and developing norms that transcend geopolitical boundaries and undermine the 'logic of Westphalia'.[9] The present challenge in teaching World Politics and Peace Studies is to reconcile these two political realities.

The European Community best exemplifies this approach to world peace and order. Its philosophical development over the centuries and the actual institutional development and maturity since the 1950s indicate that the institutionalization of peaceful settlement on a permanent basis is at least as possible as the institutionalization of military-industrial complexes. Although by no means a foolproof defense against violence (as the resurgence of xenophobia and extreme nationalism demonstrates), a changed set of expectations have emerged regarding 'proper' behavior in the Community. Such international functional arrangements can work so long as the benefits of membership, especially on the economic side, are commensurate with expectations.

Peace Studies: Teachers and Students

As an additional challenge confronting the teacher, both traditional and new approaches to World Politics and Peace Studies have assumed that our students are well-equipped to understand the significance and complexities of the issues involved. Teaching these courses, however, has become especially daunting, at least in the United States, because so many students are ill-prepared even for introductory work; they tend to know and care all too little about remote areas and peoples. American secondary schools, for example, even when they cover world history, often do so as part of Western Civilization. Their textbooks are woefully lacking in coverage of Afro-Asia and Latin America. Further, the study of foreign languages in American high schools has dwindled tragically.

Unfortunately, as preparation has slipped, the need for students to think critically about the world around them, and about the interpretations analysts and national leaders put upon "events," has risen in conjunction with citizen responsibilities to evaluate alternative policies and their outcomes for human life in various parts of the world (note the efforts to equip East European citizens for democratic decision-making). Among other pressures, the struggle of many countries for a share of the global marketplace and growing ethnic diversity require the teacher to guide students through the maze of history and research literature about the settlement of disputes at different levels of analysis.

The challenge, then, is to impart basic concepts of world politics and analysis in a comprehensible and realistic fashion to students, along with a sense of individual and collective confidence that power and struggle can be both understood and managed. David Barash poses a controversial assessment and challenge: "Our situation — whether to be at peace or at war," he writes, "is ours to decide."[10] The contemporary system's transformation and continuities have heightened both the importance and potential of this educational agenda by affording teachers the opportunity to link concepts ever more clearly to outcomes and consequences. Teachers must take advantage of this era of transformations to ask whether a decentralized world system will produce greater periods of peace. Students should be challenged to determine when and under what circumstances Barash's assertion is true, and when, on the other hand, large forces inflict war on people.

To find answers, it is incumbent upon the pedagogy of peace science to address in great detail a wide range of questions. What aspects of the international system have change, and with what effects? Is the rise and decline of bipolarity likely to increase 'peace', 'stability', or 'equity'? Is global or regional hegemony either desirable or possible? Is there a fatal clash between the idea of global order and regional autonomy? Did deterrence or some structural or economic factor (for example, division of Germany or Franco-German interdependence) account for 45 years of peace in Europe? Do individual leaders (Gorbachev, Saddam, de Gaulle, Thatcher, Mao) make a greater difference for peace than the roles and environments within which they operate? Can the paradox of having to fight to preserve peace under collective security regimes be overcome? Does the potential for planetary environmental disaster invalidate the quest for power, dominance, and prestige that has exemplified world politics for ages? What are the implications of redefining 'security' from political to physical survival, and of economic exhaustion for arms races inherent in the dilemma of finding security? Under what circumstances can or should the international arms trade be limited?

If students cannot now be made interested in and qualified to tackle these vital questions, then we will have abjectly failed as teachers, since the link between concepts and headlines has never been more sharply defined. From the perspective of peace pedagogy, students' intellectual and career development in a setting unencumbered by international and domestic violence is an investment in their own careers and hence a more reason to be interested in a peaceful world.

It is also worth noting that while some have heralded the 'end of the cold war' as a completely new era, even an 'end of history' in the 'victory of capitalism', very old policies and crusades have reemerged: arms races, ethnic rivalries, quests for dominance, trade disputes, regional alignments, and security pacts. Capitalist, as well as socialist, economies are struggling. We must, therefore, acquaint our students with the abiding aspects of domestic and international politics, and help them sort these from transitory, albeit important, structural and policy transformations. In the process, it is to be hoped that our students will be able to draw conclusions about their proper role as citizens, their careers, and their country as interventionist, hegemon, conciliator, or benefactor.

Pedagogical Objectives: Reading Scripts

Overall, then, as mentioned in an earlier study, teachers of Peace Studies must pursue four inter-connected objectives, equipping students to: 1) think critically and examine conceptions of morality and values as related to war and peace in world politics; 2) conceptualize clearly and measure concepts; 3) test generalizations and assertions empirically, offering evidence for conclusions, and assessing the implications of their findings for the future of the world system; and 4) develop theories that explain, predict, and perhaps even rectify international behavior and policies in order to maximize the potential for peace rather than war, and prosperity rather than poverty.[11]

Presumably, students would be brought along gradually and sequentially in building such analytical skills, beginning with exposition of myths and beliefs, practise in comparison and contrast, enunciation of alternate perspectives based on the study of history, economics, and geography, and proceeding through familiarity with concepts useful in understanding political behavior. In advanced work, explanatory or predictive models of such behavior, policy choices, and outcomes would be examined and developed.

While these remain valid aspirations inherent in the intellectual enterprise, they need to be supplemented with an appreciation that behavior is contextual, conforming in a sense to dramas or scripts defined for political need.[12] Scripts calling for Franco-German or U.S.-Soviet or Arab-Israeli rivalry will produce concepts and even law-like theories (such as those concerning 'balance of power') enunciated on the stage set by the political script. Different scripts and different stages can lead to different useful concepts and theories. As part of their critical thinking, students must be able to read and interpret the scripts, to analyze them for dominant themes, to understand when scripts change (à la Gorbachev, for example), and to see some of the 'laws' of behavior within scripts as potentially transient.

If the international system is evolving toward a 'New World Order', a new script, so to speak, new or revisited theories of governance, become relevant. As in all developing polities, here too the pursuit of *liberty* will come into conflict with the pursuit of *order*, and students of Peace Studies must be trained to distinguish between those trade offs that promote peace and others that provoke war, even with the best of intentions (revisiting the concept of appeasement, for example).[13] We cannot escape the main issues of politics; they present themselves over and over in local as well as global settings. It is the teacher's responsibility to enable students to grapple with these fundamental issues even as they are distracted by the transient structures and paradigms of the day. For example, nuclear deterrence theory, developed in the context of the U.S.-Soviet conflict *cum* morality play, may have renewed but modified relevance to the India-Pakistan context, as the two regional rivals pledge not to attack each other's nuclear facilities. Also, as the aftermath of the Gulf Crisis has shown, it is easy to overlook the fact that war itself is a political, and not just a military script.

The realities about which we teach and the concepts and theories we propose to discuss are extremely complicated and necessarily cosmopolitan. We must somehow make the intricacies of international finance and trade, international conflict, war and peace, comprehensible even to those students essentially illiterate in foreign cultures, languages, and psychology. The predominance of the power paradigm in our analysis does not help this endeavor, since it has left relatively little room for curiosity about the 'powerless', for example, the masses of Africa, Asia, and Latin America. Yet, of course, it is among the relatively powerless that many of the abiding social and political problems conditioning international relations as well as most of today's wars reside.

Within this context, such critical subjects as nuclear and conventional deterrence, arms control, disarmament, 'low-intensity' warfare, terrorism, and conflict resolution, to name but a few, undergirding the pedagogy of peace must be taught. For in order to understand and believe in prospects for peace, students not only must be able to grapple with traditional abstractions of 'power', 'power struggles', and 'balance of power', but they must also be able to sort out the stratified layers of international influence and decision-making, as with the tripartite (North America, Europe, Pacific rim) OECD dominance at the apex, and the regional upheavals of the Middle East, Southwest and Southeast Asia, and Sub-Saharan Africa, along with economic privation and frustration below. In one sense, these constitute distinct and largely separate realms; in another sense, however, they are intimately interconnected worlds (the availability of key resources being only one such connection). Students' familiarity with and understanding of the nature of such world-systemic, structural arrangements and the threat the latter pose to world peace might enable our "best and brightest" to do better than their 1960s predecessors in eliminating the sources of what Johan Galtung has called "structural violence"[14] and arrive at a more just world order.[15] That some American officials in the post Cold-War era evidently aspire to prevent the emergence of any new rival superpower shows how persistent the misreading of historical trends can be.

As noted earlier, in posing these complexities, the teacher therefore must also encourage students to distinguish long-term from short-term trends, secular vectors from perturbations. Of course, such distinctions elude even the seasoned researcher or policy analyst, but we can at least begin by guiding students in analyzing relatively long periods of time, detecting the direction or cyclical nature of social developments and missed opportunities for peaceful resolutions of conflicts throughout 'long cycles'. Thus, perhaps it is fortunate that interest in long cycles has reemerged after the early efforts of Toynbee and others, not so much for the validity of such analyses *per se* but for the encouragement they give to longitudinal approaches desperately needed in Peace Studies.[16] There is no inevitability to history that we know of, but major social forces have produced repeated revolutions (French, Soviet, Chinese, Iranian) with similar antecedents and consequences (war, reaction, terror, and so on). Knowing this, students might be less tempted than some of their learned instructors to think in such apocalyptical terms as the 'end of history' when in fact the international system is merely changing. Construed as systemic transformations rather than culminations, students might realize that with every such change comes an opportunity, a new global-psychological environment conducive to the construction of new and more peaceful scripts. Indeed those witnessing the end of the Second World War seemed to have a better sense for such opportunity than those agonizing for a response to the Soviet decline of the late 1980s.

Conclusion

It is a basic and somewhat simple plea we make, then, for our students to be more seasoned and sophisticated about international developments, to see and gauge underlying trends and forces (for example, the abiding influence of nationalism). Some students will pursue careers wholly removed from this form of study, and will need this seasoning mainly to be more responsible newspaper readers and voters. Others will become journalists, analysts, teachers, and business, legal, or diplomatic professionals. They may require more specific skills, but no less seasoning. And we cannot ignore adult education as a refresher for those already in public life, a means of coming to terms with debates about world order, security, welfare, ecology, and human rights.

To equip students for international life and peace in the 1990s and beyond, we must include the conceptual fundamentals as noted, and where necessary add supplementary materials in history, ethnic studies, and economics so that graduates can deal with variants of international politics, political economy, political psychology, regional studies, and so forth. Students will also be required to review the literature on international ecology and demographics, sources of international conflict and cooperation, and alternative conceptions of global order and the viability of the nation-state system given the integrative and disintegrative forces at play. The study of war and peace must inevitably entail the study of justice and equity as both concepts and issues in world affairs.

Finally, it seems clear that we are not now doing a good enough job of exciting undergraduates and even graduate students to spread international awareness and understanding widely in our communities. In view of varied student aspirations, we might begin to structure our advanced classes in World Politics and Peace Studies along more flexible lines, allowing students to pursue projects — whether research, journalistic, or policy-analytic — attuned to the types of careers they envision. Prospective teachers, for example, might be encouraged early on to develop lesson plans incorporating global studies or intercultural education so that they in turn begin to translate these notions for their students and in doing so engender greater awareness of and confidence in dealing with the possibility and difficulties of peace.

Notes

1. See, for example: Harry B. Hollins, Averill L. Powers, and Mark Sommers, *The Conquest of War* (Boulder CO: Westview Press, 1989); Kenneth E. Boulding, "Stable Peace Among Nations: A Learning Peace," and Vicenc Fisas Armengol, "Ten Bases for a Culture of Peace," in *Peace Culture and Society: Transnational Research and Dialogue* (Boulder CO: Westview Press, 1991); the special issues entitled "The Pedagogy of Peace," *Peace & Change* 15, no. 3 (July 1990); and "Peace Studies: Past and Future," *The Annals of the American Academy of Political and Social Sciences* 504 (July 1989).

2. Mike Forrest Keen, "Introduction: Peace Studies and the Pedagogy of Peace," *Peace & Change* 15, no. 3 (July 1990), pp. 219-222.

3. *Ibid*, p. 220.

4. See Ole R. Holsti, Randolph M. Siverson, and Alexander L. George, *Change in the International System* (Boulder CO: Westview Press, 1980); Robert O. Keohane, *After Hegemony: Cooperation and Discord in the World Political Economy* (Princeton NJ: Princeton University Press, 1984); Robert O. Keohane, ed., *Neorealism and Its Critics* (New York: Columbia University Press, 1986); and Robert Gilpin, *War and Change in World Politics* (New York: Cambridge University Press, 1981).

5. See, for example, John Searle, "The Storm over the University," *New York Review of Books* (6 December 1990), pp. 35-43; Immanuel Wallerstein, *The Capitalist World Economy* (Cambridge: Cambridge University Press, 1979).

6. April Carter, *Peace Movements* (New York: Longman, 1992).

7. Chris Mitchell, "Mediation," in Paul Smoker, Ruth Davies, and Barbara Munski, eds., *A Reader in Peace Studies* (Oxford: Pergamon Press, 1990), pp. 26-32; Thomas Keefe and Ron Roberts, *Realizing Peace: An Introduction to Peace Studies* (Ames: Iowa State University Press, 1991), especially Chapters 12-15.

8. Robert N. Irwin, *Building a Peace System: Exploratory Project on the Conditions of Peace* (Washington DC: ExPro Press, 1989), pp. 63; 77-85, *passim*.

9. Stephen D. Krasner, ed., *International Regimes* (Ithaca NY: Cornell University Press, 1983); Richard Falk, *A Study of Future Worlds* (New York: Free Press, 1975); and his *Human Rights and State Sovereignty* (New York: Holmes and Meier Publishers, 1981).

10. David P. Barash, *Introduction to Peace Studies* (Belmont: Wadsworth Publishing Company, 1991), p. 25.

11. Frederic S. Pearson, "The Educational Objectives of International Relations Texts," *Teaching Political Science* 1 (April 1974), pp. 169-201.

12. Michael G. Dillon, "Policy and Dramaturgy: A Critique of Current Conceptions of Policymaking," *Policy and Politics* 5 (1976); and *Britain and the Falklands: From Peace to War in Defence Policymaking* (London: Macmillan, 1986).

13. See, for example, Melvin Small and Otto Feinstein, eds., *Appeasing Fascism* (Lanham: University Press of America, 1991).

14. Johan Galtung, "Violence, Peace, and Peace Research," *Journal of Peace Research* 6 (1969), pp. 167-191; and "A Structural Theory of Imperialism," *Journal of Peace Research* 8 (1971), pp. 81-117.

15. Samuel S. Kim, *The Quest for a Just World Order* (Boulder CO: Westview Press, 1984).

16. See, for example, George Modelski, ed., *Exploring Long Cycles* (Boulder CO: Lynn Rienner, 1987).

PART THREE

Classroom Pedagogics

9

Teaching World Politics (as Well as Teaching for It)

Ralph Pettman

I have long been of the opinion that you can't teach anybody anything. It is possible, however, to create opportunities for others to learn.

This is not just a play on words. The educative process, as I understand it, entails meeting students at the point they begin whatever course is being taught and then leading them out into some more knowledgeable domain. Students can, of course, be led 'from without'. They can be drilled in the body of information and the analytic techniques believed to be beneficial. Their short-term memories, and hopefully their longer-term ones as well, can be stuffed with the 'facts' and frameworks that will serve them (in the teacher's humble view) in the very best stead. They can also, however, be led 'from within', and allowed to explore the subject for themselves. Doing so means offering them the tools the teacher believes they need. The teacher is then more of a resource-person than someone who prescribes and predetermines what is to be known.

I favor the latter approach since every student is different, having had different life experiences and having typically taken prerequisite courses that sometimes relate to teaching for world affairs but often do not. Leading 'from within' allows me to account for these individual differences between students while still making available the data and the analytic advice I think will be most helpful to them. Some, of course, will not take up the offers I make in this regard and the resources I provide, or they will take them up only selectively. But these students tend to be the most resistant to teacherly, top-down, chalk-and-talk drilling techniques too.

Students know different things, in other words, and some of these things will be of relevance to the course. Creating opportunities for students to learn in a less formal, more open-ended way means as far as possible tailoring the course to the individuals in it by providing learning experiences that are relevant to each person. This means (while remaining always mindful of your ultimate objectives) providing the opportunity for students to take the steps that are most appropriate for them.

These opportunities can be impoverished ones. You can, as I have hinted, use assessment systems and the desire for academic credentials to make students learn the historical information and the analytic organizing devices you think provide the best basis for discussing the subject. This is a time-honoured system and the easiest to use given contemporary institutional expectations and the large numbers that crowd the modern-day classroom. It is, though, far from the best we can do.

In my experience, good teachers start with each student, to try and discern what the individual student knows and feels. This opens the way for each student to develop his or her own learning process.

This may require more personalized tuition than usual, and given the pressure of student numbers, it may only be practicable as one element in a more conventional approach that leads 'from without'. Most academic institutions, for example, require you to give a course of set lectures. Now, all the educational research literature I know is pretty scathing about lectures and what they can achieve.[1] While lectures may impart much useful information they are no better than alternative ways of doing so, and they are notably less successful than alternative teaching techniques for changing attitudes or teaching students to think. Given that the adult attention span is only twenty minutes at best and most lectures are scheduled to run for fifty minutes or so, we also have the mental problem of people cutting in and out once their capacity to concentrate peters out. Nonetheless we grind on giving lecture after lecture, and though we can all recall favorite lecturers who kindled our interest in particular subjects or who were particularly engaging in some way, it is the interest or the engaging manner that we remember rather than what they said. So given that we are obliged to use such an imperfect pedagogic instrument, how can we make the best of it?

One way seems to me to give a short series of context-setting lectures at the start — a series which is non-negotiable — and then to allow the students themselves to determine, within the terms of reference set by the course title, the subject matter of the rest. This can be done at the very beginning by holding a class 'brain-storm' and noting down what the class decides. By weaving the various ideas the class comes up with into a coherent program (that follows on from the introductory lectures) you get a course that is relevant to student concerns. By formulating the program yourself you also get to weave in your own ideas as well.

The brainstorm can be done towards the end of the introductory lecture series as well, when students have a better idea of the scope of the course. I have used both methods with success. At very least students come to feel they 'own' the course having had the chance, however limited, to craft its content. At best students are encouraged to consider what the course is about and to take some responsibility for their own learning.

Another way of coping with the conventional pedagogic expectations of universities and of students themselves is to require students to set their own essay topics. I regularly do this, naming a date well in advance of the essay submission deadline by which students have to give me a specific essay title to endorse. Many find this a daunting task. They are used to having all this done for them. Lecturers commonly provide lists of essay topics from which to choose, and students do as they are bid and make their selection. As a consequence, however, they get no practise in thinking of a topic of interest to themselves or in translating general issues of personal interest into viable research proposals.

I was the end-product of such a system myself. I remember reading at random for six months in a blind panic trying to formulate a research topic for my doctoral thesis, a task for which my undergraduate training had left me utterly unprepared. It was a terrifying time. It was only much later that I realized how much I was not to blame; how much, that is, the fault lay with an educational system that had systematically failed to foster my intellectual confidence and creative autonomy.

Many students feel the same panic faced with the task of formulating their own essay topic. As a consequence I always tell them not to worry. I encourage them to come and talk about even the vaguest notion they may have of what they want to do. I invariably find that within five minutes I can bring that notion into focus and formulate a specific question for them to answer. The conversation we have provides practise for them in articulating their thoughts and they can see for themselves how the process of specification works.

Even with large classes this is not an unduly onerous task. It can also be great fun. Some students will have a clear notion of what they want to do and won't need this kind of help. At most they might seek some bibliographic assistance. For the rest, however, it is a chance to meet their instructor personally and to explore together what they find interesting.

There are many beneficial spin-offs. I always learn something in the process about what attracts students to my courses in the first place. The diversity of the work I ultimately have to mark is also considerable, which from my point of view makes the marking task much more interesting.

It also relieves the pressure on limited library resources. Furthermore the average class will often throw up a number of ingenious topics that I would never have thought of myself, which extends my own understanding of the subject. My students, in this respect among many, have much to teach me.

Both course-setting and essay-setting are predicated upon a 'hologramatic' conception of world politics. By this I mean that everything about world affairs is connected to everything else, and that a fuzzy representation of the whole subject is apparent in any particular part of it. Accepting this assumption means it does not matter where a student starts studying the subject, since the systematic appraisal of any specific aspect or issue will lead to all the rest. Likewise a lecture program that is not structured in a developmental sequence, of the kind that a class may come up with given the chance to participate in what they study, can still be used to explicate basic principles and processes. That the explication occurs in a non-linear way does not mean students don't end up understanding the how and why of world affairs.

Context-setting lectures are crucial in this regard since it is these lectures that provide the reference points to which you can return throughout the course, and that can be used to orient student readings of particular aspects and issues. In this regard I always depict myself as something of a map-maker. Since courses are rarely long enough to develop a comprehensive account of world politics in any detail, the maps I draw are rather crude ones. They are more akin to those early explorers made as they searched, for example, for the source of the Nile; they are not like those found in a good contemporary atlas.

Explorer's maps show the major features of the landscape as these are experienced on the ground. They are rather different from the sort of maps drawn with the God's-eye clarity of satellite photos from space, even assuming such a God's-eye view is possible in doing social science (which is an assumption many contemporary theorists now reject). The latter show no hand-etched chains of little mountains made of marble or alabaster, no dotted lines that represent the caravan routes from the Sudan to the Niger, no hand-written notes that say 'here is good water' or 'here is bad water' or 'here my camels died with cold' or "here is the 'simoome', or poisonous wind of the desert." The former are no less useful as a consequence. With some suitable up-dating you could still use them to get around. They are certainly more evocative of time and place.

In this context-setting regard, I also depict world politics in terms of three basic domains — a politico-strategic, a politico-economic, and a politico-social one.[2] The politico-strategic domain is the conventional account of the subject. It talks of state-making and the interstate system, and it does so in terms of national interest defined by the global competition for power. The realist (Hobbesian), rationalist (Grotian) or revolutionist (Kantian) readings usually attempted here all see strategic capacity and the balance of power (in the limited, martial, sense) as a key concern, whether that power be used to promote and protect territorial sovereignty or to underwrite inter-state cooperation.[3]

State-making and the interstate system are embedded, however, in a politico-economic domain of wealth-making, markets, and modes of production that condition, even determine what goes on there. The history of state-making and the state system cannot be told without telling that of capitalist industrialisation as well.

However, the story of capitalist industrialization is not a singular one. The details of any analytic narrative of it will depend upon the ideological perspective employed. The neo-mercantilist, the classical and neo-liberal, and the classical and neo-Marxist readings of this history diverge sharply. All attempt, however, to account for the balance of productivity that complements the strategic balance of power.

The balance of productivity refers to the struggle for material preponderance in the world. Like the strategic balance of power the balance of productivity is a highly uneven affair prosecuted (depending upon one's ideological perspective) by state-makers, by individual or corporate entrepreneurs, or by socio-economic classes (that is, by owners of capital versus wage laborers) defined in terms of modes of production.

The politico-economic domain is embedded in turn in a politico-social one. It is here that all those marginalized by the world's state-making and wealth-making live. Whether they be women, progressively 'housewifized' on a global scale as 'development' proceeds apace; street-dwellers in Los Angeles or slum-dwellers in Lima; environmentalists or indigenous peoples or peace activists or one of the many spiritual casualties of the rationalistic materialism of contemporary life; they form the social movements that keep the moral flame of world affairs alive. They have little in the way of guns or money. They do, however, have values and ideas with which they can assail the preponderance that state-makers and wealth-makers enjoy in terms of the global balance of ideologies.

Statism (the idea that all people should live in territorial domains) is one such ideology people contest. The balance of ideologies has also swung of late in favour of capitalism over 'communism'. More generally we can see such modernist values as individualism prevailing over the communal concerns of peoples designated 'traditional', despite the attempts by 'traditionalists' to fight back, and despite the questioning from within modernism itself of modernism's own most fundamental assumptions.[4]

I have found this tri-partite map a good way to point out the breadth of world politics (which clearly includes much more than the relations between political institutions like states) while providing categories concise enough to direct attention to the major ideological concerns of the day. With due regard to the history of world affairs, I have found that students quite quickly feel sufficiently well oriented not to be overwhelmed by the amount of information they typically confront, and yet not so channelled or corralled by the categories that their own ideas can't be given free play.

Obviously, having set the context you prefer, you can talk about world politics for the rest of the course without any student intervention. I find it easy to explore the simple conceptual skeleton-key outlined above by discussing further the relationships between strategic and productive power, between productive and ideological power, and between strategic and ideological power.

Talking to students about world politics in this or any other way for a whole course has well-attested educational outcomes. It is also readily testable. There is a great wealth of historical and analytic data to be provided in a more or less pre-digested form. Well-chosen information gives solid content to world politics courses. It also makes world politics look more like the established disciplines of sociology, anthropology, or psychology. Germane to teaching world politics, in other words, is a wealth of historical and analytic 'facts' which are hard to define because the value frameworks we use to select them are so varied, but which we can plough ahead and provide nonetheless. Students and institutions will be duly impressed by whatever selection we make.

Equally germane, however, to teaching world politics — in my book at least — is the feel of these facts. Teaching about world politics is not enough. To do the subject justice it is necessary to convey an abiding sense of what 'world politics' entails, and to do this you have actively to teach for it. This means confronting world politics as it occurs within the classroom itself.

There are many ways to do this. One that I have found leads well 'from within' is to start with class members as individuals-in-the-world, where 'the world' has been and continues to be made in each individual. This approach, however, leads directly to the ideology of individualism and to world politics as social practices that define a world political economy that shapes in turn a world of states. This may not be to everyone's taste.

If it is, the results can be startling. Explaining individualism involves a deep discussion of the concept of the self as the abstracted entity at the heart of Western culture and of the civilization the West would make universal. One dimension of this ideology (the politico-strategic one) is the individual as the citizen of a state. There is much more to it than this though. How are we as citizens made into nationalists too? How and to what extent are we cosmopolitans as well? Questions like these can bring the experience of living world politics very alive indeed.

In politico-strategic terms, in other words, individualism denotes state-defined individualism (citizenship), or nationally defined individualism (patriotism), or globally defined individualism (the cosmopolitan). Students embody all three roles themselves and can be encouraged to explore them in depth.

Another dimension of individualism is the politico-economic one. In this the individual is either the patriotic defender of his or her country's material strength (the neo-mercantilist view) or the marketeer, the 'economic man', the entrepreneur who creates demand or generates supply (the liberal view) or the one who owns or controls the means for making global wealth, or who sells his or her labour for a wage (the Marxist view). Assessing the roles students play in any one or all three of these views also reveals the extent to which they embody world politics in themselves.

In politico-economic terms, therefore, individualism denotes economic nationalism in both its protectionist and imperialist varieties. It can also denote 'possessive individualism', which is the concept — essentially liberal — that selfish individuals will promote collective values without even being aware of it. This is the 'hidden hand' that regulates the market. To a Marxist, however, the hidden hand serves only to conceal the boot of bourgeois exploitation and the class-structured individualism that comes with owning and managing (world-wide) the means of production, or with world-wide wage slavery. Which of these individualisms do students recognize as representative of their own attitudes and behavior? Assessing the global reach of politico-economic individualism can be a most educative experience.

The third dimension is the politico-social one. Here it is apparent how much of world politics does not just happen, but is made, and is made at the level students themselves actually live. The critical reading of a daily newspaper will quickly reveal how actively we are coached in seeing the world in terms of reified entities (*e.g.* 'Japan', 'the U.S.A.'), concepts that have long since ceased to serve as an analytic shorthand for the contending groups concerned but have become unitary actors in their own right.

Why should this be problematic? For one, it dulls our sense of states as contingent and temporary. We come to think of them as preferred. We lose the capacity to think of alternatives to them. We become conservative by default.

I tend to forget myself that though state-making in its contemporary guise has been going on for over three hundred years, the modern state system is younger than I am. It began as half a hundred more or less sovereign territorial domains in 1948. It has increased since then to nearly four times that number. Furthermore, the system continues to grow and change. With economic transnationalism, the collapse of the last of the European empires (the Russian one), and the claims of a plethora of sub-state nations for self-determination, we can hardly expect things to stay the same.

The sense that they might stay the same is only the sort of illusion that comes from growing up in a particular world at a particular time. When we add to this the conditioning we get from those with vested interests in keeping the system unchanged, it is no wonder that we have a sense of fixity. Like the mayfly who is born in the morning and who dies at dusk, knowing life only in terms of a single day, our mental horizons are heavily circumscribed. Many have much to gain by keeping them that way. This would not be a problem either if it did not make us so conservative. Conservativism itself would not be a problem if it did not blunt our capacity to cope with the one systemic constant: change.

Why do we spend so little time exploring the limits to the world in which we live, or exploring what could or should be the alternatives to it? Why do we think so little beyond what we think we know? Why do we recognize the names of so many prime ministers but not the names of the heads of the major multi-national corporations? Why is it so hard to see the politico-strategic citizen, or politico-economic individualism, as masculinist constructs, though by some feminist lights at least they are the consequence and the continuing cause of a male-built, male-dominated world?[5]

Another critical and all-too-little discussed dimension of this world is its rationalism. Rationalism is part of the patriarchal process. This process is evident in every student group and can be explored in its own right. Rationalism is also essential for the pursuit of science and for sustaining a world of capitalist industries. It also, however, generates a virulent form of moral relativism that is clearly apparent in most contemporary class-rooms and is another way of showing how much students may embody world politics in themselves.

'Student relativism' has its own little niche in the academic literature. Only philosophers have talked about it so far, since it seems to crop up in courses on ethics. The phenomenon is evident across the social sciences however. The following statements typify the response with which we are concerned: "there is really nothing true or false — or nothing really good or bad — it's all relative. One person has an opinion or feeling, and another person has a different one. What is true for one person might not be true for another. After all, who's to say? Everybody has their own feelings."[6]

Mostart defines student relativism in terms of two fundamental beliefs. The first is the idea of 'universal tolerance'. This is basically what the statements above are about: "Everything is allowed and everybody is free to consider anything to be right. There is only one restriction: the values somebody else is free to believe in should not limit my freedom to believe in my own values. Given this restriction, nobody has the right to tell somebody else which value one should prefer . . . Values are a strictly personal affair."[7]

Mostart discerns a second dimension to student relativism, however, which is that of 'private dogmatism': "In a relativistic society it is hard to find values you can sincerely believe in yourself. Once you have found them, you are eager to keep them. Therefore, why should you discuss your own values? Everybody has his [sic] own ones; you want to stay with the values you have, and you are not willing to have them openly criticized by other people."[8]

Satris argues that this sort of relativism is not a philosophical position at all, since to have a philosophic position you have to engage with questions and issues, and student relativism is a device for not doing so. It is a device for preventing or closing off thought or feeling. It provides defensive platitudes. It encourages complacency. It is an emphatic refusal to tackle real moral dilemmas.

It is a combination, in other words, of scepticism and dogmatism. It is a cultivated mental pose meant to deal with 'non-scientific' judgements — that is, ones where there is controversy over values and over how to make evaluations. And it does so in a reactionary way.[9] "Many people come out of a public school background," says Satris, "having learned that 'value judgement' or 'controversial issue' simply means a judgement or issue with respect to which there is no right response or answer and about which (since it's all a matter of personal opinion and not of scientific fact) we may all conveniently believe as we wish while remaining error-free."[10]

In my experience, students recognize at once the phenomenon of student relativism as defined by Satris and Mostart. Furthermore, most readily acknowledge themselves to be proponents of it. We could, of course, choose to ignore such monolithic nihilism. That would be to leave students entrenched in their moral bunkers, if not to reinforce these bunkers even further. Is that such a bad thing?

Should we choose to show students some alternatives to their self-imposed moral insularity, however, what is to be done? Firstly, we can point out that student relativism provides no mental defense against might making right, that is, against power creating the morality convenient to its cause. Might doesn't make for right, however. It only makes for compliance, which may or may not be right as assessed by some other standard than that of enforceability. The point of student relativism is that it preempts all prospect of acquiring the mental skills needed to fight might with right, though rightness alone will always lack the physical capacity to enforce itself.[11]

Secondly it is worth asking: why does our culture seem to reinforce relativism in this way? Is it because relativism is true? Or is it for some other reason?[12]

Thirdly, it is worth actually engaging in moral discourse just to see what progress can be made on difficult moral questions, student relativism notwithstanding. There is really no better way of discovering that some things are more important than others. There is no better way of discovering that though no absolute reference point may exist to validate intellectually the moral choices one makes, choice is still possible. Choice may even be desirable, despite the rarefied, intellectualized atmosphere of the university classroom, and the far cry it can be from the refugee camp, or the torture chamber, or villages of dispossessed peasants.

The moral discourse I use at this point is that of 'human rights'. It is not always easy to induce student relativists to try and arrive at universal moral claims that anyone anywhere might make by virtue of their human status alone. My own way of getting students to think about moral universals is a version of John Rawls' 'veil of ignorance'.[13] I ask the class — either in a lecture or in seminar groups — to imagine it will soon be joining a new colony in space. I then say that the beam designed to transport them to this colony is defective. As a consequence they cannot know, until they get to the colony itself, whether they will be old or young, male or female, homosexual or heterosexual, rich or poor, clever or stupid, disabled in some way, black or white or some other color, the member of an alien culture or religion, or the adherent of some system of ideas they don't believe in now.

The task is to devise, in groups of three, the basic rules for this colony. These are the rules under which all those in it will be expected to live. These are the rights all will be able to claim as colonists, and the responsibilities all must be prepared to meet when claims like these are made upon them.

The student response to this task can be very interesting. Some students, imbued with a hierarchic concept of society and without the experience of the pain of systematic discrimination, may opt for a similarly hierarchic society in space. Some will insist that conversion to a particular belief system will provide a universal panacea. These are in line with the standard criticisms of Rawls' idea.

Most students, however, will opt for toleration. Most can imagine themselves as potential 'underdogs'. So they write the rules required in such a way as to minimize the treatment of people as lesser beings for qualities people can't help or for beliefs they aren't really responsible for. They arrive for themselves at the equivalent of the Universal Declaration of Human Rights, a document promulgated by the United Nations in 1948 and one that has received near universal agreement from member state-makers.

It can be interesting at this point for students to compare their own rules with those written in their own name, without their connivance, over a generation ago — to compare, that is, the rules they have written with the Universal Declaration itself. For, of course, we already live on the space colony the thought experiment posits. It is our own earth. And on that earth, since the end of the last world war (and in no small part because of it) there has been a concerted effort to define the fundamental grounds on which any society, regardless of culture or religion, must rest for it to be called civilized or humane.

The Universal Declaration embodies the beliefs of those who drafted it. It views human beings as separate, isolated individuals, who live apart from their social context. This has caused considerable problems for people from outside the Western tradition, for whom the idea that people possess a non-communitarian identity is inconceivable. It is hardly surprising, therefore, that many outside the Western tradition have sought to establish the concept of collective rights. It is a much discussed point whether these complement or contradict the individualistic ones.[14]

The classical Western conception of human rights requires liberation regardless of community — even liberation from the community. But what if liberation is only to be had by communal means? The human rights idea, true to the objectifying individualism it has helped articulate, is bound up with a particular idea of human existence, that of existence as a person. You have to invent the idea of the individual, in other words, before such a being is entitled to rights. Rights are only possible when you have the idea of the individual to attach them to. In so far, though, as existing-as-a-person has a social dimension, in so far as the individual-in-the-world also represents the world-in-the-individual, in so far as socially shared or common goods are essential for individual self-realization, then both sorts of rights may exist.

Where they conflict, the conflict may only be resolvable by respecting both. The ambiguity as to which takes precedence may be inescapable since the ambiguity is actually in us. We are both individual and social beings, and a rights doctrine that reflects the complex, compound quality of human life will be a complex, compound doctrine too.

Providing opportunities for students to wrestle with dilemmas like these not only shows them ways in which they embody world politics. It also helps lead them 'from within' to a greater awareness of world affairs, individually and collectively.

Though I have been working in just one domain, the politico-social one, it is evident how quickly things turn out to be not as they seem. The world's moral map is a patchwork of uneasy compromises. The ideology of individualism currently dominates that map; but does it do so because individualism is more true? Or is this just another case of might making right? Is it a step forward towards a moral universalism of benefit to the whole species? Or is it just hegemony again, in its socio-ideological guise?

The questions go on, and so they should. The point here is to show how starting with the simple premise that students themselves embody world affairs led me to explore a phenomenon close to most of my students' hearts ('student relativism'), which led me in turn to craft the chance for them to explore the whole question of moral universals. This is no small part of world politics, regardless of how much of a realist one may be.

I have given one practical example of the method I am advocating and its substantive implications. There are many others. There is a sense in which none of this matters, however. I find that more important than what I teach is how I teach it. This is not to advocate classes that are style-rich but content-poor. This can disadvantage students just as effectively as mindless drilling does. It is to draw attention to the importance of classroom climate.

Inviting students to participate in their own learning is one part of what I am advocating. It demonstrates a level of respect on the part of the teacher for his or her students that is a lesson in itself. More important than democratic course construction, however, is teaching personality. Here there is no substitute for enthusiasm. '*En theos*' — to 'be with God' — it is no wonder that the word has divine connotations. Whatever I teach about, if I can teach for it too, and if I can do so with some degree of enthusiasm, then I don't seem to go far wrong.

At worst I always recall the words of my doctoral supervisor, as he sent me forth into the academic world to take up my first job as a lecturer. "Never forget," he said, "no matter how little you think you know, they will know less." He wasn't always right, as it turned out; but by the time I had learned that fact I had discovered another. If in doubt, ask the students. They may not have the knowledge they want or need or even have a right to. At best, however, several heads are better than one, especially when it comes to the responsible job of creating opportunities for students to learn the fact and the feel of world affairs.

Notes

1. D. Bligh, *What's the Use of Lectures*, 3rd ed (Harmondsworth: Penguin, 1972).
2. See: R. Pettman, *International Politics: Balance of Power, Balance of Productivity, Balance of Ideologies* (Melbourne and London: Longman Cheshire, 1991; Bouldern CO: Lynne Rienner, 1991).
3. See: M. Wight, "Western Values in International Relations," in H. Butterfield and M. Wight, eds., *Diplomatic Investigations* (London: Allen and Unwin, 1967).
4. See: J. George and D. Campbell, "Patterns of Dissent and the Celebration of Difference: Critical Social Theory and International Relations," *International Studies Quarterly*, 34, no. 3 (September 1990) pp. 269-293.
5. See, for example: J. Tickner "On the Fringes of the World Economy: A Feminist Perspective," in C. Murphy and R. Tooze, eds., *The New International Political Economy* (Boulder CO: Lynne Rienner 1991); and Varda Burstyn "Masculine Dominance and the State," in Ralph Miliband and John Saville, eds., *The Socialist Register 1983* (London: Merlin, 1983).
6. S. Satris, "Student Relativism," *Teaching Philosophy*, 9, no. 3 (September 1986) p. 193.
7. P. Mostart "Understanding Students' Relativism," *Metaphilosophy*, 17, nos. 2 and 3 (April/July 1986) p. 201.
8. loc. cit.
9. Satris, "Student Relativism," p. 199.
10. loc. cit.
11. This a key point in E. H. Carr's, *The Twenty Years' Crisis* (London: Macmillan, 1962).
12. M. Goldman, "On Moral Relativism, Advocacy, and Teaching Normative Ethics," *Teaching Philosophy*, 4, no. 1 (January 1981) pp. 4-5.
13. See, for example, John Rawls "Justice as Fairness," *Philosophical Review*, V. 67 (1958) pp. 164-194; cf. B. Barry, "The Liberal Theory of Justice: A Critical Examination of the Principal Doctrines," in John Rawls, ed., *A Theory of Justice* (Clarendon Press, Oxford, 1973).
14. See, for example, J. Berting et al (eds), *Human Rights in a Pluralist World: Individuals and Collectives*, (Westport: Meckler, 1990).

10

Discourse Analysis: Teaching World Politics Through International Relations

Bradley S. Klein

The semi-annual ritual of ordering textbooks for my undergraduate introductory courses is a painful reminder of some serious dilemmas that cannot be avoided these days. The issues go far beyond the immediate task of selecting reading material appropriate to an introductory course. They extend to the whole realm of living in and acting upon world politics today. The world historical epoch ushered in with the demise of the postwar world order has brought with it a fundamental reorientation of perspectives regarding inquiry into global politics. Whether such thinking has led, followed, or merely accompanied, the changing order of things is a question that cannot be settled here. But this essay does explore how innovative modes of thinking about world politics can be brought to bear in the classroom. The motivating hope is that in sharing with our students a concern about thinking critically, we can enable them to appreciate the several different dynamics at work in contemporary world politics.

An engagement with the academic field of International Relations is, I believe, indispensable. But it is not enough to stop there, as if mastering the formal language of the discipline constituted sufficient knowledge of contemporary affairs. For in world politics, the terms offered through the academic enterprise of International Relations are but one of several ways of making sense of global life. To be sure, the terms of the discipline need to be taken seriously, but not because they represent the gospel truth. The real reason the discipline deserves our attention is because IR stands as an historically important attempt, perhaps the most globally ambitious, to organize and codify human identities. IR thus needs to be taken with the utmost seriousness because it is the pre-eminent discourse of power. In effect, International Relations needs to be read symptomatically, as a discursive constellation of forces whose worldwide consequences cannot be ignored, but which itself needs to be interpreted.

To say this, of course, is already to adopt a critical approach to the discipline. The question to be explored in this essay, then, is how to convey to students a critical approach towards the discipline that is also a respectful one — not reverent, but serious. The answer, as I hope to show, is by working through a variety of debates regarding world politics that historicize the whole IR project.

The Textbook as a Genre

A recurring disappointment when teaching is to realize how great the gulf is between the promise of state-of-the-art academic insights and their embodiment between two covers for $42.95. I am referring, of course, to the comprehensive textbook — the kind that organizes a whole discipline, chapter by chapter, subject by subject. Such a promising text is customarily large, mailed without asking on a complimentary basis, comes with a little card asking for reader's comments, and promises to contain a synthesis of the latest theoretical advances with up-to-date material.

With few exceptions, books in this genre offer an opening theoretical excursus in which can be found a boiled-down version of 'what is theory?', followed by a rehearsal of various frameworks of analysis. There then follows a series of chapters that move from conventional state-centered approaches towards war and peace through the neo-realist literature on decision-making, followed by a brief look at international law, diplomacy, international organizations, and then on through such basic topics as security, deterrence and arms control, and terrorism. The final third of the text is usually devoted to issues of interdependence and international political economy, with trade and currency exchange given foremost attention, followed by the multinational corporation, international development, the Third World, and finally, a parting look at population and the environment. There are many variations, of course, but the basic pattern is more or less recognizable. These are, after all, texts with ambitious claims to comprehensiveness and exhaustiveness, and there are not all that many ways to make a text both complete and useable to scholars in the field already comfortable with dominant modes of disciplinary inquiry.

In considering adoption of such a text, I frequently find myself torn between two seemingly opposed points of view. On the one hand, I am searching for the perfect text which will serve students as a meaty bone to chew while I go on ahead and lecture the way I want to. On the other hand, when I realize that this or that latest offering is not the Holy Grail, I am tempted to fall back into the view that so long as the text is comprehensive, it almost doesn't matter which one I choose. The problem, in short, is that I find the whole genre of the IR textbook frustrating.

To some extent, the problem can be attributed to timeliness. A textbook is limited, after all, to the exigencies of research, writing, editing and production, so that even the most contemporary text is automatically two years out of date the day it appears in print. Yet this, in itself, is not a crippling problem, since there is always the possibility of culling articles from journals and popular weeklies in order to update the readings. Such a supplementation is all the more necessary in these days of dramatic change and instantaneous international communication. It is impossible to distinguish these days between the rapidity of history and the incessant demands of modern consciousness for relevant, up-dated information. The massive textbook has trouble competing on both counts.

A more fundamental shortcoming, certainly not limited to the IR textbook, and endemic to many of the social sciences, is that so much of the scholarly literature in the field is horrendously written and unsuitable for assignment to undergraduates. Temperament and writing style, after all, are indispensable elements of a text's appropriateness. Could there, for instance, be something to the recurring student complaint about readings being 'dry'? What I take this to mean is that there is a curious abstractness, a lack of envisagement. Passive modes abound. Three quarters of all verbs are variations of 'to be'. And no one or no identifiable agent *does* things; historical developments seem to hang there, happening without human input, structured simply on their own. The clearest (*i.e.* murkiest) example of this lifeless prose can be found in Parsonian structural-functionalism. Harold Lasswell[1] and Morton Kaplan[2] legitimized such a style (or lack thereof) for IR, and despite the considerable theoretical merits of these arguments, they have left behind an enduring legacy of desiccated prose. On the whole, IR scholars have been notoriously indifferent to concerns so basic as a text's readability. How else to explain the writing found in the articles poured out in the name of the behavioral revolution?

Beyond the issue of writing, there is also the way in which textbooks present an argument. In judging the appropriateness of IR texts, an important consideration is less the explanatory superiority of realism or critical theory than the stylistic dimension of how one goes about constructing and illustrating theoretically informed arguments. I have found it is far more effective to teach a book written from a sustained and identifiable point of view rather than to have to rely upon a flat presentation of the world, as if the argument emanated from an objectively speaking author unwilling — or unable — to acknowledge and elaborate upon the perspective that gives the text its life. One point of teaching, after all, is to convey a sense of a good argument. Only when students learn to recognize a coherent perspective will they be able to develop their own. Textbooks that abound in 'the complexities' of a 'pluralistic world' and that hedge their analysis 'on the one hand, but on the other' perpetrate a peculiar kind of liberal marketplace view of ideas. When students are encouraged to believe that they have the run of the bazaar and can purchase anything they find in the stalls, the whole enterprise of teaching is undercut. The assumption is one of empirically detached intellectualism devoid of issues of ideology, power, discourse, culture and historical dominance. Choice, after all, entails commitment. Such an approach to knowledge in world politics works best when students are encouraged to engage the strongest and most sustained version of a good representative argument.

The claim here is not to proliferate bias for its own sake, since that would merely be to perpetuate opinions for the sake of multiplying differences. That would be pedagogically irresponsible and politically naive, since not all statements merit the same consideration and not all social practices are able to mobilize comparable resources. After all, one does not have to rely upon the single arbiter of an Absolute Truth in order to make judgments about the relative strength of explanations. Rather, the issue is one of promoting sensitivity towards carefully elaborated, theoretically-sophisticated yet empirically-rich analyses. This is how students learn what it means to develop, defend and elaborate a compelling perspective. In this manner, students can be encouraged to develop and fill in their own points of view.

The choice of a textbook also entails a decision about scope. Is it more valuable to expose students to the widest possible range of views at the cost of sophistication in detail? Or, in contrast to the shopping market approach, is it preferable to emphasize detailed elaboration of the most influential perspectives, paradigms or theories?

There is a further danger inherent in the very species 'textbook', namely that it perpetrates upon 'the consumer' the illusion that the relevant spread of knowledge on the field can be more or less pre-packaged, digested and tested. This assumption, problematic in its own right in any era, is especially troubling today, as the very phenomena crying out for explanation seem to evade intellectual containment. Those appended little teachers' guides, replete with dehydrated chapter summaries and hundreds of short answer questions for exams, may serve some institutional needs, especially in hard times when budget lines are tight. But this scarcely begins to do the subject matter, or the student, any justice. It also presumes to write off as irrelevant one of the most important components of the classroom experience, namely, what the professor learns from the students in the course of going over the material. There is no need to romanticize the joys of teaching. Some of it, especially those blue books, can be sheer drudgery. But there's enough possibility for constructive give and take in the classroom that the teacher, in the course of elaborating a point or responding to a particularly thoughtful question, has the chance to experiment with an answer or to venture into new territory. Without such moments, teaching would lose that excitement that distinguishes it from so many other professions. One good reason to use challenging texts, then, is to keep the teacher on his or her toes.

At the same time, this begins to erode a basic cultural presumption that, I fear, increasingly influences the classroom. My sense is that many students are not accustomed to developing a point of view, nor are they encouraged to. It is not, of course, that they don't have points of view, but that a whole range of cultural pressures manifesting themselves through peers, the media, and through the norms guiding everyday life exert a certain debilitating influence.[3] Students don't like to disagree for fear that they will stand out. In an age when newspaper articles are shrinking and giving way to little pre-digested pieces of news, and when television programming assumes the form of 'info-tainment', it is not surprising that students today have trouble recognizing what a point of view looks like. Pressures toward conformity here need to be subtly but persistently countered.

A Light Touch of Theory

The immediate question of selecting texts rapidly expands into the more important issue of how to organize a semester-long syllabus designed to orient students to basic issues of war and peace, economic development, and power and powerlessness in the contemporary world. This dilemma opens up to a yet larger puzzle concerning the adequacy of the basic explanatory categories available to those of us who teach. There are a variety of ways to describe this intellectual ferment: as a paradigm shift, a search for a new and improved comprehensive theory, a crisis of representation, or the breakup of the old order and the not-yet-coming-into-being of the new. A substantial and worthy literature has emerged from the standpoint of each of these several perspectives on the debate within the IR community.⁴ If attention to these issues is unavoidable today, so, too, is their spillover into the classroom.

A critical approach requires a more interactive, dialectical classroom dynamic than might be presumed under classical doctrines of teaching and learning. The emergence of more interactive approaches toward knowledge today extend to the very conduct of pedagogy — questioning, for instance, the propriety of the lecture format as the organizing principle of instruction. Such a monological mode is structurally incompatible with the more dialogical enterprise of critical engagement and ongoing interpretation called for by contemporary approaches.⁵

One way to highlight a critical approach is to differentiate between the modernist claims of empirical investigation and the contemporary claims of an interpretive enterprise. This shift, to be relied upon throughout this essay, plays itself out when structuring an introductory course. It results, for instance, in recognizing an inescapable tension between the formal disciplinary field called International Relations and the ongoing social practices of world politics. Should a basic IR course in attempt to convey the prevailing terms of debate that constitute the field? Or should it initiate students into an appreciation of the complexities of the subject matter? Of course, the disciplinary apparatus itself is worthless if not construed in terms of its ostensible subject matter. At the same time, the subject matter itself has no independent empirical standing and only circulates within a theoretically informed perspective that allows one to identify its peculiar dynamics and dilemmas. So much, then, for the false dichotomy between theory and practice, between methodology and case study.

In this sense, all intellectual inquiry occupies that space in which theory and practice mutually enable each other. A general norm to be followed, then, might be that wherever a practice appears, we should enquire as to its animating ideas. Not even nuclear warheads speak for themselves. They only make sense — as weapons of peace, deterrence, war or Armageddon — within a set of social practices or discourses that give those weapons of mass destruction some meaningful purpose or significance in world affairs. Within the liberal-technical discourse of deterrence, for instance, the presence of nuclear weapons has a pacifying function, reducing the likelihood of war because they raise the price of aggression. Within the critical discourse of militarism, however, 'the same weapons' stand condemned for contributing to the mutual exterminism of a hostile international system. The debate about the function of these weapons is thus a debate about their description. And that, in turn, is part of a larger theoretical debate about the explanatory categories one brings to bear when accounting for world politics.⁶

The precise relationship between theory and practice remains, of course, problematic. Neither a crude materialist empiricism, nor an equally simple-minded rationalist idealism, is an adequate account of the ongoing relationship between intellectual inquiry and everyday life. My own thinking on this question has been influenced by debates about representation and discourse.[7] The modernist, Enlightenment view of knowledge sees inquiry as a tool for prying off the lid of the universe in order to gaze at its inner reality. The world has a pre-given structure, and the task of theory is to gain access to that realm. The rationalist variant of this would have us spend most of our time honing our methodological scalpels. The empiricist version, by contrast, would willingly abandon the whole pretense of theory and ask us to jump headlong into "just the facts, ma'am." Behavioral social science hastily oscillates between these two modes: obsessive theoretical refinement to the point of paralysis; and an impulsive grasping for 'events data' and 'behavior' without theoretical articulation.

In the view of those who talk about discourse and representation, by contrast, ideas are culturally circumscribed understandings that are only meaningful and available insofar as they are manifest in social practice. There can be no purely objective description of events. Reference to the constitutive ideas that enable participants to act they way they do is indispensable. Without it we cannot even properly identify what it is we are talking about. All of the basic political struggles of our day concerning democracy, nationalism, fundamentalism, and emerging new world orders are political contests in which ideas and understandings by the participants themselves are part of the object of inquiry. Thus the historic problems of idealism and relativism are at least partially overcome because a limiting condition of all explanation is that they must make contact with the ideas and beliefs that are held by those whose actions are being explored. There is, of course, no need for students in introductory world politics courses to confront these works directly. But teachers attempting to convey a thoughtful and critical approach will hold a deeper, more reflective, position if they have worked through the post-Wittgensteinian tradition of social theory.[8]

At the same time, one of the great tasks of teaching is not to belabor one's own perspective. Here and elsewhere, much of a teacher's success comes by knowingly holding back the intricacies of a well-worked out theoretical position. Such a knowledge, worn confidently but carried lightly, is a crucial way to avoid the kind of obsessive theoreticism that plagues all too many courses, and that can be especially crippling when iterated in a post-structural mode.

Debates introduced by Max Weber on value-neutrality have continued to exercise a hold on the imagination of IR scholars.[9] The concern was especially prominent in the late-1960s and early 1970s, when pedagogical styles exercised a new-found independence through a curious form of sincerity. I first experienced this as an undergraduate, and have witnessed or heard about it all too often since. The faculty member will spend the second half of the first class hour explaining — or confessing — his views. Yet a teacher laboring under the influence of this style is working with a fundamental misconception. The confessional mode is no guarantor of intellectual virtue. On the contrary, such facile intimacy can readily color everything that follows in the classroom. At least one of two possibilities is likely. The first is that students, since they have been forewarned of where the teacher stands, will prejudge issues in light of what the professor thinks — or worse, yet, what students anticipate the professor will think. In other words, their responses, both in class and on written assignments, may well become an attempt to give the teacher what they think he or she wants to hear. The only way to avoid this is for the teacher to make it clear that his or her views are to be challenged, not regurgitated. This requires an enormous intellectual tolerance on the part of the teacher, a willingness, in fact, openly to cultivate views at odds with his or her own in an effort to convince students of the importance of their developing their own arguments. And this goal cannot be achieved through a ritualistic unveiling of the soul in the opening few hours of a class.

The second problem created by 'fessing up' at the outset concerns the teacher's ability to make convincing arguments contrary to his or her professed beliefs. The teacher who has conceded this position will be handicapped in making arguments that are at odds with his or her confessed commitments, since the students will know the instructor is being disingenuous when positions are advanced that the students know the teacher does not personally hold.

My own practice in this is to act as something of a moving target throughout the semester. Moving, not in the sense of a zig-zag, but in a more developmental, linear, fashion, working through a succession of arguments in some logical progression. At first, I try to present an argument in the most convincing fashion. Then I start pulling on a few loose threads until the whole thing unravels. Then I re-construct it via another, more powerful, explanatory framework, and then keep doing this until finally arriving, with about a month left in the semester, at some reasonable version of the position I really hold. I invariably begin with a defense of the realist position, move toward the neo-realist critique, pose for a while as a critical Marxist and then move toward — without expressly defining the elements of — a position influenced by certain post-structural attitudes. In this manner, I take seriously the discipline, work through the most influential arguments, draw upon a range of critical perspectives, and encourage students to continue their inquiries. By selecting literature that at each stage represents the approach I want to illustrate, I can give concrete evidence of what different points of view "look like" rather than have to refer to them abstractly and at a distance. Students are thereby required to take seriously each of the succeeding positions since they won't know exactly where the narrative is heading. This frees me to make the best possible arguments for a position, and then the strongest possible critique.

Historicizing World Politics

Surely the most important task confronting teachers of world politics today is to convey to students some sense of the relationship between contending perspectives and the great political contests of the day. Realism, for instance, had its moment with the great powers; neo-realism enjoyed its greatest plausibility as a discourse of liberal hegemony.[10] Likewise, post-structuralism speaks to a fragmentation of political power and to the de-territorialization of social space, away from sovereign state-centered geopolitics and toward multiple dimensions of identity in time and space.[11] Thus the clash of perspectives *about* world politics is given palpable reality through a confrontation of competing claims by participants *within* world politics. In this manner, methodological debates now raging through the discipline cannot help but have a tremendous impact on what goes on in the classroom.

In considering these questions, one has to keep in mind the particularly dramatic, indeed, world-historical, dimensions of these concerns recently. We face today an exhilarating variety of sea changes, having to do with the epochal collapse of communism, the apparent 'triumph' of modern Western life forms, and at the same time a diminution in the organizing power of major states to patrol and discipline world affairs. Thus the disintegration of the Soviet Union gives rise both to democratic experimentation in eastern Europe and to a fissiparous politics of ethnic, nationalist and religious differentiation in neighboring regions where democratic institutions are just achieving institutional expression. At the same time that the United States celebrates its successful prosecution of a coalition war against an outlaw aggressor in the Middle East, it finds itself in a heightened state of internal disarray, unable to house, educate, and employ significant sectors of its own populace and deeply embedded in fiscal crises that extend to every state and local government. Meanwhile, the great promise of economic development, heralded thirty years ago as the dawn of a new age for vast stretches of the world's peoples, remains largely chimerical for most countries, and for most peoples within those newly industrializing countries where the Rostovian engine of relentless modernization had begun to pick up steam.

The end of the last great world war was supposed to usher in an era of peace, but that peace has proven to be frighteningly transitory. Classical models of nation-state warfare hardly seem to exhaust the spectrum of overt conflict wracking world politics today. Moreover, security can no longer be measured in terms of the (momentary) absence of war, but has come to include a far ambitious social agenda, including questions of ecology, economic sufficiency, and human rights.[12] Finally, there is the increasingly complicated question of the relevant actors in world politics. In an age when classical realist principles were considered intellectual manna, the sphere of relevant actors circulated within the very closed circles of the sovereign state's power. But today, such a view is considered antiquarian, and even the most dedicated realist is forced to address the emergence of a whole panoply of non-state actors, including social movements organized around such constellations of identity and power as gender, race, culture, religion and class. It may well be that the most revitalizing intellectual force at work upon International Relations is coming from the many schools of thought that generally fall under the heading of 'Feminist Studies'. Particularly influential here are debates about the phallo-centric quality of strategic discourse, the gendered nature of the development paradigm, and the patriarchal basis of the modern state.[13]

In such a world, the teaching of world politics becomes enormously complicated, particularly as leading scholars in the field explore different perspectives by which to understand recent developments. There cannot, then, be a more opportune moment to open up methodological and pedagogical questions about IR. The last two years or so have taken us through a breathless series of events. The dismantling of the Berlin Wall has itself passed into history. Now it remains to be seen what precisely will be the nature of those successor states that had been cowering behind the Iron Curtain. The makeshift Commonwealth of Independent States may prove no more perdurable than a Yugoslavia or a Czechoslovakia. The great bipolar conflict between two hegemonic superpowers has finally — or so it seems for now — played itself out. Once again, but this time for real, the Cold War is over. It is not clear, however, what will replace the old familiarities — whether something called a New World Order, or a new economic order centered on Japan and the European Community, or perhaps a revived Pax Americana venting its fury upon the same 'ungrateful' competitors it had helped revive a half century earlier. But in any case, it can fairly be said that even if the new has yet to be born, the old has died out.[14]

Of course, that isn't necessarily something to celebrate. In 1989 the talk was optimistically about 'the end of history'. Now we turn again to popularizing journals and wonder, in the words of John Mearsheimer, whether we will all soon miss the Cold War.[15] No sooner do we begin to enjoy the benefits of a 'peace dividend' than war erupts, yet again, along the Persian Gulf, bringing with it a whole spate of questions concerning nuclear proliferation, regional arms races, the agony of military regimes, and the specter of renewed cultural and social conflict.

Moreover, for vast stretches of the globe, the breakdown of the older world order offers no visible hope for the future. The talk of building a New International Economic Order has subsided as the Western world, politely referred to as the 'multilateral trading system', has refused to acquiesce in a series of structural reforms.[16] The result is that many national economies are stagnating, mired in growing debt. With the collapse of primary commodity prices on the world market, some of these countries now find it more attractive to turn themselves into tourist outposts or to export drugs to the industrialized world.

The resilience of the classical Atlantic-centered order sustains those who see in classical realism timeless principles for the discipline. There is, it must be acknowledged, something powerful about the appeal of a doctrine that speaks so consistently about the nature of power and the role of competing states in the international system. Yet, however ill-defined a new world order may be, this does not warrant confident reliance upon the versions of realism that have been deeded to us today. For the basic animating concepts of this perspective — power, the state, the state system — can all be seen to be far more internally complex than presumed by standardbearers of the idiom. One need only confront the primary works of those who have created the pantheon of realism to see that their thinking is, in fact, far richer and more ethically ennobled than as seen within contemporary textbook versions. Machiavelli wrestling with modernity, or Hobbes invoking religion in order to secure civil society — these are but two examples of thinkers whose intellectual richness threatens to break out of the Gothic straight-jacket into which they have been fitted by current champions of the tradition.[17]

All of this has meant something of a crisis for those of us who teach IR. The fundamental issue is that, like the Cold War and all the other old formulas for organizing world politics, the prevailing paradigms no longer seem flexible enough to accommodate the extraordinary changes that are taking place throughout the world. At the same time, we need to allow ourselves the frightening possibility that the inadequacy of prevailing modes of thought pertains not simply to contemporary reality, but to the received wisdom about historic reality as well. If things aren't what they used to be, perhaps they never were.

The premise of the essays in this volume is that teaching world politics is tougher than ever because the prevailing forms of thought derived to organize global experience no longer accord with the palpable complexities of everyday life. Under such a condition (of postmodernity?), it becomes all the more important to prepare students for thinking carefully and critically about the future which they face.

Teaching IR theory these days is difficult. To pose the issue, for instance, in terms of our searching for a singular new paradigm contains a number of assumptions that can be misleading and counterproductive when applied in (or out of) the classroom. There is, for example, the very idea of a paradigm as a singular way of examining the world and for arriving at demonstrable truths about its nature. The ease with which the term paradigm circulates in academic discourse, of course, owes itself to Thomas Kuhn — or at least to the Kuhn of 1962. But in subsequent editions of *The Structure of Scientific Revolution*, and in the hands of other philosophers of science, such as Imre Lakatos and Stephen Toulmin, 'paradigm' assumes a less definitive form.[18] Instead of serving as a theoretical approach within a carefully circumscribed research agenda, paradigm functions in a more relaxed manner, something on the order of a set of questions whose assumptions are themselves subject to criticism and revision in the course of research. Thus when we teach about theory and paradigms, we need to be careful about now demanding, as Aristotle reminds us, too much rigor from our concepts — or from any concepts, including those of 'theory' or 'paradigm'.

I have heard all too many stories from undergraduates exposed to the rigorous teachings of determined junior professors whose demand for scientific rigor and precision leads them — and their somewhat overwhelmed students — into a seven or nine point recitation of the criteria by which contending paradigms or theories are to be appraised. From this first step, usually undertaken in the first two weeks, it is a short step to the bowling alley, and to an approach toward 'contending perspectives' that may be fairly described as 'set them up and knock them down'. 'Bowling for paradigms', this is: an exercise made all too easy by those mail-order textbooks whose opening chapters are filled with equally rigorous recitations, replete with charts and point-by-point comparisons, of the definitive features of Realism, Idealism, and Modernism, also known as Pluralism, and sometimes critically dissected as 'Corporate Globalism'.[19] This is the kind of reductionism that makes a mockery of thinking and that forces students to make choices among differences that are artificially intensified.

A more helpful approach toward teaching, and toward encouraging student sensitivity concerning theoretical differences, can be found not in making wholesale judgments about realism/idealism/pluralism/world systems, but in looking at how key operative concepts circulate within a field of practice. The technical term for this might be called discourse analysis, but I personally have found it wise to avoid such talk in the classroom and instead, just to go ahead and do it quietly. Instead of going through theoretical gymnastics, it is usually more effective merely to rely upon some examples and discuss them. For instance, in spending a few weeks talking about global political economy, I find it helpful to walk students through the first half of Rostow's *Stages of Economic Growth*.[20] The oppositions set up there, between tradition and modernity, backwardness and progress, the pre-Newtonian limits on production and the cornucopia made available through the capitalist miracle of compound interest — delivered with the most astonishing un-selfconsciousness — are more than enough material by which to identify the whole culture of modernity and its concomitant representation of a relatively impoverished Third World.

Philosophies of language and of social inquiry these last twenty years have continually eroded away a set of distinctions that were previously part of the social sciences enterprise. The distinctions, for instance, between objective and subjective, real and ideal, reason and passion, and most importantly, between the knowing subject and the object under consideration, have all been placed under critical scrutiny by a literature that scholarship cannot afford to ignore. The difficulty comes in mediating such debates to undergraduate audiences. And here my approach is simply not to try, but instead to make an honest effort to convey to students, without the intellectual baggage, what it means to take seriously contending conceptual frameworks and to see how some crucial concepts operate within sets of assumptions that continually need to be explored.

After spending some time on the making of the modern world, I turn to issues of war and peace. This is a section that I usually call 'The World Military Order', and my intent here is to begin with the most familiar and seemingly accessible debates and to use them as a jumping off point for exploring the meaning of war and peace. Starting the discussion with debates about arms control, deterrence and major wars is fine insofar as it seems to speak to student's views about the inevitability and timelessness of conflict: there always was war, there always will be war. But there is, I believe, a need to historicize the production of those global dilemmas which to students today can seem all too naturalized. These are, after all, post-nuclear students; and they are no more accustomed to life without nuclear weapons than to life without television. It helps, then, to convey to students how nuclear weapons were introduced into the world and how they became so pervasive a part of modern life. The best way to do this, I am convinced, is to ask them to empathize with those men and women who made fateful decisions about the advent of the nuclear age. Thus a careful study of the Manhattan Project and the first decade or so of US-Soviet nuclear relations brings to bear the ideas of something fundamentally different having happened. Here I find it far more helpful for introductory students to read *In the Matter of J. Robert Oppenheimer* than, say, the literature on prisoner's dilemma.[21] To historicize is to politicize, for in explaining how things came about, there is automatically introduced into the equation the assumption that things might have been worked out differently had different conditions prevailed.

This is not to say that history is sheer contingency. But opening up questions of historical construction is, I believe, the most effective way to get students to appreciate the mechanisms by which political structures are created. In this sense, the problem I have with the structural approach as developed in its most sophisticated form by Kenneth Waltz, is precisely that it freezes out of consideration the processes, both micro and macro, by which structures are constructed and reproduced.[22] The result is a lifeless ossification, a reification of world politics, which depoliticizes critical inquiry and reduces it to a technical mechanism of systems adjustment.

Here and elsewhere, I avoid asking questions starting with the term 'why?'. Such a question, when posed on an exam, for instance, presupposes that there is some single and originary source of political history, which can be known, mastered, and judged true or false. Asking 'how', by contrast, opens up students to questions of historical process and to the multiple paths of human events whereby contending social forces clashed and resulted in certain outcomes.

A final point — an appeal to be 'post-hegemonic'. There are serious problems in searching for a new form of dominance. We don't need, and can't have even if we wanted, a new dominant paradigm for our discipline. Indeed, I doubt whether we can have anything as systematic and as self-contained as a paradigm at all. Instead, we should ask interesting questions that speak to, and that listen to, ongoing social and political struggles. In this sense, the task of social science is to give voice and clarity to the multiple forces and social movements that help constitute world politics.

Notes

1. Harold Lasswell, *World Politics and Personal Insecurity* (New York: Free Press, 1935).

2. Morton Kaplan, *System and Process in International Politics* (New York: John Wiley, 1957).

3. Helen Lefkowitz Horowitz, *Campus Life: Undergraduate Cultures from the End of the Eighteenth Century to the Present* (Chicago IL: University of Chicago Press, 1987); and Michael Moffatt, *Coming of Age in New Jersey: College and American Culture* (New Brunswick NJ: Rutgers University Press, 1989), are indispensable reminders to teachers today of the many ways outside the classroom by which students learn to learn.

4. Robert W. Cox, "Social Forces, States and World Orders: Beyond International Relations Theory," *Millennium* 10 (Summer 1981), pp. 126-155; Robert O. Keohane, ed., *Neorealism and its Critics* (New York: Columbia University Press, 1986); Robert O. Keohane, "International Institutions: Two Approaches," *International Studies Quarterly* 32 (December 1988), pp. 379-396; Mark Hoffman, "Critical Theory and the Inter-Paradigm Debate," *Millennium* 16 (Summer 1987), pp. 231-249; Richard K. Ashley, "Untying the Sovereign State: A Double Reading of the Anarchy Problematique," *Millennium* 17 (Summer 1988), pp. 227-262; Ernst-Otto Czempiel and James N. Rosenau, eds., *Global Changes and Theoretical Challenges* (Lexington MA: Lexington Books, 1989); James Der Derian and Michael J. Shapiro, eds., *International/Intertextual Relations: Postmodern Readings of World Politics* (Lexington MA: Lexington Books, 1989); Thomas Biersteker, "Critical Reflections on Post-Positivism in International Relations," *International Studies Quarterly* 33 (September 1989), pp. 263-267; Jim George, ""International Relations and the Search for Thinking Space: Another View of the Third Debate," *International Studies Quarterly* 33 (September 1989), pp. 269-279; Joseph Lapid, "The Third Debate: On the Prospects of International Theory in a Post-Positivist Era," *International Studies Quarterly* 33 (September 1989), pp. 235-254; K.J. Holsti, "Mirror, Mirror on the Wall, Which are the Fairest Theories of All?" *International Studies Quarterly* 33 (September 1989), pp. 255-261; Jim George and David Campbell, "Patterns of Dissent and the celebration of Difference: Critical Social Theory and International Relations," *International Studies Quarterly* 34 (September 1990), pp. 269-293; and Yale H. Ferguson and Richard W. Mansbach, "Between Celebration and Despair: Constructive Suggestions for Future International Theory," *International Studies Quarterly* 35 (December 1991), pp. 363-386.

5. Tzvetan Todorov, *Mikhail Bakhtin: The Dialogical Principle*, trans. Wlad Godzich (Minneapolis: University of Minnesota Press, 1984).

6. William E. Connolly, *The Terms of Political Discourse*, 2nd ed. (Princeton NJ: Princeton University Press).

7. James Clifford and George E. Marcus, eds., *Writing Culture: The Poetics and Politics of Ethnography* (Berkeley CA: University of California Press, 1988); and Michael J. Shapiro, *The Politics of Representation* (Madison: University of Wisconsin Press, 1988).

8. Peter Winch, *The Idea of a Social Science and its Relation to Philosophy* (London: Routledge and Kegan Paul, 1958); Charles Taylor, "Interpretation and the Sciences of Man," *Review of Metaphysics* 25 (Fall 1971), pp. 3-51; Steven Lukes, "Methodological Individualism Reconsidered," in Alan Ryan, ed., *The Philosophy of Social Explanation* (Oxford: Oxford University Press, 1973); Hannah Fenichel Pitkin, *Wittgenstein and Justice* (Berkeley CA: University of California Press, 1973); Fred Dallmayr and Thomas McCarthy, eds., *Understanding and Social Inquiry* (Notre Dame: University of Notre Dame Press, 1977); William E. Connolly, *Appearance and Reality in Politics* (Cambridge: Cambridge University Press, 1981); and Connolly, *The Terms of Political Discourse*.

9. Max Weber, *The Methodology of the Social Sciences*, ed. and trans. Edward Shils (New York: The Free Press, 1949).

10. Robert Cox, "Social Forces, States and World Orders"; and Stephen Gill, *American Hegemony and the Trilateral Commission* (Cambridge: Cambridge University Press, 1990), 11-32.

11. Benedict Anderson, *Imagined Communities: Reflections on the Origin and Spread of Nationalism* (London: Verso, 1983); David Harvey, *The Condition of Postmodernity* (Oxford: Basil Blackwell, 1989); Arjun Appadurai, "Disjuncture and Difference in the Global Cultural Economy," *Public Culture* 2 (Spring 1990), pp. 1-24; James Der Derian, "The (S)pace of International Relations: Simulation, Surveillance, and Speed," *International Studies Quarterly* 34 (September 1990), pp. 295-310; John Maxwell Hamilton, *Entangling Alliances* (Washington DC: Seven Locks Press, 1990); John Urry, *The Tourist Gaze: Leisure and Travel in Contemporary Societies* (London: Sage Publications, 1990); Jacques Attali, *Millennium: Winners and Losers in the Coming World Order*, trans. Leila Conners and Nathan Gardels (New York: Random House, 1991); and Stephen Gill, "Reflections on Global order and Sociohistorical Time," *Alternatives* 16 (Summer 1991), pp. 275-314.

12. Carol Thomas, *In Search of Security: The Third World in International Relations* (Boulder CO: Lynne Rienner Publishers, 1987); Bradley S. Klein, "After Strategy: The Search for a Post-Modern Politics of Peace," *Alternatives* 13 (July 1988), pp. 293-318; International Institute for Strategic Studies, *Strategic Survey 1990-1991* (London: Brassey's, 1991); and Michael T. Klare and Daniel C. Thomas, eds., *World Security: Trends and Challenges at Century's End* (New York: St. Martin's Press, 1991).

13. Carol Cohn, "Sex and Death in the rational World of Defense Intellectuals," *Signs* 12 (July 1987), pp. 687-718; "Women and International Relations," special issue, *Millennium* 18 (Summer 1989); Adrienne Harris and Ynestra King, eds., *Rocking the Ship of State: Toward a Feminist Peace Politics* (Boulder CO: Westview Press, 1989); Cynthia Enloe, *Bananas, Beaches and Bases: Making Feminist Sense of International Politics* (Berkeley CA: University of California Press, 1990); Christine Sylvester, "The Emperor's Theories and Transformations: Looking at the Field through Feminist Lenses," in Dennis S. Pirages and Christine Sylvester, eds., *Transformations in the Global Political Economy* (New York: St. Martin's Press, 1990), pp. 230-253; and Anne Sisson Runyan and V. Spike Peterson, The Radical Future of Realism: Feminist Subversions of IR Theory," *Alternatives* 16 (Winter 1991), pp. 67-106.

14. Thomas L. Friedman, "Rethinking Foreign Affairs: Are They Still a U.S. Affair?" *New York Times*, 7 February 1992, shows the yearning among the country's foreign policy elite for a new 'X' article that would do for the future of American strategy what Kennan's doctrine of 'containment' did for U.S. diplomacy in 1947.

15. John Mearsheimer, "Back to the Future: Instability in Europe After the Cold War," *International Security* 15 (Summer 1990), pp. 5-56.

16. Enrico Augelli and Craig Murphy, *America's Quest for Supremacy and the Third World* (London: Pinter Publishers, 1988); and Vincent Ferraro, "Global Debt and Third World Development," in Klare and Thomas, eds., *World Security*, pp. 324-344.

17. William E. Connolly, *Political Theory and Modernity* (Oxford: Basil Blackwell, 1989), pp. 16-40; R.B.J. Walker, "'The Prince' and 'The Pauper': Tradition, Modernity, and Practice in the Theory of International Relations," in Der Derian and Shapiro, eds., *International/Intertextual Relations*. Robert Gilpin, "The Richness of the Tradition of Political Realism," *International Organization* 38 (Spring 1984), pp. 287-304, rightly acknowledges the tradition's internal complexity, yet the same author's *War and Change in World Politics* (Cambridge: Cambridge University Press, 1981) falls back on a thin version of realism.

18. Thomas S. Kuhn, "Postscript-1969," in *The Structure of Scientific Revolutions*, 2nd ed., enlarged (Chicago: University of Chicago Press, 1970). Also see Stephen Toulmin, *Foresight and Understanding: An Enquiry into the Aims of Science* (Bloomington: University of Indiana Press, 1961); and Imre lakatos and Alan Musgrave, eds., *Criticism and the Growth of Knowledge* (Cambridge: Cambridge University Press, 1970).

19. Melvin Gurtov, *Global Politics in the Human Interest* (Boulder CO: Lynne Rienner Publishers, 1988).

20. W.W. Rostow, *The Stages of Economic Growth: A Non-Communist Manifesto* (Cambridge: Cambridge University Press, 1960).

21. Heinar Kipphardt, *In the Matter of J. Robert Oppenheimer*, trans. John Roberts ((New York: Hill and Wang, 1968).

22. Kenneth N. Waltz, *Theory of International Politics* (Reading MA: Addison-Wesley, 1979).

11

Pedagogies on the Edge: World Politics Without "International Relations"

R.B.J. Walker

My understanding of what it means to teach international relations or world politics is informed by a fundamental scepticism about the pedagogical value of the literature usually designated as 'International Relations'(IR). While I have little doubt about the need and even urgency for courses and curricula that might introduce students to those broad structures and practices of contemporary world politics, including the relations among states, that set many of the conditions under which political life is possible anywhere, the IR literature does not seem to me to provide a particularly helpful basis for doing so. This is especially the case with the text-book literature specifically designed to introduce students to the subject, although these express problems that are no less apparent in many of the most highly regarded theoretical texts and research traditions.

My remarks here are therefore intended to explore some of the pedagogical implications of my ambivalence about IR. This ambivalence — about the importance of contemporary world politics and the relative triviality of IR — is compounded by the fact that I spend very little time actually teaching 'IR', though in teaching under other rubrics I am always aware of the impossibility of avoiding principles and practices that are usually fixed under this rather teasing name.

This ambivalence finds one expression in a personal division of labor. Most of my teaching occurs under some version of the grand rubric of 'political theory': early-modern political thought, contemporary social and political theory, the philosophy of social science. Much of my research and writing, on the other hand, is usually fixed under the seemingly quite distinct sign of IR. Indeed, much of my work has been devoted to a series of explorations of the conditions under which these two realms of contemporary political discourse have been articulated as separate and even mutually-exclusive jurisdictions. While I have a long-standing interest in the discourse that is conducted as a form of IR, I have very little interest in treating this work as a body of knowledge that might be taught to anyone, least of all to undergraduate students. I prefer to treat IR — the literature and pedagogical practices that have emerged under this name — as part of the modern world that itself needs to be understood and explained, not as something that might be deployed as a mode of understanding or explanation. As a phenomenon demanding explanation, IR is indeed crucial, and it is primarily in this guise that I am able to assign it any pedagogical significance.

Some of my teaching does occur under the explicit imprimatur of IR, and scepticism about material so designated makes courses intended to instruct on international relations or world politics rather problematic, to say the least. If one is to indulge in sweeping dismissals of an established discipline, it might be said, one must be prepared to identify some alternative, some other way of introducing material that is nevertheless admitted to be of considerable substantive importance. Yet the dismissal I recommend is not quite as sweeping as it might seem. I do not wish to deny that IR can tell us a lot about contemporary world politics — on the contrary. I merely want to claim that what it tells us is not quite what it is so often claimed to tell us. It does not tell us very much about how the world is, though it does tell us a great deal about the conditions under which we are able to claim to know what the world is and what its future possibilities are. Even as a phenomenon that demands explanation, it is certainly a good guide to where and who we think we are.

This, at least, is the view that guides my understanding of what it can mean to teach international relations or world politics, even under the rubric of IR, and it is this understanding and its pedagogical consequences that I want to pursue here. I will do so through some brief comments on the categories that inform so many introductory treatments of the subject, on the assumptions that students typically bring to the classroom, and on several things IR has conventionally not been expected to teach even though there are reasonable grounds for assuming that they are of some considerable significance for an understanding of contemporary world politics. The distinction between international relations and world politics will then be sharpened through a brief discussion of the principle of state sovereignty, which will in turn lead to some concluding comments on four interrelated themes that inform my own teaching practices. My general argument rests on an insistence on the significance, though inadequacy, of the principle of state sovereignty for an understanding of contemporary world politics, including the relations among states, and a claim that if this principle is to be treated seriously, many of the typical procedures of IR must be abandoned.[1]

The Reification of Categories

The obvious practical solution to the problem of knowing how to begin teaching material of such uncertain status is to make a decision about the texts that might be used. But this is immediately to encounter some of the greatest difficulties head on. The text-book market may be flooded, but it is largely a flood of trinkets, few of them usable in any classroom situation with which I would care to be associated. For most introductory and many more advanced texts simply assume, and constantly affirm, precisely those claims that seem to me to be a matter of considerable dispute in contemporary political life. Not least, they assume and then reify categories that depend upon the constitutive distinction between international relations and some other — more normal, more orderly, more progressive, more normative — form of political life, a form that is in turn assumed to occur in paradigmatic fashion within the modern state.

Here it is only necessary to think about the sheer banality of the categories that pass for theoretical starting points, for unchallengeable assumptions upon which the accumulation of positive knowledge may proceed. Perhaps even the majority of scholars in the field would admit that simple distinctions between political realism and political idealism are more than a trifle oversimplified. Many might also admit that claims about political realism cover more sins than ought to be placed in such a dignified conceit. Unfortunately, such admissions seem to have little impact on the writers of introductory texts. Similarly, it is almost impossible to avoid the effects of the crude classification of all political phenomena that has become known as the three 'levels of analysis': individuals, state and international system. Here, the great liberal reading of the ontology of the modern state — individual and state inside, state and Other (interstate system, other states, other [non]cultures) outside — is turned into a hierarchical account of the way things obviously are. So much for the critique of hierarchy that was so crucial for the achievement of modern claims to autonomy; or for the practices of states in mediating the relation between inside and outside; or for the complexities of genders, cultures, classes, economies or societies, not all of which have been successfully carved into territorial fragments of inclusion and exclusion by states.

The overbearing presence of such categories is often made all the more oppressive by the pervasive presence of various strategies through which ontological puzzles are solved by epistemological moves of varying degrees of sophistication: the delineation of different theoretical traditions among which one must choose as if between flavors of ice-cream; the demand for rigorous methodological procedures within a specific tradition; or even the old, but certainly not defunct, appeal to the way things are. It may be possible to find more critical texts in which the effects of such categories are more open for exploration and appraisal, but these, few as they are, tend to be framed as critiques of a prevailing orthodoxy, to be safely introduced only after the serious damage has been done. First get to know the basics, then introduce the theoretical qualifications; as if the basics were not already heavy with abstract and, in my view at least, very contentious theory, and as if later qualifications could undermine principles already firmly absorbed as commonsense.

Obviously not all — perhaps very few — scholars working under the rubric of IR share my scepticism about such matters. Nevertheless, I do find it difficult to expect students who have been encouraged to give some serious thought to Machiavelli, or Hobbes, or Weber, or Foucault, or to the dynamics of capitalism and modernity, or to the logics of scientific explanation, textual interpretation or ideology critique, or to the politics of classification and theory construction, to treat the usual category schemes that inform the IR text-books as anything more, or less, than characteristic refusals of scholarly inquiry. It is only in a very specific sense that individual, state, and international system can be arrayed as levels of an ontological hierarchy. It is only through the grossest of conflations and anachronisms that Machiavelli, Hobbes, and the rest can be forced into a textual coffin marked 'realism'. It is only by cartooning the flimsiest caricatures of scientific method that it is possible to pretend that all ontological puzzles can be solved by epistemological fiat. Yet frequent protestations to the contrary, these are all still very familiar landmarks of a literature that may contain the occasional oasis but is generally quite parched and inhospitable to critical inquiry. Again, this is not to denigrate the oases, which are often very fertile indeed, but it is to underline the difficulties and dangers of pedagogical ambitions limited by the prevailing textual initiations.

The other obvious starting point is the affirmation of a particular flavor, the choice of a particular theoretical perspective, or array of perspectives, which can then be presented precisely as a just perspective or choice between perspectives. This is a particularly attractive option in relation to fairly specific problems or literatures, such as international trade theory, or conflict resolution, or international law. With a careful delineation of the topic and with a relatively coherent body of literature, the development of credible course material is not especially difficult. Unfortunately, careful delineations of such material often turn out to be rather arbitrary, and theoretical coherence has to be maintained by a steady refusal to let one's attention wander too far from the specific problem at hand. Theories of international trade begin to slide into theories of international — or perhaps global — production. Accounts of conflict resolution quickly encounter murky debates about justice, violence and oppression. International law may be presented as knowledge fit for a professional career, but it can also be presented as a rapidly changing form of human experience in which seemingly established principles are far from certain. Indeed, it is the very unruliness of specific problems or bodies of literature that seems to me to be of more than passing interest in this context. It is not easy to carve the world up into parcels fit for problem solving or for 'middle-range theories' of IR because the boundaries of what we call international relations or world politics are themselves so very unstable, the categories within which one might capture its determinations and trajectories so very obscure.

My understanding of what it means to teach international relations or world politics, then, is marked by a stance of double heresy: as a so-called political theorist I have an interest in 'IR'; but my interest in IR arises from a deep scepticism about it as a mode of scholarly inquiry. The obvious punishment for such sins is to be cast into those untold depths concealed by the fine line between disciplinary categories, between the edifying moralities of life within the modern state and the worldly cynicism and incipient horror of life between moralities: a serious punishment indeed, perhaps, though one to which I have become rather accustomed. But it is also here, between the life affirming and tragically limiting discourses of the modern disciplinary academy, that I believe it possible to envision pedagogical practices that do speak to a world of global structures, practices and possibilities. For here there is no alternative but to treat international relations, and especially claims about world politics as a problem, as a fundamental challenge to historically constituted claims about what and where political life is, about who we are — claims that are simply reiterated in the categories of IR as tired answers to questions that have lost their critical, and political, edge.

The Myth of Empty Heads

This initial stance may be recast in terms of a complaint that is more often aired in this context, a complaint less about *what* than about *who* is to be taught. It is frequently said that the most serious difficulties involved in teaching international relations arise from the lack of preparation — even ignorance — on the part of students.

It is perhaps difficult to be unsympathetic to some forms of this complaint, but it often rests on a diagnosis that can bring its own dangers. Treating students as the bearers of the proverbial *tabula rasa*, it is tempting to assume that one's task is to fill the vacancy with knowledge, however this knowledge is conceived. Hence the view that more history, or more initiation into the hard nosed realities of power politics, or more objective research skills, or more basic theory, or more institutional detail, or more attention to normative ideals is required.

Although intellectual vacancy may be all too familiar, it is not the natural state implied by the epistemological naivety of Lockean legend. Enormous energies are deployed to produce the knowledge that becomes manifest as an absence. One may bemoan the parochialism, the chauvinism, the historical myopia, or the scarcity of critical skills among students, but these, too, are forms of knowledge. They are produced by specific social conditions, not given in the nature of things. Moreover, attempts to fill in the vacancy, to pour the appropriate measure of positive knowledge into the supposedly empty heads of misguided youth, can only perpetuate the problem. Youth may be misguided, but this is not because it is driven by an absence. Students enter classes on international relations having already acquired deeply entrenched understandings of history, legitimate knowledge and their place in the world. Those who teach may have a very low opinion of those understandings. This low opinion may even be shared by the students themselves. But the problem is not appropriately understood as an absence to be filled. It is a presence, the presence of historically and socially produced forms of knowledge. And it is this presence that must provide a starting point, one with which it is possible to work, to clarify, to disrupt, to enhance, to make visible as knowledge rather than to obscure as an apparent absence.

This is why I prefer to teach by helping people to understand where and what they are, and the conditions under which they have both come to be where and what they are and to take it for granted that they are where and what they are, rather than to pretend that I have a better understanding of life elsewhere or a better account of what they really ought to know or be. If I am teaching, say, Hobbes, I attempt to treat him not as a great dead white proto-bourgeois male, as an historical precursor of modern achievements, but precisely as an articulation of ontologies and contradictions that are actively at work *within* modern consciousness and institutions/constitutions. To read Hobbes is in significant ways to read oneself, even though this may not have been quite what Hobbes himself had in mind when he recommended self-interrogation as a methodological principle. (And to read Hobbes, I should add, is as good an antidote as any to all those silly claims about international relations as a Hobbesian state of nature; moreover, a few hours with the passages that precede his portrayal of the state of nature/equalitarian individualism, passages about language, science and the perils of nominalism, would provide a useful penance for all those who insist on invoking claims about science in order to discipline explorations of the historical, practical and discursive character of contemporary world politics). Similarly, if I am teaching under the rubric of IR, I attempt to show how patterns of political life that appear to be grandiose and far away, the concern of states and statesmen, of grand historical forces and structural contradictions, are in fact part of the minutest routines of everyday life, part of the familiar politics within rather than just the extraordinary relations that occur out there among the Leviathans.

Students already have many if not most of the assumptions and categories needed to work within IR: assumptions about self and other, about the legitimacy and illegitimacy of violence, about interests, moralities, about History and Progress, about the saved and the damned. Films, news and rock-and-roll are much more effective in this respect than any introductory course can ever hope to be. It may well be that students have to be introduced to more information, to more sources, to more skills, to more histories, to more experiences; or to be stripped of naive illusions; or to be convinced of other, less cynical or less self-righteous aspirations. But it is first necessary to encourage students to understand what they already bring to the practice of knowing more, or of dissipating illusions, or of formulating other aspirations. The important problems for pedagogy in this respect concern the extent to which courses on international relations should seek to question, or to reproduce in a more sophisticated fashion, those assumptions and categories that students already have when they enter the classroom.

A Discipline of Absences

If it is a mistake to presume that students present an absence waiting to be filled, it is useful, however, to think about the absences that are such an important part of IR. Four of these strike me as especially useful ways of coming to terms with what it means to engage with the complexities of contemporary politics through this particular discipline.

First, consider the fate of the concept of 'culture'. This is, no doubt, a complicated term, not least because it participates in two of the primary antinomies of modern thought: through pluralist claims about cultures as opposed to unitary claims about civilization; and through claims about the status of ideas, ideals, consciousness and ideology as opposed to claims about the material and the concrete. These antinomies are undoubtedly important for thinking about international relations. Indeed, it is in IR that the term 'culture' is likely to evoke especially crude formulations of these antinomies, usually through a not-so-subtle translation into various claims about 'values'. International relations then become a realm of irreconcilable value relativism, and thus an arena of force and violence; unless all values can be reconciled on the convenient utilitarian terrain of modernity itself, the culture beyond all cultures in which all differences, and all heresies, can be reconciled with state and capital. They also become a realm of almost pure material necessity, a discourse in which normative aspiration can only be utopian illusion. Perhaps the absence of cultural analysis in IR is not surprising. Perhaps the degree to which the critical category of 'ideology' has become synonymous with descriptive categories like 'doctrine' or 'belief' is not surprising either. But this absence does provide one telling indication of how this discourse of inclusion and exclusion, of politics inside and mere relations outside the modern state, is itself constructed through procedures of inclusion and exclusion that are scarcely recognized in its own categories and procedures.

The absence of gender is equally telling. Despite increasingly frequent calls for a convergence of feminism and IR, it is a convergence that is strictly unthinkable without a fundamental reconstruction of the categories that make IR possible. The 'levels of analysis' schema already affirms a particular account of political identity, one in which the politics of gender is erased through a reading of state and individual as abstract universals, as macro and micro versions of the modern aspiration for autonomy articulated by the early-moderns. While some forms of feminism may be content to articulate their aspirations completely within this modernist frame, others are more likely to treat this frame as at least part of the problem to be confronted, as the condition under which contemporary sexual politics have come to be as they are. At the very least, it is not at all obvious that categories of man, state and war, or of realism and idealism, or of realism, pluralism and structuralism, and so on, can tell us very much about the construction of gender relations or the gendering of political practices on a global scale.

The absence of political economy from the categories of IR has been more frequently noted, so much so that international political economy in some of its many forms has been treated as one of the contending 'approaches' now considered to be worthy of a taste test. The problem that is usually canvassed here is the apparent gap between IR and a more broadly conceived account of a 'world politics', a term that is perhaps even more problematic than 'international relations'. The most familiar form of this complaint is that 'IR' is rather narrow, concerned only with matters of high consequence in the relations among states. Most often, this complaint is issued as a claim about historical obsolescence, about political realism as a theory that may once have applied to a simpler world gone by but which can no longer grasp the complexities and interdependencies of the present. Again, something seems missing, though it is not at all clear what this missing something is. It might be simply the economy, or, less euphemistically, capitalism. IR might then be read as yet another of those political discourses that work simply by affirming capitalism as the natural order of things. But it might also be a form of politics that does indeed encompass the world, a world politics that continues to be more significant, but also more enigmatic, than the usual initiations of IR could ever hope to portray.

This problem emerges more clearly in relation to the final absence that I want to note here, an absence marked by the constant presence of claims about the principle of state sovereignty. For, this principle is constantly invoked as the ultimate source from which the necessities of political power must flow. Yet the resources that have been devoted to the examination of this principle are rather meagre, again to say the very least. There may be occasional references to some famous texts by Jean Bodin or John Austin, or famous legal landmarks such as the Treaty of Westphalia or the Wimbledon Case. There may even be several handy surveys of its historical emergence and application. But it would be difficult to argue that the IR literature offers much serious analysis of how this principle works — that is, of the conditions under which the seemingly elegant claim to state sovereignty has come to be accepted as the primary constitutive principle of modern political life.

Yet, of course, this claim was established only with considerable difficulty. It was articulated against other principles, notably those legitimizing hierarchical modes of feudal and theological order. It required the emergence of forms of human experience in which claims about autonomy, about separation, and about subjectivity, made some sense. It required — and still requires — the deployment of enormous resources to ensure that the messy edges and heterogeneity of human affairs conform to the orders of modernity within the jurisdictions of state. It required, and still requires, enormous imagination to come to terms with the new political identities that could be articulated within these novel and so very tidy jurisdictions. Not least, it required the confirmation of new forms of privilege: of the secular over the sacred, of the particular terrain over the universals of eternity, of one's status as citizen over one's status as a human, of the necessity of obligations to the state as the condition under which one might nevertheless aspire to the universal or even the eternal. And strictly speaking, of course, it required the forfeiture of any claim to a world politics, to a politics that might encompass the world, as opposed to a politics that might arise in particular places.

The sign of 'IR' teases precisely because it makes it possible to elide this consequence of the early-modern resolution of all philosophical, theological and political puzzles. Canvassing the international, it invokes the world, the global, the human. Admitting mere relations, it affirms the authenticity of the political community within. The apparent elegance of state sovereignty, and the silent contemplation that affirms its hold on contemporary political discourse, speaks to the enormity of its historical achievement. It is no surprise that it works so effectively as our great myth of origins and guide to disciplinary initiations. But it should be no surprise, either, that it works so ineffectively to provoke analyses of world politics that can do anything more than confirm the expectations of a world that affirms itself in its own contradictions, its own chasms, its own unrealizable ambitions. If the construction of traditions of realism and idealism, or those peculiar hierarchical levels stretched out across a territorial space from here to there, from within to without, project possibilities that arise from the resolutions of state sovereignty, as I believe they do, then it is absurd to expect them to reveal the contours of an emerging world politics or the dynamics of historical transformation. For state sovereignty, and the categories that derive from it, already tell us where and what politics must be, and thus where and what it cannot be. As such, it is not a fact of life, the ultimate given from which all else must follow. It is merely a practice, an historical achievement, though one that continues to play a crucial constitutive role in the way things come to be.

Pedagogies of Inside/Outside

Students already bring knowledge with them to the classroom, though this knowledge may be judged to be woefully inadequate in many respects. IR already affirms the impropriety of speaking about world politics, although this does not prevent it from transgressing its own prohibitions with some regularity. Together, these two observations provide a way of orienting myself in relation to the demands of the classroom. And despite my scepticism about IR, they should indicate why I nevertheless consider it essential to begin, as the IR texts say we must, with some understanding of how the claim to state sovereignty works both as a principle and as a constitutive practice of modern political life.

My difficulty with IR in this respect is that while it affirms the claim to state sovereignty, it fails to problematize the degree to which this claim informs the categories and procedures through which it seeks to understand what it takes a world of sovereign states to be. Permitting this historically specific resolution of all philosophical, theological and political puzzles to inform the standards of goodness, truth and beauty — not to say research methods — through which the consequences of this resolution are judged, IR can only encourage the familiar arc of self-fulfilling prophecy: states are not obsolete, so realism must be true; utopia is clearly not upon us, so we must put up with tragic necessities for the foreseeable future. A refusal to take this resolution for granted, though without in any way denying its continuing significance as a constitutive practice, permits an opening up of the questions to which that resolution has provided one immensely elegant but never entirely persuasive answer. Moreover, it is precisely knowledge shaped by claims to state sovereignty that students bring with them to the classroom. For state sovereignty is not just an abstract legal principle. It is part of the broad culture of modernity, with all its assumptions about universality and diversity, self and other, and space and time, all its assumptions about the world and how it is appropriate for people to be in it. IR offers both evidence that the world is as this knowledge suggests it is and intimations that this knowledge, so comfortably absorbed from the codes and expectations of everyday life, is vaguely — or perhaps even dangerously — unsettling.

This unsettling, of course, is the stock-in-trade of the self-anointed realists, with their well-rehearsed charade of cynicism and worldly wisdom. But it is a form of unsettling that brings its own forms of stability, a charade of cynicism that legitimizes the myopia within, a form of worldly wisdom that encourages amnesia about the place of power and violence in the goodness, truth and beauty of the polity inside the modern state. My difficulty with claims about political realism in this respect is not that it affirms the place of historicity and contingency in human affairs, or the necessary convergence of knowledge and power in games among Leviathans, but that it does so while insisting that historicity, contingency and power politics have their own special place, a place reserved for them beyond the apparent calm within. Political realism marks the line beyond which the convergence of knowledge and power must be legitimate. It also marks the line within which knowledge and power ought not to converge. As such it has always been an explicitly normative move, though one that has managed to masquerade rather successfully as a pure absence of both teleology and illusion.

The assumptions that students bring to the classroom — the possibility of unpacking claims to state sovereignty, the puzzling character of claims about world politics, the unsettling even if superficial character of claims about political realism, and the pervasive sense nevertheless that in a moment of fairly profound structural transformation the way we are is not the way we have to be — all of this is more than enough to engage with world politics and even international relations without relying on the initiations of 'IR'. Even if one relies entirely on the literature produced by this discipline — a feat akin to wrestling with one arm tied behind one's back — it is possible to animate very effective classroom techniques by emphasizing two guiding strategies that underlie these resources: the persistent return to the claim to self-identity that informs one's understanding of the world, and the insistence on the historicity of one's self-identity, and thus of one's understanding of the world. Both strategies offer the possibility of encouraging a properly critical pedagogy, that is, one rooted in an explicit concern for the conditions under which specific knowledge claims are made.

Concretely, this seems to me to imply four sets of themes that might be at work or play in a course on international relations or world politics. The scope they permit is potentially enormous, and the details of their improvisation would obviously depend on where courses would be taught and on what kinds of students might be interested. Though these four themes can be captured fairly easily within the familiar categories of IR, the way in which I try to pose them is explicitly intended to denaturalize those categories, and to insist on the need to understand the conditions under which those categories have been produced.

One would involve an exploration of the practices of state sovereignty itself. This might lead to an historical interest in the massive transformations through which state sovereignty has been established in principle or in the long and complex processes through which it has entered into the practices of particular states, or in the different forms in which it has been articulated in particular cases. It might lead on to other well known literatures about the state or about the nation, and thus to the historical construction of particular identities and communities. It might also lead to a consideration of many other literatures that either presume or seek to challenge the construction of the community from within which relations without are surveyed and condoned, not least those involving culture, gender and political economy. As far as possible, I seek to make connections with a broad range of cultural contexts, not merely to emphasize the cultural specificity of the emergence of state sovereignty, but to demonstrate its complicity with what now passes for 'common sense', at least in those societies in which IR has become a persuasive representation of the world. In this context, I am prone to make special reference to the aesthetics of three-dimensional perspective, the geometry of the Mercator map projection and the harmonic structures of rock and roll: after all, state sovereignty participates in a broad articulation of spatio-temporal relations and it is always instructive to be reminded of the extent to which this articulation informs the most pervasive practices of everyday life that one has come to take for granted.

Another would involve an exploration of the limits of state sovereignty, that is, of the practices that occur on the boundaries of established claims to sovereign identity. War offers the most obvious focus here, though a wide range of topics conventionally arrayed on either side of the domestic/international divide could also be encompassed, not least diplomacy, the practices of foreign policy and the constraints placed on, say, democratic politics by invocations of emergency or 'national interest'. Though much of this material is conventional, framing it in relation to practices at work/play at the margins of established identities tends to problematize what is so often treated as either a nice clear divide — domestic/international, here/there, community/anarchy — or as an empty category, the abstract state. Any number of complaints have been issued about the oversimplifications involved in such treatments. A relative blindness to the tremendous resources devoted by states to the mediation of relations between inside and outside, for example, seems to me to have been one of the most significant consequences of the 'levels of analysis' categorization, and the simplicity of those theories of the state that do sometimes appear in literatures informed by this categorization are hardly to be commended for their adherence to Ockham's principle of parsimony. Even so, the number of complaints has not had much effect on the grip of the straight line on the modern imagination, despite the slipping grip of the modern imagination on the spatio-temporal trajectories of the contemporary world.

In this context, I find it helpful to complement some of the better known accounts of the state with three related lines of analysis. One is concerned with the discursive framing of the outside, the Other, whether as enemy, as barbarian or as a generalized anarchy/uncertainty. One is concerned with the use of such framings of an external other in the construction of a self-identity within, a prominent theme within influential accounts of republican *virtù* but one that has been lost in theories emanating from societies more convinced of their own virtue. One is concerned with the practices of boundary maintenance/ transgression in many different settings; the analogy between the boundary maintaining practices of states and the practices of erotic transgression, for example, offers considerable opportunity for discussing the legitimation of violence in the modern world.

A third set of themes is again quite conventional and concerns the articulation of practices and institutional arrangements among states. Here I am generally content to draw upon much of the well-established IR literature, especially that which has been concerned with the historical emergence of a 'society of states', whether understood in primarily diplomatic terms or in relation to the global articulation of capitalism. I am particularly unimpressed by recent attempts to elevate utilitarian forms of liberal micro-economics to the status of paradigmatic theory in this context, and tend to treat them as more or (usually) less interesting footnotes to already rich literatures on international law, diplomacy, hegemony, historical sociology, and so on. Otherwise, my only significant deviations here derive from my prior resistance to clear cut distinctions between politics inside and outside the state. Given the theoretically contested state of the literature on the structures of relations between states/world politics, however, I consider it important to emphasize the multiplicity of conflicting accounts of what these structures are and how they work, while also attempting to relate them to possibilities already made available by certain articulations of the claim to state sovereignty and to different readings of the relative autonomy of state and capital.

These first three themes, then, are all concerned with the historical construction of and the practices involved in the reproduction of international relations or world politics as a territorial politics of inclusion and exclusion. Taking the resolution of all philosophical, theological and political puzzles through a spatial framing of political identity, community and possibility seriously, they are intended to highlight the always problematic character of that resolution. They are intended especially to avoid the specifically liberal (sovereign individual-sovereign state-other [non]sovereignties) rendition of this resolution that is naturalized in categories of analytical levels and realism/utopia. They are also intended to focus attention on both the role of the state in mediation between patterns of inclusion and exclusion and the participation of these mediating forces in the broader cultural and institutional practices of modernity.

The final theme encompasses material that is somehow concerned with patterns of historical transformation, emerging forms of 'world order', and so on. Somewhat paradoxically, perhaps, it is here that I feel most constrained by the relevant literature, extensive though it is. I feel constrained precisely because so much of this literature, while correctly calling attention to the limited obsessions of dominant forms of political realism (both historicist and utilitarian), continues to work well within the philosophical, theological and political options made available by the claim to state sovereignty. My reasons for this judgement are rather complex, but it is perhaps only necessary to consider the extent to which this literature is content to reproduce the binary options — state/humanity, fragmented/integrated, sovereignty/world order — that have been produced by the discourses of the sovereign state. It seems to me to be more useful to try to understand contemporary transformations in terms of various challenges to the resolution of all puzzles that is expressed by the principle of state sovereignty rather than to ask whether that principle is obstinate or obsolete in terms already determined by the principle itself.

Thus rather than resort to various claims about interdependence, world order, and so on, I prefer to introduce students to the apparent contradictions of the 'global city', or the challenges to established patterns of political space/time posed by social movements, technologies of information transmission or changing patterns of capitalist production on a global scale. I find it especially useful to relate the apparently global to the apparently local, to ask about the extent to which the world 'out there' is already present in the familiar world of everyday life.

It is at this point, it seems to me that it is possible to pose all the questions that must arise in a course on 'world politics' that takes the problematic character of all claims about world politics seriously: questions about who we are, about the character of our relations with and obligations to others, about our capacity to fix forms of political community and authority in a world characterized increasingly by temporal accelerations rather than spatial extensions. It may be rather paradoxical that it is precisely this possibility that arises from a pedagogy so fixated on the importance of state sovereignty; on the other hand, I find it difficult to understand why so much teaching of IR depends on a monotonous affirmation of state sovereignty without ever asking where it came from, how it works, or how it continues to inform the practices through which we come to know its effects. No matter what the official rubric may be — international relations, political theory, sociology, history, law, cultural/gender/development/interdisciplinary/literary studies — it seems to me that contemporary pedagogies concerned with a politics that is somehow international or global must seek to both understand and challenge those affirmations of self/other, human/nonhuman, and included/excluded which may insist that we do not change the world under conditions of our own choosing but which also do not preclude our capacity to struggle for other possibilities.

Notes

1. For a critical reading of the theoretical literature on "international relations," see R.B.J. Walker, *Inside/Outside: International Relations as Political Theory* (Cambridge: Cambridge University Press, 1993). Because of the scope of the literature addressed by the present argument, I rely on this text to provide explicit

bibliographical references as well as more extended argumentation in support of the position that I adopt.

12

The Classroom as Political Arena: The Making of a World Politics Experience

Lev S. Gonick

The teacher is an exorcist confronting a panoply of dybbuks.
   Ira Shor, *Critical Teaching and Everyday Life*

No culture will give
popular nourishment
and support to images
or patterns which are
   alien to its
dominant impulses
and aspirations.

   Marshall McLuhan, *The Mechanical Bride*

Ideally, what should be said to every child, repeatedly, throughout his or her school life is something like this:

> 'You are in the process of being indoctrinated, we have not yet evolved a system of education that is not a system of indoctrination. We are sorry, but it is the best we can do. What you are being taught here is an amalgam of current prejudice and the choices of this particular culture. The slightest look at history will show how impermanent these must be. You are being taught by people who have been able to accommodate themselves to a regime of thought laid down by their predecessors. It is a self-perpetuating system. Those of you who are more robust and individual than others, will be encouraged to leave and find ways of educating yourself — educating your own judgement. Those that stay must remember, always and all the time, that they are being moulded and patterned to fit into the narrow and particular needs of this particular society.'

   Doris Lessing, *The Golden Notebook*

Let me cut to the chase. We, the academy of world politics scholars, face two major disorienting challenges. The global make-over underway leaves the discipline in what orienteering experts call bush madness (no pun intended). Gone are the central organizing principles of the cold war — the bifurcation of the world into two ideological camps, what we called bipolarity. Gone is the preoccupation with massive nuclear warfare between yesterday's superpowers. Gone are Franck and Weisband's dual ghetto system with the odd power relationships that followed.[1] No longer will tails wag dogs. Just ask the Pakistanis or the Israelis. The second disorienting challenge is to move beyond the academy's own *longue durée*, the straightjacket of pre-Gutenberg pedagogy. Why do we cling to the lecture format? The lecture is a late medieval invention instituted because books were scarce. The lecture was originally a reading: one *man* reading aloud could make a single book accessible to many. Why has this ritual survived among the literate in the post-Gutenberg era?

First to the ritual of subject matter. Peter McLaren's ethnographic work, *Schooling as Ritual Performance*, from which the passages quoted above have been selected, is a study of a Catholic junior high school in Toronto. Not unlike high school, the university is an intricately structured and ritually saturated institution. Classroom rites provide blueprints for both 'thinking' and 'doing'. Through this pedagogical engagement, students are structured to think of the world in certain ways and are motivated to act upon their world according to prescribed symbols. Critical pedagogy reflects on the interrelationship between the learning process, domination, language and thought, subjective empowerment, alienation, political extension of subject matter to daily life, sexual and racial divisions, and the problem of student resistance to transformation.[2] As Shor concludes, "education is a tough and inviting medium at the heart of culture war."[3] For Giroux, pedagogy and the culture of the classroom represent "a battleground on which meanings are defined, knowledge is legitimated, and futures are sometimes created and destroyed."[4] The university classroom, especially Introductory World Politics, dedicated to exploring the making of new world futures, becomes one of the principal socializing agents in shaping our understanding of that new world order-in-the-making.

Against the background of a continuing economic crisis, the specter of ecological ruin, the weak consensus for national and global austerity, the absence of hegemonic deference among competing world capitals, and growing instability, the role of university instructor as *clerks of the empire* having taken on the *dead weight of warehouse knowledge* has been challenged to the very core.[5] Traditional classroom pedagogy is based upon what Freire calls *the banking concept of education*. When received wisdom is no longer adequate, the classroom culture — in which students are the depositories and the teacher is the depositor — runs the risk of bankruptcy. Instead of communicating, many of us, trained in just this tradition, issue communiqués and make deposits that the student continues obligingly to receive, memorize, and repeat. When inevitabilities are challenged we find ourselves in crisis seeking orientation. The two Chinese characters for crisis, that is 'danger' and 'opportunity', are symbolic of the double-edged sword facing teachers of world politics. While there are obviously no easy answers there are still available discoverable hard answers, and it is these that we can now learn to make and share.[6] Here I first make the case for a new conception of world politics. Second, I share with the reader my experience in bringing some of these themes to the classroom.

Pre-Pedagogics: Violence, Power Relations, and Change — Towards an Integrative Agenda for the Study of World Politics

After 350 years of centripetal force, the great majority of modern states are internally divided into status-groups different in culture, separate in organization, and unequal in resources. These same deeply divided states, no matter the degree of their subordination within the international division of labor, jealously reserve the right to defend and advance the 'integrity' of their state-building project against internal or external threat, real or merely perceived. The result is a study of world politics, framed in terms of the competing social and political forces, pitting those who struggle to maintain the delicate state-building project and its external projection against those imploding forces challenging the prevailing social construction of reality. One set of analytical constructs offers primacy to social forces building order, the other offers primacy to the forces of change. As has become clear in the theoretical literature, these two sets of dynamics are inextricably linked (See Figure 1). In conventional terms, such a starting point in fact amounts to a call for an integrative project between comparative politics and international relations. The process of extricating ourselves from the narrowly defined disciplinary boundaries between comparative politics and international relations is one major challenge. Rather than offering primacy to one or the other impulse, the challenge, at this level, is to conceptualize the interaction between the two dynamics as *the* contested issue.

The second challenge is the persistent question of how to organize and present an integrated enterprise to the undergraduate student. Over the past number of years I have attempted to build such a project under the general theme of violence, power relations, and change. The project

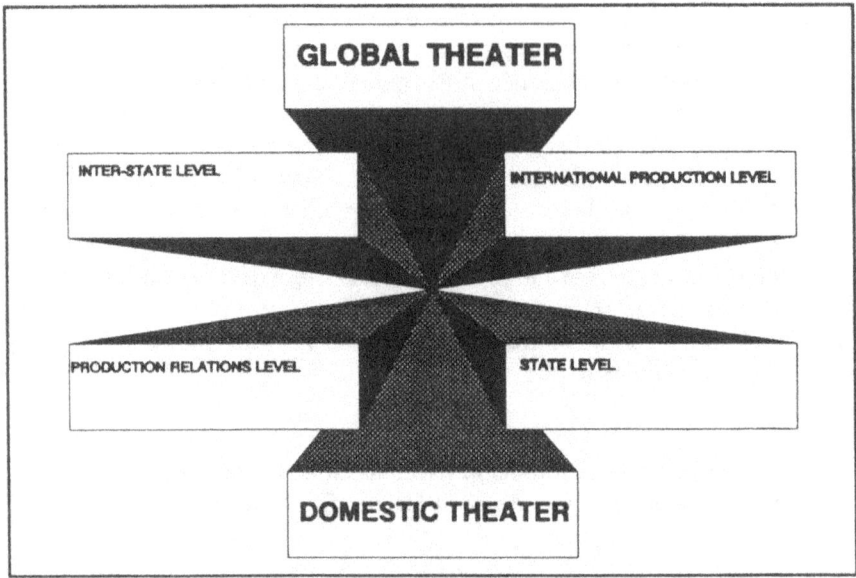

FIGURE 1: LEVELS OF ANALYSIS

is built on the edifice of a modified Galtungian matrix of theaters of violence (See Figure 2). Pedagogically, the aim is to demonstrate that external forms of violence and power struggle have an impact upon the internal configuration of social forces *at the same time* as internal forms of violence condition the external workings of the international political economy and the inter-state system.

One's starting point within the matrix is as much tactical as it is politically relevant.[7] From my modest experience I have observed that students in the introductory course bring varying amounts of information (data) to the course, a range of research skills, and degrees of theoretical sophistication. Most of our texts begin with broad historical treatments, in an effort to offer students a road map for positioning states within the international division of labor and inter-state system. As Marshall Hogdson pointed out some years ago, such orientations tend to reinforce the ethnocentricism of both our Western Historical Self-Image, and our limited and distorted Steinberg *New Yorker Magazine* Image of Geographical Space.[8] Instead of beginning with 'external' theaters of violence I have taken to starting with what most students can identify with from personal experience, namely violence, and power relations in their own families and self-defined communities. I begin with reflective

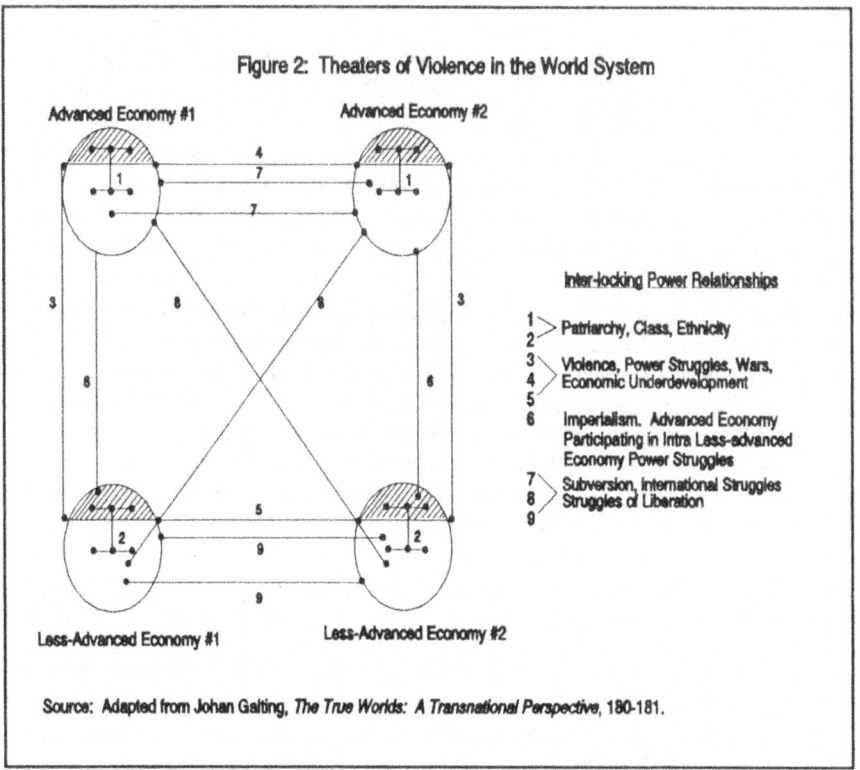

Figure 2: Theaters of Violence in the World System

Source: Adapted from Johan Galting, *The True Worlds: A Transnational Perspective*, 180-181.

consideration of the nature of violence between men and women in the context of the patriarchal and hierarchical society that is our own. In general, I am interested in developing critical thinking skills and there is no better reference point, no matter the pain and hurt involved, then the familiar. I begin the course with Cynthia Enloe's revisionist text *Bananas, Beaches and Bases*.

> It has almost become a cliché to say that the world is shrinking, that state boundaries are porous. We persist, none the less, in discussing personal power relations as if they were contained by sovereign states. We treat ideas about violence against women without trying to figure out how the global trade in pornographic videos operates, or how companies offering sex tours and mail order brides conduct their business across national borders. . . . To make sense of international politics we also have to read power backwards and forwards. Power relations between countries and their governments involve more than gunboat manoeuvres and

diplomatic telegrams. Read forward, 'the personal is international' insofar as ideas about what it means to be a 'respectable' woman or an 'honorable' man have been shaped by colonizing policies, trading strategies and military doctrines.[9]

A different form of violence is engendered when the IMF dictates that price subsidies on food stuffs must be removed by the Jamaican government. Writes Susan George:

> Fatherless households are commonplace in Jamaica. Veronica is another woman whose man left her with two small children . . . She also cares for her blind and housebound grandmother. 'Friends feed the children sometimes. We can't manage on my earning [of not quite $US4 a week, which she gets for part-time work making bags]. We eat mostly rice and calaloo [local spinach]. I used to buy chicken necks for the children, but we can't afford that any more. Prices just go up and up. It frightens me to think what will happen. Starve to death, I suppose.[10]

Admittedly, these opening vignettes stir a good deal of unease. *Whose script is the Prof reading from?* Because men out number women in the course (consistently 65:35), and because of the preconceived notions with which students come to the course, I actually accentuate my opening script by contrasting these questions with two short videoed press clippings — the first the press conference of the U.S. military spokesmen after the July 3, 1988 'accidental downing' of the Iranian airline, explaining the carnage of two and hundred and ninety people away in the language of sterile, computerized, decision-making. The other is a short segment from an International Monetary Fund video extolling the virtues of structural adjustment and export-led growth to the macro-economic prospects of third world countries and to local peoples.

There are other forms of domestic power relations. The next step is to share with students some of the conventional and important ideas in international relations such as nationalism and state-building and the rise of the Westphalian inter-state system (relations 3-5 in Figure 2).[11] A famous Canadian Prime Minister once compared the relationship between Canada and its neighbour to the south in terms of a mouse and an elephant. Canadian students are immediately suspicious of the assumptions of functional equivalence as being the basis for the Westphalian order. "*How can you separate function from capability?*" challenges one student. "*When the U.S. sneezes in the international theatre Canadians tend to catch pneumonia*" marks a second student. "*What about the independence of Canadian foreign policy-making towards Cuba and Nicaragua?"* counters a third student. As we develop the basic organizing concepts and principles of international relations, nationalism, state-building, state power, a general sense of relief pervades the class. *"At last we're doing I.R."* notes a student in her academic journal.

Just as an air of 'normalcy' returns to the class I propose that *state-building* is actually the mirrored-opposite of *nation-destroying* (back to relations 1-2 in Figure 2). This leads to an important discussion of the dynamics of group rights, ethno-nationalism, dominant and subordinate cultural groups and the prerogative of state-building. Again I begin with our own backyard and try to advance the proposition that the fragile state-building project in Canada is predicated on forms of nation-destroying (assimilation, accommodation, and genocide) of the First-Nations and the *Québécois*. Given the Constitutional crisis in the country, the proposition immediately produces reaction. I further introduce the concepts of political fragmentation, economic dependence, and cooptation of leadership as themes for understanding how dominant cultural groups attempt to reproduce order in deeply divided states. Following the work of Ian Lustick[12], and Deborah Gerner's excellent monograph-length text, *One Land, Two-People*[13], we then extend our questions to a short three week module on the Middle East. In years passed I have used the example of South Africa, India, and Yugoslavia to advance the collective breadth of knowledge on the dynamics of *state-building* and *nation-destroying*.

While the Theaters of Violence framework helps to identify additional forms of external and cross-national violence (see key), I have chosen to walk away from a systematic treatment of the framework at this point in the term and return to it only at the end. Students will often pick up on the framework through course evaluation exercises.

At this point many students begin to understand the dynamic between violence and power relations. Moreover, there is a hint that all of this introspective analysis actually connects to the relations between states (wars, economic dependence), and to the way in which non-state and state actors engage in struggles for power. Writes a student in her academic journal: *"it seems to me that all the pieces of the puzzle are out on the table. What is missing is some sense of how all the pieces fit together."* Contrary to the post-modernist impulse to resist totalizing frameworks I try to offer students a flexible framework that I refer to as a 'question generator' (inasmuch as it helps to generate forms of inquiry). I call it the *extraction and expansion cycle*. Students are socialized to think in various parochial ways. In an attempt to enlist student imaginations in the service of a WORLD perspective I want to offer them a road map that privileges an analysis of WORLD history, WORLD civilization, WORLD-wide violence and underdevelopment. The theatres of violence framework is an important anchoring point in reorienting the student; the *extraction and expansion cycle* is an helpful, historically grounded complement.

The dynamic driving the cycle is a derivative of what Choucri, North, Ashley, and others call *lateral pressure*.[14] The central point of this two week module in the course is to develop a 'question generator' based on a concrete study of comparative historical international political economy and world politics. The twin engines of the cycle are world capitalist forces and the dynamics of inter-state conflict. The basic logic of the cycle can be summarized very briefly.

The uneven amplitude of the dynamics of expanded reproduction and state formation generates a spatially unequal or *asynchronic* wave of industrialization and market networking resulting in two types of economies, one advanced and one less-advanced (again refer to Figure 2). This initial advantage, aided by the joint effects of state-directed military use in defending and encouraging mercantilism in the expansion of markets and its rationalization provided by various forms of religion, produces a crystallization of the unequal distribution of resources between advanced and less-advanced economies. While initially geographic differentiated, the ensuing advanced/less-advanced distinction not only cements asymmetric power relationships *between* geographic spheres (relations 6-9 in Figure 2) but also develops centres of powers and marginalized elements *within* states (relations 1-2 in Figure 2). These internal inequalities are products of both the expanding national market and the incorporation of certain staple goods into the fledgling capitalist world-order. The advanced country seeks to stabilize and monopolize its advantages through policies aimed at the institutionalization and routinization of this asymmetric relationship evidenced in the epochs of imperialism, colonialism, and arguably the prevailing international division of labor. Similarly and obviously related to this external form of hierarchy is the consolidation and legitimization of differentiated domestic social hierarchies. These asymmetric relationships *between* and *within* states are encrusted through an historically-informed dynamic called *peripheralization*.

As the World-Economy expanded and matured through the 18th and 19th century, non-core states were *peripheralized*. Hierarchy, based on economic function divides the economies of the world. Less-advantaged economies are not 'permitted' to converge or penetrate the advanced economies of the World Economy, not because the core has failed to diffuse its modernization programme but rather because it is not to the advantage of the advanced economies. Peripheralization has involved first and foremost the creation of a new domestic social order, in both the advanced and less-advanced economies, in which social relations are tied to the dynamics of externally-induced expansion, accumulation and periodic crisis.

In turn, the process of peripheralization carries a political and economic programme of *fragmentation*. Fragmentation refers to the relative isolation of individual peripheralized social formations in the context of the international division of labor. It also refers to the fractious nature of peripheralized forces within the internal division of labor, be they based on gender, skill, language, geography or ethno-cultural differences. Fragmentation leads to a general difficulty in building and sustaining political and economic alliances. The process of fragmentation is itself generated by hard bargaining taking place between and within the supraordinate and subordinate classes of advanced states, *bridgeheads* within the less-advanced social formations and the ensuing class struggles within the less-advanced social formations to resolve these contradictions.

Given the dynamics of peripheralization and the ensuing condition of fragmentation, it becomes useful to view the process of accumulating economic wealth based on differentiated patterns of production relations both within advanced economies and peripheralized social formations as being based upon various forms of exploitation. That is, a society's working class, far from representing a homogeneous social force, has been and remains internally divided along economic lines that are in turn both created from and reinforced by gender, racial, or ethnic differentiation. Those divisions may carry with them corresponding degrees of exploitation. Different forms of domination lend themselves to different political projects, varying tactical strategies, and distinct coalitions of social forces.

The rise, expansion, and logic of the capitalist world-system has been based upon segmentation both within the development of internal divisions of labor, and as in the hierarchical divisions of the international division of labor. The very rise of the capitalist World-System, centered in Europe and later in the United States and Japan, has embedded within it two co-evolving dynamics. These dynamics are largely responsible for both the expansive nature of capitalist development and many of its inherent contradictions.

The first of these dynamics is the segmentation of production processes. Dogmatically understood as bifurcated class divisions, in fact, segmented production relations within internal divisions of labor have been based upon more complex differentiation based upon gender and ethnic lines. While skilled and high-paying work belonged to males within the ethnically supraordinate group, a hierarchy of the less desirable, lower-paying labour engage women of the supraordinate group, men of the subordinate group, and women of the subordinate group.

The domination and exploitation by supraordinate groups over subordinate groups has led to two types of political responses. The first, the politics of inclusion, is manifestly evident within both the 20th century womens' movement (within the state) and the G-77 (between states). Women, largely responsible for the physical reproduction of the segmented basis of capitalist development, have sought to reduce the gender form of exploitation embedded in segmented development. The struggles of the suffragette movement at the beginning of this century, and pay equity at its close, offers one form of political response. The routinization of Sukarno's 1955 call for reason and the redress of historical inequities between the superordinate first world and the subordinate third world has also evolved into a strategy of inclusion. Calls for a new international economic order reflect demands made by subordinate state actors seeking a form of 'level playing field' with the First World.

The second form of political response is the politics of insurrection. This second form of political agency is about the transformation of social orders. Insurrectionism is manifested in armed liberation struggles, organized women's struggles in modern national liberation struggles, nationalization of multinational operations, and in the radical origins of the non-aligned movement. Between these dyads, the reality of segmented development unfolds. Contrary to integrationist and marxist theory, labour market segmentation has provided ideological sustenance for subordinate groups in the persistence and revival of ethno-nationalism. While the process of state building and economic development required the segmented basis of the economy to be only secondary to the call for 'nation-building', the negation of ethnic or national expression continues to bring about its own negation in the separatist, irredentist, or secessionist expressions of ethno-nationalist revivalism.

The second dynamic is the segmentation of the international division of labour. While peripheralized economies were initially supplier economies to the externally controlled World-Economy, a wide range of political economies have evolved, some of whom are now directly challenging the source of their historical condition of peripheralization and fragmentation. While, initially, advanced economies sought to build up empires by integrating peripheralized social formations into their spheres, the necessity of controlling the new colonies, coupled with the limited number of countries to be dominated, brought advanced economies into conflict with one another and afforded certain elements of the peripheralized economies access to resources — including instruments of war. As empires declined and others came to dominate, advanced economies no longer had a monopoly of or control over, the instruments of violence now in the possession of former subordinated groups. The rise of modern state forms in the Middle East, Africa, Asia, Central and Latin America all follow this pattern. More important still was to be the lingering economic ties that still had the effect of creating or underscoring the hierarchical ranking within the international division of labour between advanced and peripheralized social formations.

To lend historical specificity to the *extraction and expansion cycle* students are assigned chapters from Paul Kennedy's *Rise and Fall* and/or Eric Wolf's *Europe and People Without History*. Armed with concepts, history, and a flexible 'question generator' the rhythm of the course proceeds to include an extended treatment of war, statecraft, imperialism, conflict management, trade, internationalization of capital, debt, and foreign aid. As an introductory course, the survey of substantive subject matter is actually less important than the two primary goals: critical thinking and an escape from the parochialism and ethnocentric blinders that they bring with them. To that end, the real challenge for the teacher is pushing the threshold of pedagogy beyond the pale of Gutenberg.

In Search of a Post-Gutenberg Pedagogy

Every fall, across hundreds of university campuses, an annual ritual begins. The university comes alive when the ghosts of yesterday come back to haunt students, faculty, and administrators alike. Every year it is the same. Nothing changes. The line up at the bookstores, the annual shopping for courses expedition, and the desperate scramble to find lecture halls only to find them teaming with faceless bodies are all part of the ritual. The rites begin with the professor distributing the course outline. Quick — to the requirements of the course. The ice is broken when someone inevitably chimes in with "*exactly what do we need to know for the exam . . . will it be based on the texts or lectures?*" It is, as if, with this question, all the important questions of the course will have been dealt with and we can move on to the next part of the ritual. There is something very assuring about these rituals. Everyone has been schooled in a similar set of traditions, expectations are assumed, responsibilities are accepted, and the fear of the unknown is quickly replaced by the comforts of these well rehearsed practices. The lecture is central to the ritual and it is rarely, if ever, challenged as an appropriate mode of pedagogy.

I do not wish to dispute the centrality of the lecture. But learning, real learning, involves more than just the exercise of students taking copious notes from the lecturer. Like many other contributors in this volume I have been experimenting with extending the threshold of the traditional pedagogical instruments. To begin with, on the first day of the fall term, when my students come into the lecture hall, they are given a magazine-formatted course syllabus called the 'Survival Guide'. Testimony from students suggests that this first impression, being faced with a non-traditional, 24 page syllabus has a lasting impression. "*I'd heard about the Survival Guide but I was floored when I saw it. Who ever heard of taking twenty-five minutes to read a course outline?*"

The second element of the rude awakening and the subsequent uneasiness that permeates the class is the almost immediate realization that this course is not built on the format of a mid-term, term paper, and final exam. As a student writes "*Coming to university was just how I imagined boot camp would be. We are told to forget both what we've learned, and more important, how we've learned it. This course confused me. It was like a renegade had been let loose in boot camp.*" Before they become our students, these same people are the products of nearly twenty years of a different learning milieu. They are the products of an electronic world informed by computers, videos, and television. There appears to be a degree of Ludditism in the institutional resistance and unwillingness to build institutional capacity to engage our students in their world. Rather, the tendency is towards reverting to the comfort of the traditions and rituals that define institutional inertia. Within the constraints of that reality, students in the Introductory Course in World Politics choose among eight to ten different evaluation exercises. Students are asked to sign an academic contract outlining their choice of exercises and the relative weight they wish to accord to each (within set limits). Given the primacy accorded to the objectives of critical and global thinking, these pedagogical practices are rigorously developed with an eye to meeting those goals.

The heart of the World Politics learning experience is a Computer Moderated Conference (CMC) called WPMail. Every student in the course is given a computer account to access the computer system. WPMail is an integrated information system, that I have developed, providing students with access to an electronic mail system, a series of computer mediated roundtable discussions on topics related to the course, access to international newswire services (UPI, CP, DPA, Xinhua, Koyto, Middle East News Network, PR Newswire, Business Wire etc. . . .), and readnews capabilities for international computer discussion groups on Listserv (bitnet, internet) and UUCP-type discussions. WPMail is accessible from any terminal on campus and via modem from remote locations. As conceived, WPMail has been developed to transform World Politics experience from the traditional classroom into a potential 24-hour-a-day learning experience. Debates begun in class can shift to a roundtable discussion. Written submissions can be either circulated for draft comment to students writing in the same area, or directly to my electronic mail address for evaluation. Negotiations related to conflict management simulations or debt summits, integral parts of the curriculum, are now conducted through WPMail. All course administration is conducted through electronic mail.

Beyond the wealth of information at the fingertips of students from WPMail, the challenge is to channel the immediate intrigue and curiosity of students into evaluation exercises that allow them to integrate lecture materials, assigned texts, and WPMail materials. Day One: At the end of each student's "Survival Guide" is a tear-out page with a set of 5 randomly generated library reference questions. *Find the phone number of a Libyan Arms Dealer in Tripoli; Develop an organization flow chart of the interlocking holdings of Molson's Canada; What percentage of dollars repatriated to the Philippines comes from domestic (female) labour in the Gulf States?; Americans claim that Canadian welfare programmes represent an unfair subsidy in trade relations between the U.S. and Canada — how much of a subsidy does* the U.S. military complex represent to the U.S. economy; How much money does the average Zambian worker make? If the price of new, IMF-imposed prices for millie meal is 125 kwacha per 25 kilogram sack what is the earning power of the average Zambian worker? This exercise not only gets students into the reference library or the various information folders in WPMail, it also contributes to an immediate bonding of students who, inevitably, work together on the assignment. "*Gonick has you finding an arms dealer in Tripoli?, he wants me to find an address of an arms conversion factory in Minsk — any ideas?*" The answers to these questions must be all submitted to me on WPMail. This guarantees that students become familiar with the new enhanced mode of communication.

The core of the evaluation exercises for the course is based on a series of assignments — some required, some optional. First, all students are required to submit a 1200-1500 word academic journal every three weeks. The academic journal calls on students to draw upon lectures, assigned readings, reference materials, current affairs, and an articulation of their own opinions in an integrated fashion. This challenges the students to apply the theoretical constructs developed in class and to test the robustness of the models and related questions asked. It also provides me with a running indicator of what concepts, theories, and historical materials students have managed to grasp. As one student mentioned in the year end evaluation — "*the journals forced me to become active in the course — I liked that you actually cared what 'I' thought.*"

The second required element in each term is a simulation exercise. Simulation exercises are term-long in duration. In week two of the course country assignments (or NGO or INGO assignments) are made. Students are encouraged to use the simulation briefing dossier to begin developing their position papers. There is always a Summit or a General Assembly meeting; but the agenda for the Summit or GA is debated by the student representatives of the countries throughout the term. Private roundtable discussions are set up on the WPMail system to discuss strategy. Pre-conference news conferences are called either in class or through WPMail. The World Press, an important player in the simulation, uses video camcorders to interview representatives and holds several 'Meet the Press' sessions before, during, and after the Summit. The simulation always marks a highlight in the term. Pedagogically, the aim is praxis: developing skills for affinity, understanding the foreign policies of 'others', learning something about cooperation, and conflict resolution. A Russian Jewish immigrant in the course wrote in her journal "*I never, ever, thought I would* find myself defending the rights of Palestinians to self-determination and statehood. After a while, I found myself so emersed in the mind set of the Palestinians that I actually began to believe what I was saying." Like a good number of students, this particular student's academic career took off after the Summit on the Creation of a Palestinian State.

Other students have found their calling through one of the optional exercises. The local community radio station, CKWR FM 98.7, has granted us a 30-minute slot every week for student radio documentaries. The overall theme of the radio documentary is worked out in the course outline and hosted by a third or fourth year student teaching assistant. Pairs of students engage in a structured research programme for radio documentary-making including presenting scripts, interview schedules, and documentation. Once the project idea is approved, students place phone calls to experts, political analysts, and commentators across Canada and the United States. Together with the students' background work, the radio documentary is taped in the recording studio and aired every Thursday morning. The success of this program has led to the distribution of the series to other community radio stations across the country.

For the Spielbergs in the course the same type of project is available using video as the presentation medium. With energy and a level of determination that I have rarely seen in a traditional term paper, students spend countless hours researching, writing, producing, and editing their prize works. The whole class gets to screen the finished products in a mini-video festival along with a question and answer session with the producers. Whether the project deals with local soup-kitchens and global hunger or the sweat factories in Toronto's garment district and changes in the international division of labor, students embrace these projects and with such ownership build confidence and critical research skills.

"*And so what do you really think of the rise of nationalism around the world?*" One of the least well developed learning skills in the university setting is orations. We demand that our students read, listen, and write. We rarely develop curriculum to enhance elocution and debating skills. Great speakers are not born with oratory skills. To try and make a modest contribution to the level of public debate in Canada we have developed a "Great Issues Debate". Again, for credit, students are paired off to undertake a formal debate. "*Be it resolved that the best solution to the challenges in the Soviet Union is to allow each of the federations to form their own autonomous states.*" "*1992 will mark the end of state sovereignty in Europe as we know it.*" "*Canada's participation in the coalition against Iraq was in the national interest of Canada." "Patriotism is an anachronistic concept with no value in the late years of the 20th century."* Response to this exercise is very popular and taken very seriously. Debates take place in a theater auditorium with moderators and formal question and answer period from the audience. The series is advertised and draws students and the occasional faculty person. To introduce students to the idea (largely foreign in the formal classroom setting) the teaching assistants undertake a formal debate during class time. The topic for the formal TA debate over the past last couple years has been: *"be it resolved that women are invisible from world politics."*

There are several other smaller evaluation exercises, such as a world band radio listening exercise (integrated into the WPMail system), critical book reviews, and the creation and dissemination of a WPMail weekly electronic alternative news summary. The aim in all these exercises is to try to find explicit ways to reach out to students.

To return finally to the chase. Making sense of the new world order-in-the-making challenges us to examine the 'why', 'what' and 'how' of the subject matter we call world politics. The contested terrain is about competing central narratives we now wish to tell in the teaching of World Politics. The central motif of the world politics narrative in my class is a multi-tiered exploration of violence, power relations, and change. If we wish to help our students develop critical analytical skills, the time has come to break through the barriers of the dominant mode of teaching and learning. Lecturing is, at its very core, an hierarchical, alienating, and largely passive form of learning. It is limited by the assumptions of the *banking concept* of learning. If we want our students to become impassioned, caring, and thoughtful citizens of this globe — the process of learning about the world must be made as compelling as the problems facing the human race.

Notes

1. Thomas M. Franck and Edward Weisband, *Word Politics: Verbal Strategy Among the Superpowers* (New York: Oxford University Press, 1971).

2. Examples of Critical Pedagogy include Paulo Freire *Pedagogy of the Oppressed* (New York, Seabury Press, 1973); and *The Politics of Education: Culture, Power and Liberation* (South Hadley MA: Bergin & Garvey, 1985), Ivan Illich, *Deschooling Society* (New York, 1970); Herbert Kohl *Growing Minds: On Becoming a Teacher*

(New York: Harper & Row, 1985); Jonathan Kozol *Death at an Early Age* (New York, 1967); Henry A. Giroux *Teachers as Intellectuals* (South Hadley MA: Bergin & Garvey, 1988); Henry A. Giroux and Stanley Aronowitz *Education Under Siege* (South Hadley MA: Bergin & Garvey, 1985); Ira Shor *Critical Teaching and Everyday Life* (Boston MA: South End Press, 1980, *Cultural Wars: School and Society in The Conservative Restoration, 1969-1984* (London & New York: Routledge & Kegan Paul, 1986); Michael Apple, *Ideology and Curriculum* (London & New York: Routledge & Kegan Paul, 1979); and *Education and Power* (London & New York: Routledge & Kegan Paul, 1982).

3. Ira Shor, *Culture Wars: School and Society in the Conservative Restoration, 1969-1984* (London and New York: Routledge, Kegan and Paul, 1986), pp. 193.

4. Henry A. Giroux, "Marxism and Schooling: The Limits of Radical Discourse", *Educational Theory*, 34, no. 2, pp. 134.

5. Peter McLaren, "Towards a Pedagogy of Liberation: Peter McLaren Interviews Henry Giroux", *Borderlines*, no. 2, (1985), pp. 10,11.

6. From Raymond Williams, *The Year 2000*, pp. 268-269.

7. For example, elsewhere in this volume Weisband makes the case for beginning one's analysis of world political economy and world politics by analysing the patterns of power relations that are generated from every day work. Given the variety of settings in which work takes place (an experience that most students can relate to), and the fact that work is part of internal and international divisions of labour, here too is a strategy for beginning with the familiar as we take students into the realm of world politics.

8. Marshall Hodgson, "The Historical and Geographical-Image of the West" unpublished and undated manuscript.

9. Cynthia Enloe, *Bananas, Beaches, and Bases: Making Feminist Sense of International Politics* (London: Pandora, 1989), p. 196.

10. Susan George, *A Fate Worse Than Debt* (London: Penguin, 1988), p. 180.

11. Lynn Miller's *Global Order* makes a readable and thought-provoking presentation on the rise and workings of the Westphalian order. Elsewhere in this volume, Miller makes it clear how he understands the continuing utility of the Westphalian analytical framework.

12. Ian Lustick, "Stability in Deeply Divided Society: Consociationalism vs. Control," *World Politics* 31, no.3 (April 1979), pp. 325-344.

13. Deborah Gerner, *One Land, Two People* (Boulder CO: Westview Press, 1991).

14. See Richard K. Ashley, *The Political Economy of War and Peace* (London: Pinter, 1980); Nazli Choucri and Robert North, *Nations in Conflict: National Growth and International Violence* (San Francisco CA: W.H. Freeman, 1975); Lev Gonick and Robert Rosh, "The Structural Constraints of the World-Economy on National Political Development," *Comparative Political Studies* 21 (1988), pp. 171-199; Robert C. North, *War, Peace, Survival: Global Politics and Conceptual Synthesis* (Boulder CO: Westview Press, 1990).

PART FOUR

Normative Pedagogies in World Politics: Justice and Conviviality

13

Justice and the Challenges of Constructivist Pedagogy: Normative Perspectives in Teaching Political Economy

Edward Weisband

Political Economy and Normative Inquiry

Power and the Pedagogical Discourses of Political Economy

As teachers reflect upon the complex set of issues relevant to the teaching of world politics and political economy, we all would do well to remember that undergraduate students often, too often perhaps, are driven by careerist ambitions and that a job at the end of the college rainbow is a primary force in sustaining student interest and fortitude throughout their educational experience. Teachers interested in demonstrating that the study of political economy relates to the personal goals and objectives of students might start by suggesting something like the following to their class:

The First Lecture

We all work. We all labor. Often, work is measured by outputs, that which derives or results from labor. Labor is measured as input or time devoted to producing outputs of work. One speaks of labor-time and of work output. We try to understand the relations between them in order to examine such social indicators as productivity and exploitation. Some of us play away from work at least some of the time. Most of us in our adult lives take work home with us. Our families and our doctors warn us against becoming workaholics. Work and labor occupies our lives, as no other form of activity. In a sense, labor consumes us as we consume the outputs of work. Work and labor are thus embedded in the social fabrics that surrounds our lives. The phases of our life are often denoted in terms of work, getting a job, retiring, and the like.

For the most part, work and labor remains a collective enterprise involving institutional and hierarchical, authoritative and cultural, cooperative and oppositional, socio-economic and political, orders of all kinds. Thus without work and labor, our lives sometimes seem devoid of meaning.

For many, however, labor is unrewarding, unsafe, and insufficiently remunerative; for still others, even more unfortunate, better jobs are blocked by labor markets that channel privileges toward some and away from others in ways that can and do involve exploitation. Jobs and the labor markets that dispense them are thus mechanisms that distribute values. Some gain more from work than others in terms of financial resources, social status, a personal sense of gratification. Access to labor, access to labor markets and jobs, represent major avenues through which many individuals define their lives and have their social existence defined for them.

Thus the strictures of labor and the demands of work often threaten to squeeze those most vulnerable to their dictates. Work and labor can be fearful masters filled with fatigue, boredom, risk, humiliation as well as challenge, drive and ambition.

Must it be so? Must unequal distributions of labor and work opportunities or outright unemployment oppress so many individuals. Is this exploitation? If so, what are the forms of exploitation? Under what sets of circumstances does it arise and why? What is the relationship of exploitation to injustice?

Answers to these sorts of questions permits the instructor of world politics and of world or international political economy to point toward the mediations of political, economic, social, and cultural forces. They also permit a teacher to underscore the central significance of normative and ethical issues, especially distributive issues, in applying social theory. That exploitation and injustice serve as core units of analysis in the study of political economy, also allows teachers to develop the crucial linkages between social science and moral philosophy.

Exploitation as an analytical concept fosters coherence as well as normative relevance by requiring students to confront the social dimensions of power in terms of ethical considerations raised by notions of justice.

A focus upon work and labor in political economy thus permits teachers to review the realities of economic life through the prisms of social and political power. It enables students to explore how such prisms refract, indeed, distort the energies of economic and social life. Such emphasis encourages students to think and to reason in terms of distributive justice.

The concept of power — in all of its guises and modes — along with the concept of justice — in all of its standards and forms, enable teachers to 'contextualize' the contested terrains of political, economic, and normative theory. What informs the pedagogical enterprise of international or world political economy is its prior and overweening commitment to a normative praxis dedicated to the defense of justice. This holds true whether the substantive issue at hand be the vectors of poverty or the trajectories of development, and whether the analytical compass a teacher is pursuing points toward the arcs of post-industrial capitalism, or to the lattices of a coming world order. Teaching political economy thus becomes part of an emergent emancipatory exercise borne of and by the conviction that social and distributive justice need not be the enemy of political freedom, any more than political stability requires economic exploitation.

Poverty, Labor, and Differential Growth: From the Cannons of Power to the Guns of Exploitation

The study of political economy concentrates upon the interaction of political and economic structures and distributions. Outcomes of such interactions are relevant to students for what they reveal about the nature of power. From a pedagogical point of view, the field of political economy contributes to student understanding of how power in political form intersects with power in economic form. This applies whether power derives from state institutions or through class structures or as a consequence of social norms and mores. But more than this, international or world political economy as a form of pedagogical inquiry and classroom reflection, requires, on the part of teachers and eventually, students, evaluative judgments that fall within the cultural, social, and, ultimately, the normative.

The seminal themes in political economy, adumbrating, on the one hand, the structures and dynamics of power, introducing, on the other, contrasting visions of justice and economic freedom, define an intellectual landscape characterized by three major substantive concerns — poverty, work/labor, and differential growth. The task of teachers in this field is to convert these analytical discourses into an appropriately unified pedagogical and instructional discourse. Students must understand how poverty, work/labor, differential growth are connected.

Differential growth, after all, reproduces certain structures of work and divisions of labor. How work is distributed provides a key to how, why, and in what ways, poverty accelerates. Indeed, the familiar concepts of theoretical explanation in political economy provide useful instructional terms for demonstrating how poverty, work/labor, or differential and uneven growth, operate. Thus, they may well serve as the focus of classroom investigation. Such standard concepts as pauperization, marginalization, feminization of poverty, for example, help teachers to portray uneven growth, while such terms as the degradation and deskilling of labor, "Bloody" Taylorism, the principles of scientific management, Fordism and Post-Fordism, facilitate student understanding of work, labor, and exploitation in industrial capitalism.

Additionally, neoclassical liberalism as well as classical Marxian and neoclassical materialist theory has bestowed upon political economy an instructional vocabulary relevant to student understanding of how both wealth and exploitation analytically relate to work or labor. The theoretical language of neo-Marxian materialists as well as neo-Ricardian liberals underscores the relations of labor, on the one hand, to market exchange, modes of production, regimes of accumulation and distribution. Such political economic discourse, tempered by decades of contrivance and controversy, now etches the contours of mainstream sociological and political economic theory. This is evidenced by the common acceptance of such analytical constructs as 'forces of production', 'modes of production', 'social relations of production', and 'regimes of accumulation'.

Teachers interested in comparative political economy may thus depict the uneven emergence of hegemonically contrived socio-economic zones by relying upon such formulations as underdevelopment, disarticulation, economies of scale, and market disequilibrium theory. What converts these concepts and explanations into a unified pedagogy is their focus upon work, labor, unemployment, and the character of exploitation.

In particular, if one distils the residue of analysis presented by neo-classical liberalism and by the Marxian labor theory of value, for the purposes of defining a pedagogy in political economy that remains sensitive to the value of both, a teacher is left with such instructional questions as the following:

- How do labor markets function — within different societies, within different historical episodes of power, within different modes of production, within different regimes of accumulation?

- Is the structure of labor markets relevant to exploitation and, if so, how, according to neoclassical liberalism, materialism, etc.?

- How does the labor process operate to extract value from labor or, conversely, to enhance labor productivity — within different societies, within different historical episodes of power, within different modes of production, and within different regimes of accumulation?

- Does class cleavage, surplus value, forced and unpaid labor, as enumerated by Marxian principles of surplus value, accurately depict the vectors of exploitation?

- What is the relevance of exploitation to injustice?

- How does capital circulate? Is capital circulation and consequent distributions of private property and wealth crucial to explanations of exploitation or injustice?

Each of these questions requires students to examine the relationship of capital to work and labor within a context framed by a normative concern regarding justice, injustice, and exploitation. Nor is the validity of neoclassical liberal or materialist analysis the basic issue here. Methods, approaches, explanations, and values differ among teachers of political economy who grapple with these issues. What is shared among those who do teach world politics and political economy is the common, sometimes, tacit conviction, that economic and social injustice tends to grow out of the cannons of power, just as these serve as the guns of exploitation.

Teachers of political economy thus perceive a window of pedagogical opportunity. They are able to show students how structures of power corrode the values of justice. Theoretical explanation in the teaching of political economy must operate, I suggest, against the dramatic standards of social and distributive justice. Such problematics imbue the teaching of political economy with its peculiar normative coloration whatever the ideological commitments of any particular teacher or practitioner. A range of questions arise that link theoretical explanation to normative evaluation: why do people work and how do they labor; under what conditions do people work or labor and in what forms of production; what wages, profits, rewards, or meanings do individuals or households or classes receive from work and labor; what does work or labor represent culture to culture, or society to society, or region to region?

These questions enable teachers to encourage even introductory level political economy students to reflect upon the relations of work to economic productivity, the linkages between productivity and income distribution and rates of exploitation. Therefore, a commitment to a pedagogy in political economy that is molded by a concern for ameliorating conditions of exploitation stresses the ties between theoretical explanation and normative examination. More than ever this, such an instructional commitment permits classroom exploration of the great issues relevant to international markets, competitiveness and industrial versus post-industrial growth. In an era of manifest structural decline in U.S. productivity when the rise of part-time jobs becomes the stellar achievement of what Harrison and Bluestone have called, 'The Great American Job Machine', this orientation hits students 'where they live' imaginatively. Teacher are thus empowered to reveal the emergent political realities in world politics, such as the forces of economic regionalism in Europe and throughout the Pacific Rim, but in the context framed by concepts of comparative and competitive advantage, labor markets, job creation, and income distribution.

Teachers of world politics do not necessarily renounce their traditional interest in explaining the structures and dynamics of balance of power, conflict and peace. Nor do they abjure the role of law, norms, regimes and intergovernmental organizations in sustaining peace and security. But those teachers who wish to treat issues of conflict comprehensively must now confront in the classroom a vastly expanded array of economic and political economic matters, matters which point not only to the problem of order but involve standards of justice as well.

Relativism and Rationalism: The Quest for Normative Contexts in the Teaching of Political Economy

What, then, is needed in the classroom is the construction of a language of justice attesting to the validity of normative standards, but a language that operates alongside units of analysis reflecting the scientific discourse of world politics and world political economy. There exist, however, certain pedagogical traps along this yellow-brick road to successful teaching.

For one thing, the language of political economy derivative of rational or public choice perspectives focuses upon exploitation, but its syntax and logic revolves around a formalist logic. This often prevents lower division students from envisioning the problems of exploitation or injustice in terms of concrete historical or cultural settings. Such an approach to the teaching of political economy, encourages students to 'contextualize' justice by universalizing its standards, a contradiction in terms. Students specify the conditions that prevail in situations of exploitation, but they fail to refer to the norms or values of identifiable cultures and societies in which exploitation occurs. The implicit assumption that pervades this ahistorical formalism in pedagogy is that exploitation is exploitation once the standards or criteria for exploitation can be rationally and thus universally derived irrespective of culture or the modes of exploitation that reflect culture.

Other instructors in political economy fall into a contrasting pedagogical trap. Comparativists tend, like historians, to think in idiographic terms. Such an instructional approach so relativizes culture that the universalist language of social justice or normative philosophy becomes irrelevant. Standards of justice become exiled to the moralists and thus relegated to a realm beyond comparative political economy. The pervasive pedagogical assumption here seems to become simply that culture is what culture is. Cultural relativism, however, need not devolve into an ethical relativism, one that eschews moral principle and judgment. *What is pedagogically wanted is a normative language in political economy that renders universal the cultural experiences of exploitation by applying in relative terms the principles and standards of justice.* What teachers require, therefore, is an ethically informed language in political economy, one focused upon work and labor within specified historical, cultural, regional contexts and thus a language attached to concrete modes of production such as capitalism.

Capitalism remains the historical mode of production that continues to create, destroy, recreate the world in its image. This force gives rise to broad allegations of exploitation but to even a wider range of support grounded in testimony to the capacity of capitalism to generate both freedom and prosperity. It is the very capacity of capitalism to produce more, to accumulate more, to incorporate more, perhaps to exploit more, that generates both devotion and antipathy. Instructors only occasionally explore relations between exploitation, however defined, and standards of justice, however defended, within the capitalist mode of production.

Classroom debate over exploitation and injustice must ultimately, it seems to me, focus on the impact of capitalism as a mode of production, as a regime of accumulation, as a work and labor process, within, above all, specific settings. Yet capitalism too rarely receives the classroom attention it deserves on the part of undergraduate teachers. Teachers tend to speak 'neutrally' by adopting the language of liberalism. This leads to a serious disjuncture between research and teaching. For purposes of research, political economists perceive capitalism to be everywhere, the winds of its creative gales shifting everything that is cultural, social, economic, and political, leading to a world nation, to a single homogenized culture. Yet such concerns too seldom, it appears, enter the classroom.

Serious research effort has been devoted to depicting the impact of capitalism. Such analysis tends, however, to remain irrelevant to American education. The assumption here appears to be that student conscience and consciousness must not be sullied by the challenges entailed in discussing capitalism seriously. Yet classroom discussion of capitalism, in all of its forms and complexity, is never more needed than now as market approaches to economic development become more widely accepted than ever with the extensive incorporation of the communist or Second World into the First World of capitalist industrialism.

The question becomes how to do this. What might be the most effective way for teachers to engage lower division world politics and world political economy students in a discussion designed to evaluate capitalism?

I suggest that, in specific terms, teachers wishing to explore the nature of capitalism within the framework of political economy, may select from among at least three narratives or stories in political economy. The first of these configures roughly around the process usually referred to as development; the second around industrial work or industrial relations; the third around the recent phenomenon of postindustrial capitalism. Each offers an instructional opportunity that links social science in general and political economy, in particular, to philosophical debate regarding exploitation and distributive justice.

More than this, each provides a method for universalizing debates over culture, while contextualizing the applications of normative standards. Teachers of political economy may adopt what I shall refer to as a **Constructivist Pedagogy**. Such a pedagogy is designed to reveal how people shape the circumstances of their lives, especially in regard to conditions of exploitation and injustice. This represents an important message for students to take with them after the final exam is over. For it reminds us all that the linkages between political economy and moral philosophy stem from the decisions and choices that individuals make in regard to their own lives.

Constructivist Pedagogy and the Question of Exploitation

Three Stories of Exploitation: Peasant Agriculture, Industrial Labor, and Informationalized Networks

Contemporary analysis in political economy, focused on work and labor, has tended to construct three contexts based upon three production worksites: peasant agrarian, industrial, and post-industrial or informational. Within some theoretical frameworks these sites are treated separately and comparatively. Within others, especially those developed by world-system perspectives, these three sites tend to be conceived as stages or as articulations of a singular capitalist labor process. To the extent that teachers wish to stress the predominant character of transnational capitalism as it operates within and across many different societies, the three major narratives may be presented as but monolithic episodes in a capitalist labor process. Students learn to grapple with the proposition that capitalist exploitation at any one site is linked to exploitation at all others.

On the other hand, any attempt to apply normatively conceived standards of justice to the structures and dynamics of exploitation requires scrupulous attention to concrete worksites or production sites. As we have suggested earlier, such a conceptualization requires students to emphasize the importance of cultural settings and environments. This requires teachers to differentiate the various worksites or modes of production and to link each of them to exploitation. Such an attempt might proceed as follows:

The Second Lecture

In the case of peasant agriculture, exploitation arises through devalorization of peasant labor-time, under conditions at least partially determined by the incorporation of primitive modes of production into new social divisions of labor; this process tends to be predicated upon capitalist commodification and specialized forms of production.

In the case of modern industrial labor, the devalorization or exploitation of industrial labor arises through processes that involve, first, a systematic degradation of labor; work and labor processes become increasingly shaped by the 'advances' of knowledge and technology; such trends displace the need for labor initiative or worker skill in accordance with Taylorist precepts of scientific management. Labor tasks become routinized in keeping with both Taylorism and Fordism in a massive process of deskilling. Secondly, the devalorization and exploitation of industrial labor is manifested by an increasing erosion of worker control through bureaucratic or structural mechanisms; this attenuation of worker control within the employment relationship reflects how capital circulates in a spatial division of labor that leaves labor subject to an extractive squeeze generated by capital's ability to move to new locations in search of a cheaper or more abject labor force. Thirdly, even in those situations where worker oriented quality control groups or worker councils promote the cause of sound industrial relations, labor is subject to exploitation as a consequence of the structural decline of trade unionism and the rise of the informal sector or the 'casualization' of work throughout the industrial world; workers in lesser skilled capacities face increasing marginalization by losing control over the workplace, over working conditions, over compensation, as evidenced by increases, throughout the industrial world, of part-time work, employment of immigrant labor, and the pandemic rise in several global urban settings of sweatshop populations.

Post-industrialization promotes segmentation of the labor force and thus it tends to accelerate various forms of structural polarization within the labor force. This is revealed by a new set of class relations including a labor aristocracy composed of highly skilled information processors who service the productive functions of postindustrial industries. This segment functions alongside a massive underclass which tends to work and labor under highly vulnerable and oppressive conditions.

Teachers of international and world political economy interested in forging an instructional language attuned to the normative implications of exploitation may refer to concrete examples in regard to these prototypical production worksites or locations. This enables teachers to develop a pedagogical approach that combines theoretical and normative categories. Indeed, an appropriate pedagogy geared to classroom discussion of exploitation, one punctuated by the concepts of justice, should suggest to students that there exists in the nonperfect but real world the possibilities of actively pursuing standards of justice within the various settings that define and manifest these modes of production.

Student activism, however desirable, is not the immediate aim here. Rather, the overall objective is to reveal to students that a fundamental mediation exists between how we perceive the world and act upon it, and how the world or the society in which we live imposes certain determinants upon us. Specifically, teachers might pursue a double-track agenda in outlining the central issues of international or world political economy: macroanalysis of exploitation in terms of justice, microanalysis of exploitation in terms of moral agency. This double-track agenda suggests to students that individuals create the social worlds in which they live, just as the social worlds in which we all live, tend to mold our lives, our perceptions, our values, and our causes. Such assumptions indicate the potential value of a pedagogical approach that associates moral agency, concepts of cultural life and activity, standards of justice — all with political economic theories of exploitation. This instructional approach and method, with its emphasis upon the social constructions wrought by human autonomy may be termed as *Constructivist Pedagogy*.

Edward Weisband

Constructivism and the Quest for the Meanings of Truth, Identity, and Social Reality

Constructivism goes by many names and many reference points as the task of social construction and reconstruction changes. In the insurrectionary hey-days of the 1960's, the code term that passed for constructivism was liberation. We spoke of gay, gray, black, and women's liberation. The specific spin that the language of liberation gave to the constructivist project tended to emphasize the role and nature of the self. This was the era, after all of the *me-generation*. If liberation was our enterprise, the task we faced was the liberation of self. We liberated our individuality from the objectivist essences imposed upon us by the artificial constructions of society. Our objective was a more authentic self and a more genuine state of collective belonging.

Thus the liberation movement thrived as a collective political effort precisely because it spoke to us as individuals and told us that we no longer had to accept the social reifications that distorted and skewed our ability as persons to define and determine our own being.

Today this langauge of liberation conveys an aura of a living language, but one that is antiquated in style, sound, and substance. Like the classical versions of English or French or Japanese or German, the lexicon and the grammar of such a language sounds familiar to our ears. After all, it is our own language, the mother of our mother-tongue. But is also alien to our ears and inaccessible to our instinctive feel for what is our true linguistic home. We know that the imprint of the past upon this early language reflects a distant age of assumptions and thus the very phonetics of the language seem strange. For this reason, we become estranged from it, even as we recognize it to be our own.

Language changes as our social constructions change. Thus liberation, as a linguistic framework for discussing politics and pedagogy, has given way to postmodernism. Postmodernism is constructivist to the barest of its conceptual bones. But gone are the trappings of authenticity, truth, and the self-as-project. Now they are replaced with the hermeneutic probabilities and probes of Gadamer, Derrida, Lyotard, Foucault, Bourdieu, Baudrillaud, Debord and others of the new canon who so vehemently reject all status, canonical or otherwise.

No longer is the self a self in the new reading. We become the replicas of standardized discourse machines programmed by hegemonic rules to speak and to listen in particularized ways, ways that require and receive deconstruction and reconstruction. Thus there is no authentic text. Indeed, there is no authenticity. Truth disappears into a miasma of postmodernist possibility. Here, method is the only clarity; now, nonsituational speech and vision represents the truest form of centeredness.

In such moments, textual interpretation becomes more rather than less important. Postmodernist interpretation thus constructs an etiology of discourse. It investigates the designs of language. It prosecutes the ways language reinforce social opportunity and intellectual privilege. In so doing, it replaces the language of liberation, with the language of empowerment.

Empowerment represents *the* new constructivist mandate. It exhorts us to cut through and into the networks of articulation and expression that advantages some forms of discourse while disempowering others. Above all, postmodernist empowerment invites struggle and resistance against the hierarchical, the vertical, and the center of social as well as intellectual authority.

Empowerment as a pedagogical framework thus requires instructional emphasis upon the *decentered classroom*. The very authority of the instructor must give way to a multiplicity of participations. The classroom becomes a vehicle for connected and activist learning. Pedagogical discourse thus seeks to achieve a decentering of the collective academic authority in favor of the concentric, the unbounded, the interlinked.

With this arrives an entire set of concomitant projects not the least of which is the systematic denuding of sexist and racist forms of suppression and the stripping away of discourses of oppression. Race and class become part of a reconstituted cluster of concepts, one that now includes gender, to stress how color and status become refracted through the prisms of sexual identity or orientation and, in turn, how gender-driven reifications still shape the everyday world.

Constructivism in teaching world political economy underscores how and in what manner people alter the circumstances that affect their lives. Within such an instructional framework, teachers may find it useful to portray moral agency in terms of resistance and rebellion. Countless examples, including several identified below, abound. Normative standards of justice shaped by a constructivist pedagogy thus represents a way to encourage students to grapple with the full violence that is exploitation but in terms of the choices available to persons and groups subjected to it.

Classroom teaching, crafted by constructivist pedagogy and thus sensitive to the basic epistemological premises and methodological assumptions of constructivism, is designed to counter the ethical insouciance and normative cop-out implicit in a variety of determinist assumptions that students often reveal. Constructivism rejects all forms of determinism and seeks to identify the impact of human autonomy on the human condition. Constructivism seeks to discern the role of human agency in order to lend credence to human intentionality in a social world deemed amenable to human imprint. From this perspective, once constructivism is ignored, an analytical fatalism and a moral relativism creeps into discourse. This is like a paralyzing malady that disorients students and carries them away from the central concerns in studying political economy. When this happens socio-economic and political structures begin to loom larger than life. Human autonomy and intentionality, social constructivism itself, the very assertion of normative standards, all seem futile. The relationship between culture and social change also tends to fade away, like an 'old soldier' no longer relevant.

All this points to the necessity of careful regard to culture in the teaching of international and world political economy. I illustrate these propositions below by reference to certain constructivist contributions in pedagogy and teaching, contributions that link culture to collective action grounded in normative presupposition. I categorize this material in terms of the three production sites or work-locations identified above, namely, peasant, industrial, postindustrial. But, first, let us explore the meaning and significance of constructivism in order to identify the character of a constructivist pedagogy in the teaching of international political economy.

I begin with reference to Margaret S. Archer's indictment against 'industrial society theorists', who envision a coming world order in terms of inexorable determinants tied to technological change.[1] Industrial society theorists, she declares, suffuse the coming information society with a misguided objectivism, what she calls 'culpable scientism'. Her condemnation focuses on their "fallacy of amoral objectivity,"[2] that is, their tendency to use fallacious grammars that "make ethics superfluous. . . reduce morality to a mere by-product of social forces, in this case the powerful constraints of technological change, and therefore. . . promote moral agnosticism within the social science community."[3] But Archer goes beyond allegations of positivism for itself or technologism as an end in itself. She stresses the importance of elevating the stature and role of normative orientations in social science pedagogy which, she asserts, must reveal a sensitivity — not to moral universalism — but to moral particularism. If social theory is to "pay its real respects to the morality of actors," she writes, "this means more than a simple acknowledgement that people think and. . . act in terms of what is good, right and proper, for so does the morally determined humanoid. It entails both a respect for moral differences *and* the human capacity to endorse different morals."[4] Social theory, she concludes, must 'concede' some degree or element of autonomy to the moral realm and thus to human ability to alter and redefine right and wrong, good and bad.[5] This quality or element is essential to the shaping of a constructivist pedagogy and to the study of culture.

Not only is social science, in general, and political economic pedagogy, in particular, subject to the sanitizing assumptions of sociological objectivism, so too is the study of culture. Culture becomes readily reified, by what Archer calls the myth of cultural integration. This myth asserts that cultures manifest high levels of monist homogeneity. It derives, Archer claims, from the positivism of Comte, German historicism, the anthropological interpretations of Benedict, Malinowski, and Kroeger, the structuralism of Parsonian sociology, and from materialism which argues that Western capitalism represents a hegemonic culture and thus a single 'dominant ideology'.

Archer concludes that the task of contemporary social theory must be to revive a conception of culture that stresses how beliefs shape cultural change and how cultural change reflects culture and cultural contradictions. "The subordination of culture in theories of industrial society rules out a priori any significance of cultural contradictions," she writes. "Viewing culture as subordinate is really what makes for an industrial society theorist — they have a limited 'industrial imagination' which conflates structure with culture, instrumental rationality with morality and technical advance with social progress."[6] What Archer alleges to be true in the case of industrial society theorists, also holds true in the case of many political economic theorists, who refuse to look at cultural distinctions and contradictions as relevant features in analyzing exploitation and who thus refuse to operate within a pedagogical framework guided by constructivism.

The full implication of constructivism as a framework for teaching and pedagogy in political economy may now be directly addressed. Constructivist pedagogies originate with a commitment to the study of recursive mutualities that arbitrate between collective actions born of human autonomy and the organizing realities of the world. A constructivist pedagogy in political economy would thus orient students toward an understanding of the role individuals and groups play in defining the conditions and circumstances of their lives. This holds especially true in the case of the central issues of work, labor, distribution, standards of living, poverty, development, modes of production, markets, exploitation, oppression, justice.

One sustained treatment of constructivism relevant to the social sciences and, in particular, to the study of international relations, law, and international political economy, is Nicholas Greenwood Onuf's *World of our Making: Rules and Rule in Social Theory and International Relations.*[7] Onuf locates his analysis within postmodernism by advancing a 'constructivist' approach to social reality. Onuf's constructivism is particularly relevant to pedagogy in political economy, since it helps to reveal the intimate connections between normative philosophy and theorization regarding exploitation — all of which is as an antidote to the kind of social theory and pedagogy Archer deplores above.

Onuf's account of constructivist pedagogy, indeed, constructivist hermeneutics, argues against naturalism or objectivisism, reification or essentialism, dualism or structuralism, in favor of analytical perspectives that assume social change occurs through endless moments of recursive self-invention on the part of persons and society as a whole. "In my view," Onuf declares, "people always construct, or constitute, social reality, even as their being, which can only be social, is constructed for them."[8] Onuf declares that his is a "bounded rather than grounded" constructivism. "Human beings, with whatever equipment nature and/or society provides, construct society, and society is indispensable to the actualization of whatever human beings may 'naturally' be. . . . "[9]

Like Archer, Onuf demands that constructivism be recognized as elemental in how we formulate our epistemological concepts and thus our pedagogical categories. Constructivism seeks to breach the Cartesian dualities that have afflicted Western epistemology. It seeks to bridge the standard divide between subject and object in Western images of truth and reality and it punts across Western symbols that bifurcate language, thought, expression, and interpretation. The social reality we know, the truths any of us can teach, the works that all may contribute, are mutually grounded in neither mind nor matter, but both, are reflective of neither the subjective and objective, but both, and are permeated by neither the imaginations of one nor the many, but by both. The constructivism that Onuf defends "does not draw a sharp distinction between material and social realities — the material and the social contaminate each other," he writes, "but variably — and it does not grant sovereignty to either the material or the social by defining the other out of existence."[10] It is this emphasis upon the intermediation between what is given or received and what is taken and remade, this stress upon what is immovable and what is subject to change, this focus upon arbitrations of human will and social destiny, all of this, that characterizes the constructivist perspective within postmodern letters. The human condition is fated by both free will and the forces of determination and, as a consequence, the life of each person is absolutely unique and absolutely universal. Within the context of social theory and teaching, therefore, students of political economy must seek to reveal the structures that position social fate, the dynamics that produce collective destiny, in order to understand and explain the dimensions of human freedom.

Constructivism thus proceeds along a narrow methodological divide between historical materialism and philosophical idealism. It operates between the shoals of essentialist forms of structuralism and those generated by nihilist versions of existentialist poststructuralism. As Onuf argues, it rejects the poststructuralism of Derrida and Lyotard which suggests that "all grounds are groundless, all foundations are specious"[11] but, on the contrary, it recognizes the "logocentric content" of the dualities that have characterized Western thought. Thus Onuf declares that constructivist historiography, constructivist epistemology, constructivist methodology, and, by implication, constructivist pedagogy, seek to "overcome these dualities by treating people and society as each the product of the other's construction."[12] Thus history becomes a given, but also a contingency. "The logocentrism I concede, Onuf states, "is this: The act of construction, the co-constitution of people and society, makes history."[13] Thus Onuf rejects, what he describes, as Richard K. Ashley's 'totalizing duality', that we are either in history or outside it.[14] "I can have it both ways," he proclaims. "We are always within our constructions, even as we choose to stand apart from them, condemn them, reconstruct them."[15] For teachers, the implication is obvious. We teach the standard canons of received wisdom so that the canons of truth no longer become merely received. We represent the authority of truth, so that categories of truth might be challenged and transcended by new insight and interpretation. We reaffirm the validity of derivation, in order to legitimate innovation. We revel in continuity, in order to reveal the truest possibilities for change and discontinuity.

If social phenomena are all collective human constructions, as constructivism holds, the status of normative philosophy becomes both problematic but 'activist' in any historical moment of social development. Once social rules, norms, or practices, are conceived, not as cultural givens, but as contingencies in the never ending process of being defined, they become matters of social choice and collective decision-making as well as major instrumentalities for social reconstruction. If people create history, as history creates us, then part of any historical narrative, indeed, the basic elements of any seminal social dialogue, are the very normative rules and practices that guide, shape, and constrain our behaviors, our visions, our commitments — and in the present context of political economy — our views of exploitation and distributive justice.

In constructivism, therefore, an act of individual creation or defiance, an event of history, a cultural symbol, a social practice, a regime of control and power, serves to enable teachers in many fields, from literary criticism to social theory, to demonstrate and explain how theoretical concepts enables us to stand, in ever greater degrees of, what Martin Buber once called, distance and relation to reality. Constructivism requires that we distance ourselves from the 'Other', from each other, from art, from law, from mores, from truth, from politics, from authority, from science, from meaning and identity, from life, love, or culture, from God, only to return in new, radical, and imaginatively closer ways. So too must this be the case in respect to the destitution of others and the need for normative categories to define the moral violations perpetrated by both visible and unseen forms of labor exploitation, distributive injustice, and what Johan Galtung once aptly called 'structural violence'. Herein lies the ultimate aim of constructivist pedagogy in the teaching of international or world political economy.

Ultimately constructivist pedagogy offers the opportunity for teachers to invite students into a common educational project designed to rewrite the texts students are assigned to read, to redesign the syllabus that steers student learning, to reform their education by learning how to teach themselves. Just as teachers begin to learn once they start to teach, so too must students be asked to begin to teach, once they start to learn.

Constructivist Pedagogy and Heteronomy: Market Liberalism and Its Illusions

For many political science teachers of political economy, one of the more troubling aspects of the emphasis upon distributive issues is that it tends to devolve either into an exercise in public choice theory, ethical philosophy, international sociology, or neoclassical economics and rarely involves the appreciation of politics. Students might well wonder where is the *political* in political economy.

The field of political economy, indeed, is inherently interdisciplinary. It is thus readily possible for instructors to incorporate multiple frames of analysis central to several disciplines into the teaching of political economy. The neologisms of rule-based utilitarianism, for example, may be used to link public choice methodologies, grounded in logics of rational self-maximization, to ethical principles predicated upon universalizable normative precepts. Sociological units of analysis in international and world political economy establish class oriented configurations within society, whereas neoclassical economic models tend to impose markets categories upon identical phenomena. To the political scientist teacher, all such categories and concepts — rational choice, normative standards, class analysis, market principles such as supply, demand, and economies of scale — are relevant to what a student should be required to know and to understand in the study of political economy. But neither the diffusion of disciplinary perspectives, nor the profusion of conceptual orientations, need breed confusion among students regarding the analytical fusion that is possible once the political becomes conceptually associated with rule and with exploitation.

Political economy as a field of study and as an intellectual exercise is ultimately political in character precisely because it seeks to establish the links between power and justice, governance and exploitation. This points toward the need, in the teaching of political economy — particularly, teaching geared to normatives issues pertaining to justice — to compare regimes of regulation and accumulation, in order to assess how they promote exploitation or oppression. Heteronomous regimes may exploit but how they do so, under different conditions of rules, constitutes a major feature of comparative pedagogy in the field. This relates to pedagogical treatment of the allegation that capitalism is exploitative or unjust. The pedagogical task of examining capitalism within the frames provided by the field of political economy entails comparison in relation to alternative forms of exploitation. If exploitation is inevitable in any episode of rule, and on the assumption that rule cannot be dispensed with, how are we to measure injustice in capitalism as opposed to injustice under any other regime of accumulation or regulation. Answers in the classroom grounded in constructivism must only be derived comparatively and in cultural contexts.

Constructivist pedagogy in political economy, once oriented toward the character of injustice, thus orients teachers and students alike to a comparative perspective designed to examine the role of culture in defining status or standing, the role of power in defining notions of security, the role of class in defining wealth and equity. Students at various levels of academic advancement and intellectual maturity come eventually to confront the problem of exploitation under differing cultural, political, and socio-economic conditions.

A teacher of political economy, seeking to stress the importance of comparison relative to exploitation might raise the following propositions in the classroom:

Propositions To Guide Classroom Discussion Of Exploitation

Rule exploits through rules;

- Modes of production, such as slavery, feudalism, capitalism, socialism, sustain moments of exploitation, but differently in terms of who gains, who loses, how and in what ways, to what extent, and under what conditions;

- Application of standards of justice relevant to exploitation within the context of a constructivist pedagogy requires evaluation of choices available to those who work or labor and thus an examination of the degree to which persons in any society are forced systemically and structurally to lose as they earn in relation to the alternatives;

- A worker in capitalism might be exploited, but would he/she regard herself, or would we from a universal and philosophically neutral posture, wish to claim that he/she is more exploited than the slave under slavery, than the servant during the not so chivalrous days of chivalrous feudalism;

- How and to what extent does private property conduce to exploitation, if at all, and on a comparative basis given different forms of rule, especially variations within regimes or conditions of heteronomy;

- To what extent is exploitation in liberal or capitalist societies a matter of disparity in distribution as opposed to asymmetrical structure; and related to this, is the question of reform, in terms of what is required for the amelioration of exploitation, an issue that requires distributional realignment or structural transformation;

- How does exploitation operate at different levels of development, accumulation, and in different modes of production;

- To what extent is capitalist exploitation, unjust, given alternatives under the normative standard established by the proposition that choice is essential to justice and that injustice or exploitation revolves around the standard of **no choice but to lose as one labors or works**.

Here then we have the outlines of a major heuristic debate regarding the nature of exploitation in capitalism focusing upon the above formulations and others similar to them which together require students to reflect upon a normative oriented agenda in the study comparative, international, and world political economy. To avoid unnecessary and confusing abstraction, the teacher of political economy may wish to use the pedagogical device of depicting poverty and exploitation in terms of concrete worksites or moments. One way for teachers to set out to discuss these issues in the context of the real world is to conjure up the image of representative worksites or workplace and to explore with students the linkages among culture, rule, rules, poverty, social change, and exploitation within each. It is to this task that we now turn.

Pedagogical Discourses on Development and Peasant Modes of Production: Resistance and Rebellion

Professional students of political economy have long been aware of the dangers of Westernism and of orientalism. Objectifications of the cultural realities of non-Western, especially, of developing societies, has long been rejected, yet the problem of reification remains. Western values, Western perspectives, Western ways of doing things, so deeply infuse Western developmental theory, that often insufficient sensitivity to the relations of culture to economy informs Western portrayals of peasant societies, especially in the classroom. Developmental theory along with developmental aid often operates intrusively and without adequate attention to the social consequences of economic change.[16]

Many antidotes have been proposed and developed both in the field of developmental studies and in the classroom. The range of curricular issues in American higher education pertaining to multiculturalism (for example, the rejection by many teachers of what now appears to some to represent the doctrinaire perspectives of Eurocentrism, the call for empowerment based on cultural diversity) all reflect a new appreciation of the role of culture and cultural continuities amidst change. Constructivism, with its emphasis upon the role of persons and groups in shaping the conditions that in turn shape their lives thus establishes the importance of an interpretative approach to culture that stresses hermeneutic methodology, communication, performative speech, intersubjective realities and meanings.

A pedagogical perspective based upon such constructivist assumptions requires that students approach culture, not as a given, but as an historically derived and uniquely contrived set of human artifacts and social precepts. The philosopher Charles Taylor recently posed the problem in terms of the importance of historical memory, but even more than this, the historical memory of historical memory. What students of culture must seek to understand is the historical memory of ourselves and of others as we all remember history. What we must grapple with is the historiographic problem in teaching: how certain memories embed particular views of the world and how, recursively, particular views of the world mold historical memory. "What we need to do is to get over the presumption of the unique conceivability of the embedded picture," he writes. "But to do this, we have to take a new stance towards our practices. Instead of living in them and taking their implicit construal of things as the way things are, we have to understand how they have come to be, how they came to embed a certain view of things."[17] Such concerns and approaches appear directly relevant to the instructional needs of those who teach in the area of development or whose teaching touch upon topics relevant to the political economy of developing areas.

In particular, the study and the teaching of peasant societies, or of societies at levels of development involving simple commodity production, should require students to confront how such societies embed a certain view of things. Students must deal with questions of 'development' within the context of the cultural frameworks that hold society together. They should be invited to consider how technical and political programs of development have impact upon groups and individuals in society in terms of how these same individuals and groups have functioned in the past and in terms of how they will function in the future. From a constructivist perspective, the emphasis throughout must be upon people, how they shape their own social universe, as the social world helps them to define themselves.

This constructivist pedagogy geared to the needs of teachers engaged in teaching topics relevant to development, especially of poor agrarian or peasant societies, may be illustrated by reference to three analyses discussed below. Each implicitly incorporates a constructivist approach. Each represents an example of the kind of text that demonstrates for students how development, poverty, and exploitation all are embedded in cultural habits and assumptions. Teachers interested in adopting a classroom or instructional approach more amenable to the requirements of constructivism might use such materials as to show students that the social scientific examination of political economy requires neither cultural ignorance nor normative abstinence.

Henry Bernstein,[18] for example, develops a constructivist methodology by indicating that depiction of peasant forms of production remains ahistorical and thus devoid of theoretical significance if not rooted in historically based contexts.[19] Neither a free-wielding definition of 'peasants' nor a free-yielding conception of the 'peasant mode of production', he suggests, suffices in political economic research or pedagogy. "One conclusion — that there is no single and 'essential' peasantry — means," he writes, "that it is impossible to talk about peasants as a 'class' in general terms. Discussions of the 'revolutionary potential' of the peasantry in the abstract. . . are basically misconceived."[20] Thus the very term, 'peasantry' or 'peasant agriculture' may be misrepresented if not moored upon a constructivist foundation geared to the intersubjective realities of those whose lives and way of life are being described.

Although Bernstein explicitly adopts a materialist framework of analysis, he advocates — partially at least a constructivist pedagogy. Bernstein reveals his constructivism, by calling for theoretical emphasis upon the recursive causalities or mechanisms of mutual articulation built into the social relations of peasant production. Bernstein's analysis unfolds within the basic framework of materialist categories: the nature of capitalism as a mode of production, the destruction of pre-capitalist modes of production, the subordination of traditional household economies by commodified forms of production. His materialist methodology retains its sensitivity to the need for cultural specificity in research and teaching. "This provides, in principle," he declares, "the means for using the necessary abstractions of theory to provide a concrete analysis of the concrete situations of contemporary peasantries, their location in particular social formations and in the global circuit of capital. . . ."[21] Nowhere, however, does Bernstein explicitly refer to the concrete elements of culture or to the possibilities of moral autonomy. In this sense, he appears to separate his materialist analysis from his constructivist pedagogy. Bernstein's analysis, although highly useful for teachers interested in presenting a systematic method for grappling with the political economy of peasant societies, therefore, only partially reveals a constructivist commitment to pedagogical discourse grounded in the primacy of culture and the ways in which human beings shape, mold, or 'construct' the political economic and social circumstances of their lives.

Any failure to fuse materialism with constructivism might operate, if incorporated into teaching, to prevent teachers and students from examining how different peasant communities perceive the different socio-economic or political conditions in which they live and work. It might tend to prevent an assessment in the classroom of the extent to that these perceptions include feelings of loss, oppression, and exploitation. It might impede adequate exploration of how and in what ways individuals who perceive themselves to be exploited respond to such circumstances. Nor does Bernstein's perspective encourage the adoption of a pedagogy that stresses the immediacy of choices available to individual households within specified cultural contexts. This not only leaves the issue of exploitation unresolved, it works to prevent teachers from linking exploitation to normative concepts relative to agent autonomy and morality.

Bernstein does make an important passing reference to the possibilities of autonomous moral agency on the part of peasants caught in a production squeeze when he refers to resistance strategies available to peasant households. According to Bernstein, these include: rejection of new forms of cultivation or their sabotage; peasant strikes that disavow plantation of certain categories of crops, that engage in practices designed to reduce yields, that 'withdraw' from markets engaged in commodity exchange; migration; avoidance of market rules, prices structures, state regulations to obtain higher returns; and, finally, in Bernstein's words, "political actions, including individual or collective acts of violence, against agents of capital and state functionaries in the rural areas."[22] Such actions may be deemed by teachers and students alike, to be illegal, criminal, or the highest acts of moral autonomy against injustice. But such a judgment call depends upon an understanding of the socio-economic, political, legal, and, ultimately, cultural contexts in which such actions occur, and a constructivist pedagogy that emphasizes what people do for themselves as autonomous moral agents.

Constructivism would ask that students consider the possibility that such forms of peasant resistance are profound ethical acts designed to revise the 'rules of the game'. Such actions of rebellion or resistance might be considered as acts of civil disobedience, that is, as legitimate responses to increasingly illegitimate sets of conditions. But, true to constructivist perspectives and pedagogies, the validity of such judgments cannot be established by a nonhistorical materialist forms of analysis alone. Teachers must ground student evaluation within the context of cultural meanings or social identity and this requires exquisite attention to history and, again, to the role of individuals in history in shaping their social universe.

In adopting Bernstein's partially materialist, partially constructivist framework, teachers of development and of comparative political economy might encourage students to come to see, in historically as well as theoretically informed ways, that there tend to be winners as well as losers in the process of peasant 'development'. As Bernstein stresses, internal differentiations begin to emerge and assume the form of a peasant class structure, that is, the emergence of a 'middle', 'rich' or kulak, as well as a poor peasant class in the course of capitalist incorporation. Bernstein attributes the internal formation of a stratified peasantry to the process of intensification of commodity relations. "Differentiation in the materialist sense is tied to the condition in which wealth becomes capital, when it is not consumed individually but productively through investment in means of production. It is this which gives a content to the classification of 'poor', 'middle', and 'rich' peasants in terms of the relations of production."[23] But such dynamics may equally be applied to a description of the mechanisms of growth, productivity, the emergence of a middle class, and the sustainability of Third World agriculture, etc., in the process of development. The arguments Bernstein uses to condemn the effects of commodity production upon peasant households, from the perspectives of a fully evolved constructivist pedagogy, insufficiently reviews the issue of alternatives in rural or agrarian development, or at least fails to account for the peculiar mix invariably created economy to economy, culture to culture, whenever commodity and peasant forms of production confront each other.

Bernstein's approach to peasant societies does lend itself to a more fully engaged constructivist pedagogy, however, given its methodological emphasis upon household and household forms of production. Bernstein draws a distinction in respect to how peasants are exploited as opposed to how proletarianized workers are exploited, one that revolves around the role of households in development. "The position taken," he states, is that peasants have to be located in capitalist relations of production, but in conditions less determinate than those of the proletariat to the degree that household production is not subject to complete expropriation nor to the particular modes of regulations and discipline of labour. . . ."[24] The household thus represents the fundamental unit of analysis in his materialist interpretation of peasant society. Indeed, the entire framework of Bernstein's theoretical project regarding peasant society and the exploitation of peasant agriculture revolves around household forms of production. But nowhere does he call for specification of the cultural modalities in which household production occurs or in which it becomes subordinated in the transition to capitalism by what he calls commoditization. "By this we mean," he writes, "that the destruction of the reproduction cycle of natural economy gives way to a different process of social reproduction in which the reproduction of households takes place increasingly on an *individual* basis through the relations of commodity production and exchange. The relations between individual households, whether at the village level or at the level of the regional, national, or international division of labour, are increasingly mediated through the *place* each household occupies in the total nexus of relations of commodity production and exchange."[25] But the incorporation of household production into this nexus involves cultural forms of displacement and resistance, ones that go unaccounted for in Bernstein's account.

Nonetheless, Bernstein's examination of the process of capitalist exploitation of peasant work and labor as peasant households confront commodified forms of production remains highly suggestive for teachers of comparative development interested in creating a constructivist pedagogy and teaching approach. He demonstrates why peasants must, in response to capitalist forms of production, engage in commodity production of their own in a kind of 'commodify or perish' environment where capital attempts to regulate and rule the processes of peasant production. He describes the process of exploitation in the following terms that stress a notion of 'squeeze'. "By the simple reproduction 'squeeze,'" he writes, "we refer to those effects of commodity relations on the economy of peasant households that can be summarized in terms of increasing costs of production/decreasing returns to labour."[26] The squeeze results in increasingly unfavorable terms of trade between the income of the peasant generated by what peasant households are able to produce and sell, on the one hand, and what it costs to live and produce those goods for sale, on the other. It is this combination of reduction in consumption and intensification of commodity production, which involves increasingly more expensive inputs, the depletion of land resources to the point of exhaustion, the literally back-breaking extension of the work and labor process, that Bernstein associates with exploitation. And as part of this process of exploitation, he includes a cycle of indebtedness which peasant households must face, and consequent starvation rents. This combination of forces and factors thus amount to what Bernstein calls a 'devalorization' of peasant labor-time.

Is such devalorization unjust according to the standards of justice? Bernstein's analysis, and its avoidance of the cultural contexts in which such devalorization occurs, leaves teachers — for purposes of pedagogical clarity, on contested terrain. Diminishing terms of trade, decreased amounts of consumption, intensification of peasant production appear to simulate representative conditions of exploitation. Before analysis can render a normative judgment, however, teachers and their students must assess the costs to individual households as they arise within specified social or cultural contexts. Conceptions of work and of labor differ. So do the social relations of production differ in keeping with various cultural presuppositions regarding the production of value. If students are to be asked to reflect upon the economic conditions of exploitation, then they must also be challenged to consider the cultural conditions that renders forms of exploitation so varied across the many kinds of peasant cultures. As a consequence of such constructivist teaching methods and emphases, students gain insight not only into the universal nature of capitalism and peasant agrarianism as modes of production, but, rather, they come to understand how modes of production such as peasant production come to be articulated through history within the context of specific cultures.

Perhaps the most sustained treatment available in the contemporary political economy literature of peasant resistance and its implicit relevance to constructivist conceptions of culture, morality, and justice is that developed by James C. Scott. Scott presents an elaborate ethnographic tableau that vividly details the character, process, and structures of peasant resistance to exploitation.[27]

The specific production site Scott investigates in *Weapons of the Weak*, for example, is also rice producing village, one named Sedaka located in rural Malaysian society. His emphasis is upon changing social and economic relations resulting from double-cropping and introduction of mechanization into the productive process. But the struggle he identifies is more than a random series of events. The struggle is for and against capitalism itself and thus over the social relations destroyed and the social relations reconstituted for good or ill by the encroachments of capitalism upon traditional ways of life.

In this, his analysis parallels that of Carney and Watts' study of women rice workers in the Gambia.[28] He writes, ". . . we are dealing herewith the undramatic but ubiquitous struggle against the effects of state-fostered capitalist development in the countryside; the loss of access to the means of production (proletarianization), the loss of work (marginalization) and income, and the loss of what little status and few claims the poor could assert before double-cropping."[29] Citing the work of E. P. Thompson and Barrington Moore, Jr., Scott shows that the significance of poverty resides in its symbolic as well as material consequence for those who experience it. As is the case in so many parts of the less developing world, relative poverty, rather than absolute poverty, represents the most silent pain and most salient evil. For Scott's Sedaka villagers, how could it be otherwise in a culture built on pillars of shame and standing. "Poverty is far more than a simple matter of not enough calories or cash. . . . For most of the village poor, poverty represents a far greater threat to their modest standing in the community."[30]

Scott also explores an emerging stratification of rich, middle, and poor farmers commensurate with the observations reported earlier by Bernstein. But most relevantly is Scott's repeated observation that 'face', 'honor', 'reputation', represent the currency of human relations in a system of values and norms clearly oriented, by what might be cautiously termed, 'a shame culture'. The relationship between land owners, large farmers, and poor peasants revolves around reputations for "respect, loyalty, and social recognition. What is involved," Scott comments, "to put it crudely, is a kind of 'politics of reputation' in which a good name is conferred in exchange for adherence to a certain code of conduct."[31]

Scott outlines the vocabulary of exploitation used by Sedaka peasants to describe reactions to perceived injustice. It is a grammar of moral agency and resistance as well. "**What is demanded, ironically, is patronage that is not patronizing.** The poor of the village attempt, symbolically, not only to enjoin the charity and assistance but, simultaneously to negate, the 'social premium' the rich might expect to extract as compensation for their generosity."[32] Scott evaluates how stratification and income are evaluated by villagers as they 'fix' normative expectations regarding patron-employer relations. Shame is the name of the game. "Just who is well-off, just how generous they should be, just what forms their generosity should take, just which forms of help are compatible with dignity, and just what behavior is arrogant and shameful are questions that form the substance of the drama."[33]

Scott's analysis of the confrontations between rich and poor in cases of perceived exploitation by the poor constitutes the bulk of his analysis.

Citing Hobsbawm, he reveals how peasants "work the system to its disadvantage." Resistance occurs in all shapes and manners, and more often than not without great revolutions in mind. And yet the consequences of such acts of resistance can often prove to be momentous even when those who act do so with a pervasive sense of futility in the face of overwhelming odds. Scott saves some of his best writing for the end as he brings his discussion of peasant resistance to closure by sounding this theme: "All the more reason, then," he concludes, "to respect, if not celebrate, the weapons of the weak. All the more reason to see in the tenacity of self-preservation — in ridicule, in truculence, in irony, in petty acts of noncompliance, in foot dragging, in dissimulation, in **resistant mutality**, in the disbelief in elite homilies, in the steady, grinding efforts to hold one's own against overwhelming odds--a spirit and practice that prevents the worst and promises something better."[34] [Emphasis added.] What better way to encapsulate the epistemological and theoretical orientation suggested by constructivism than the phrase, 'resistant mutuality'. For it contains the core of constructivist precepts regarding how human beings shape the world through resistance.

Political struggle against exploitation, even if measured in terms of material causes and events, is best understood in symbolic, ultimately, normative terms. Exploitation, however structural, must be converted into normative issues relevant to an understanding of injustice. Exploitation and injustice must be examined in terms of the victims themselves. Victims must no longer be seen as victims but rather as the subjects of politics who live in a broad range of cultural contexts, and who take their historical lives 'into their own hands' to assert their ethical dignity. The language of materialist exploitation must thus become a language of justice. The language of justice and exploitation must be shaped by constructivism and constructivist pedagogies if the issues of both exploitation and justice are to reach a student audience who must learn to care before they learn how to understand.

Pedagogical Discourses on Industrial Relations: Labor, Skill, and Control on the Factory Floor--In Search of Constructivist Mediation

A vast and important literature has focused on work and labor during the modern industrial era. Harry Braverman in 1974 opened a major new chapter in the debate over the nature of work and exploitation within the modern labor process.[35] Subsequent contributions by a wide array of talented authors, including Burawoy, Rubery, Edwards, Zimbalist, and many others, have generated a discourse around two basic issues: the deskilling of work, and increasing discipline and control of workers by forces of capital and management. Such topics are especially ripe for constructivist treatment in the classroom on the part of teachers wishing to outline a course of instruction on modern labor processes within the context of industrial sociology or comparative political economy focusing upon industrialization. Here, too, the linkages between world politics and world political economy emerge clearly. After all, if productivity and competitiveness are the keys to political as well as economic order, the role and nature of industrial labor retains a cultural concern for students interested in security as well as prosperity.

Let us encapsulate briefly the central arguments of this debate over deskilling and modern industrial forms of labor in order to elucidate how research regarding the rules and authority that govern the shop floor and constructivist pedagogies can effectively become aligned. As before, constructivism and constructivist pedagogies require certain emphases, in particular, an emphasis upon how agents, factory workers, for example, shape the working conditions that surrounds them, just as the world of factory life molds the character and meaning of their lives.

The structural status in capitalism of industrial labor represents an essential focus in any discussion of work, exploitation, and injustice, especially if linked to materialist or Marxist conceptions of class relations in capitalist modes of production. Pedagogical discourse applied to these issues lends itself to a constructivist orientation, however, insofar as the deskilling of labor can be viewed in terms and in terminologies that recognize or lend credence to the fact that workers can and often do take their situations into their own hands.

Those who argue that industrial work is becoming deskilled, mean to suggest that labor is experiencing a major form of degradation by becoming ever more divorced from the rational elements that dominate the industrial labor process. Workers, in a word, are required by the rationalities of industrial manufacture, dominated as they are by economies of scale, to do increasingly mindless work on the industrial factory floor. Linked to this is the claim by those that advocate the deskilling proposition that managerial, bureaucratic and/or structural techniques of control over the workers is accelerating within the labor process thus further attenuating the autonomy of workers and their capacity to enlist their own mental and ethical resources in the service of work. Such views tends to portray labor as the victims of structural decline, technological change, and capital domination and thus of exploitative labor subordination.

Constructivism would alter the terms of debate, however, by viewing deskilling against the possibilities of worker resistance, which, like the resistance of Sedaka peasants, may not eliminate the system that exploits them, but which, at the very least, does behoove us to recognize in workers more than the passive victims of industrial capitalism, but rather the autonomous agents capable of transforming the very character of the labor process in which they are enmeshed. As in the case of peasant societies, a literature on work and labor in the industrial setting exists which lends itself to constructivism and to constructivist approaches to teaching and learning. A few examples below might help to illustrate the kinds of resources available to teachers interested in discussing industrial labor processes in a variety of intellectual contexts but essentially from a perspective permeated by constructivist pedagogy.

Paul Thompson, for example, in his overview of the debate over the nature of industrial work, points out that even in the face of deskilling, industrial workers can and do find space for autonomy and subjective discretion.[36] "As Burawoy perceptively points out," Thompson declares, "**Despite** the separation of conception and execution, the expropriation of skill and the narrowing of discretion, studies like Braverman's have 'missed the equally important parallel tendency toward the expansion of choices within narrower limits. . . . ' The growth of internal labour markets can therefore act as a counterweight to skill degradation, and this opens up the whole area of the subjective components of deskilling."[37] Thompson also observes, after considerable discussion of methods of worker control in the industrial workplace, that workers continue to retain elements of control especially with regard to working conditions. "The essential confusion," he writes, "is between the ability of workers to retain skills and job control. There is considerable evidence that workers can exercise the power to determine elements of working conditions and rewards, **after** deskilling has taken place."[38] This continues to be the case even as the industrial workplace or production site changes to accommodate new mechanical techniques. "In fact deskilling can sometimes **confer** bargaining power in circumstances where mechanisation replaces craft labour with semi-skilled workers have been previously unskilled. . . . The lesson is that no amount of deskilling or mechanisation can lead to the **complete** domination of capital over labour."[39] This is the lesson which teachers dedicated to student understanding of the political economy of industrial labor processes, an understanding, that is, as interpreted in a constructivist perspective — invariably choose to convey.

None of this denies categorically explanations of exploitation of the modern industrial workforce based upon the classical labor theory of value, so central to Braverman. What it does suggest is the importance of retaining a conception of modern labor that allows for human autonomy and moral agency. Only in such pedagogical frameworks, can teachers and their students relate theoretical explanation to normative exposition, that is, only in so doing can we mobilize explanations of exploitation and press them into the service of advancing normative standards of justice. That teachers do precisely this, that they encourage their students to do precisely this, represents not only sound normative reasoning, but sound instruction in political economy as well.

This theme is perhaps most explicitly introduced into the political economic literature by Michael Storper and Richard Walker's *The Capitalist Imperative*.[40] Taking their intellectual cue from David Harvey, Storper and Walker attempt to develop a geopolitical economic perspective grounded in a conception of differential or uneven economic growth organized along the geographical contours of a spatial division of labor. They reject the neoclassical liberal view of capitalist growth on the grounds that the liberal perspective incorrectly emphasizes equilibrium market forces and reduction of input costs of factors of production, whereas capitalism introduces technology in ways designed to stimulate demand through new and innovative output thereby generating 'superprofits'. Growth in capitalism is thus linked to the profits generated by outputs. Storper and Walker argue that models stressing disequilibria brought about by the endless and thus 'normal' search for profits more accurately reflect the dynamics of capitalist growth. And on the basis of this emphasis upon the search for profitability of outputs, Storper and Walker conclude that the consequence of growth in capitalism is an unceasing pattern of uneven growth among economic regions and cities within and across national borders.

But the thrust of Storper and Walker's thesis is to reconceptualize the role of labor in the labor process. And here they implicitly attack not so much the neoclassical equilibrium model as much as materialist conceptions which in their view liken the role of labor to that of a commodity. "Laborforces exhibit a high degree of geographical differentiation owing to labor's unique nature," they write. "Labor differs fundamentally from real commodities because it is embodied in living, conscious human beings. . . . Labor takes a commodity form, but it is not a true commodity."[41] Storper and Walker proceed to develop a theoretical approach to labor as a force in production in terms of four dimensions: conditions of purchase, performance capacity, actual performance, and reproduction in place.

The implication of their framework of analysis is the central role of culture and agency in the relation of capital to labor within the industrial workplace, a constructivist theme albeit without its pedagogical implications. Thus Storper and Walker, while working the mines of industry manufacture from the perspective of geopolitical economy, also help to define the pedagogical linkages between exploitation and injustice in teaching political economy whether from the perspective of neoclassical liberalism or neoclassical materialism. "The politics of production... need to be set within the larger frame of labor markets and broader processes of social reproduction," they write. "People in different labor market or national contexts will practice production politics differently. Employers and workers use the conditions in the labor market and in the larger community and society as a way of influencing life within the workplace. This wider relationship between workers and employers," they conclude, "is the employment relation, and it is only in the context of employment relations that real demands for labor are defined and supplies of labor produced."[42] Different cultures thus sustain different 'factory regimes' which must be understood as specific or concrete cultural artifacts that affect the nature of politics at the factory or industrial worksite. Application of the labor theory of value without regard to these specified cultural modalities cannot attend to the full nature of exploitation let alone lead to student comprehension of the injustice such exploitation entails. This represents a call to interdisciplinary 'discipline'. The sociology of the workplace as practised by Studs Terkel, the politics of the workplace as defined by the analyses of Cloward and Piven, the anthropologies of the workplace as explored by Foucault and several authors previously cited, all converge into a singular political praxis designed to investigate how people shape their working lives.

Pedagogical Discourses on Postindustrial Civilization

What is true of instruction regarding the industrial labor process in modern capitalism holds true for pedagogies designed to present students with insights into the implications for work, labor, and class stratification of advancing postindustrial technology and society. Here too a constructivist pedagogical perspective guides instructors in terms of the materials presented and the concepts discussed. Of particular interest in this context is the relationship between informationalized flows, discussed in the analysis included elsewhere in this book by Timothy W. Luke, and the socio-economic impacts of the telecommunications process measured in terms of labor markets, labor process, and labor segmentation.

These linkages, relevant to a constructivist pedagogy geared to a course of instruction regarding postindustrialism and postindustrial society, is demonstrated by Manuel Castells' study of labor, *The Information City*.[43] Castells' study represents an example of several recent monographs that depict the future of work and labor in the face of advances in telecommunications technology. Castells, for example, examines how telecommunications technology is resulting in ever freer flows of investment capital and how this in turn is tending to generate segmentation in the labor force. Industries mounted to the wheels of global telecommunications operate transnationally and, in so doing, sometimes directly, often indirectly, also create slums of exploitation within marginalized domestic labor markets or segments of labor markets.

The pedagogical language adopted by Castells is strongly prophetic in that he speaks of new ages and of new cities. "The fundamental contemporary meaning of the dual city," he writes, "refers to the process of spatial restructuring through which distinct segments of labor are included in and excluded from the making of new history."[44] He speaks — correctly but ironically — of new ghettoized communities where youths have no prospect of work in 'upgraded economy', of formal and informal labor economies, of upgraded and downgraded forms of work. He depicts the bimodal distributive patterns of work, labor, employment, income so symptomatic of largescale migration. "The articulation between socio-economic restructuring and the diffusion of information technologies, both in factories and in offices," he says, "is transforming labor and the labor process. . . . While a substantial number of jobs are being upgraded in skills, and sometimes in wages, in the most dynamic sectors an even larger number of jobs are being eliminated in key manufacturing and advanced service industries, and these are generally jobs that are not skilled enough to escape automation but are expensive enough to be worth investment in technology to replace them."[45] For Castells there is an advancing new world order and that order is of increasing bifurcation between labor and capital. "Capital," he writes, "has two main goals in pursuing the restructuring of labor. . . . The first is to change qualitatively the power relationships between management and organized labor in favor of business interests. The second is to enhance substantially the flexibility of labor at all levels, through deregulation, sectoral and geographical mobility, networking and subcontracting, and constant redefinition of working conditions according to the changing strategies and interests of firms."[46] Castells envisions the introduction of telecommunications technology as the key instrumentality in achieving both aims. Teachers of world politics and of world political economy wishing to address the future of industrial civilization must, therefore, confront the implications of telecommunications upon labor and the labor process as well as upon state relations writ large.

Castells, in constructivist fashion, appears to recognize, at least partially, that exploitation attached to the massive restructuring of labor brought on by telecommunications, which he describes, occurs within concrete cultural contexts. Modern telecommunications may destroy the sense of place, but the exploitation which occurs as a consequence, must be presented by teachers of political economy in terms of place, or what

Castells calls 'social fabric'. High technology contributes to the polarization and segmentation of the labor force, he suggests, "by contributing to the dissolution of the social fabric that for decades protected wage-earners from the unrestrained imposition of the logics of capital. Otherwise it would be difficult to explain why clerical work is less well paid than assembly-line work, or why the wages of electronics production workers do not match those of their counterparts in the automobile industry."[47] The analysis offered by Castells, however, does not develop the full theoretical or pedagogical significance of the cultural modalities or social artifacts he is discussing.

What is forgotten in Castells' analysis, and others similar to it, is that social relations at the workplace involve cultural and symbolic meanings, intersubjective understandings, imaginative moments of self-reflection, or what we earlier called, recursive mutuality. These alter the very coin of workplace transaction. Castells devotes an entire monograph to a description of the new telecommunications order without peering into that order to assess the nature of human or social relations within it. He is prepared to argue that global telecommunications will transform labor markets, international modes of production, world divisions of labor, the capitalist circulation of capital and its regime of accumulation, but never systematically studies the cultural or symbolic character of social relations within the organizational worksite. He fails to do so, since his analysis of work and production does not include normative categories nor constructivist units of analysis. For Castells what counts is the march of autonomous capitalism as the music of global telecommunication plays on.

A constructivist pedagogy would seek to amend such methodological crimes of omission. Social consciousness, cultural ideology, conceptions of male and female apply to social relations in the peasant, postindustrial or informational civilizations. Clerical workers are less paid in Castells 'information city' because they are overwhelmingly women. Electronics workers — and garment industry workers — are paid less well than automobile factory workers, because they too are women, and despite the fact that both garment and electronics manufacture tends to be more complex and more demanding on the industrial floor than is automobile manufacture. Such forms of discrimination and oppression have cultural roots that require self-reflective interpretation by students seeking to understand political economic relationships.

One study attempting to strip away the levels of mystification that surround the organizational workplace of tomorrow is Shoshana Zuboff's *In the Age of the Smart Machine: The Future of Work and Power*.[48] Zuboff examines the mix of technology, hierarchy, and authority under differing moments of capitalism in order to understand the potential impact of advanced telecommunications and information technology upon work as it is lived at the workplace. Her conclusions are startling. The workplace of the future, she suggests, may be conceptualized as a text. Hierarchy and authority at the workplace become subordinate to the ability, in any instance, to read the text and to respond to it. Formerly relevant, indeed, crucial distinctions between manual labor and intellectual work, begin to fade away, as each permeates the other in new and previously unsuspected ways. "When the textualizing consequences of an informating technology become more comprehensive, the body's traditional role in the production process (as a source of effort and/or skill in the service of **Acting On**) is also transformed," she writes. "The rigid separation of mental and material work characteristic of the industrial division of labor and vital to the preservation of a distinct managerial group (in the office as well as in the factory) becomes, not merely outmoded, but perilously dysfunctional."[49] The hierarchical lines of traditional production organizations disintegrate. "Earlier distinctions between white and blue 'collars' collapse." The reason for this reflects fundamental changes in the distribution of responsibility for knowledge and for textualizing problems at the workplace. "Even more significant is the increased intellectual content of work tasks across organizational levels that attenuates the conventional designations of manager and managed."[50] Differences among employees remain, but no longer serve to conflate authority, hierarchy, and responsibility. "This does not mean that there are no longer useful distinctions to be made among organizational members, but whatever these distinctions may be, they will no longer convey fundamentally different modes of involvement with the life of the organization represented by the divisions of abstract and physical labor. Instead, the total organizational skill base becomes more homogeneous."[51] Contrary to the polarizations predicted by Castells, Zuboff thus indicates that a great levelling will occur among managers and workers as the electronic text "becomes a vast symbolic surrogate for the vital detail of an organization's daily life."[52]

Zuboff recognizes that the significance of this transformation in social relations of production resides in the changes such a transformation promises in the symbolic meanings that help to define the subjective and intersubjective understanding of work. Human relations take on new forms of solidarity, new kinds of identities, new kinds of devotions. "The textualization process moves away from a conception of information as something individuals collect, process, and disseminate; instead, it invites us to imagine an organization as a group of people gathered around a central core that is the electronic text. Individuals take up their relationship toward that text according to their responsibility and their information needs. In such a scenario, work is, in large measure, the creation of meaning. . . ."[53] Zuboff envisions the need for a new division of learning to support the new division of labor. Since "an informated organization is structured to promote the possibilities of useful learning among all members and thus presupposes relations of equality," members of the informated organization will require a new pedagogy and a new instructional mode.[54]

A sense of the productive significance of learning, of emancipatory education, of a pedagogy that enhances the recursive self-reflections of a workforce capable of determining the conditions of work as well as the product of its labors, appears, if only by implication, to be at the core of Zuboff's conception of the informated organization. "The informated organization is a learning institution," she writes, "and one of its principal purposes is the expansion of knowledge—not knowledge for its own sake (as in academic pursuit), but knowledge that comes to reside at the core of what it means to be productive."[55] And in so writing she appears to aim a criticism at contemporary modes of education and instruction as well as contemporary conceptions of what learning and education entails. In the informated context, "Learning is no longer a separate activity that occurs before one enters the workplace or in remote classroom settings. Nor is it an activity preserved for a managerial group. The behaviors that define learning and the behaviors that define being productive are one and the same. Learning is not something that requires time out from being engaged in productive activity; learning is the heart of productive activity."[56] Zuboff concludes on an especially important note within the framework of this paper: "To Put it Simply, Learning is the New Form of Labor."[57]

The labor of learning, the relearning of work will not occur immediately nor automatically. We remain the captives of our own vocabularies and imaginative constructions regarding work, labor, the meanings of hierarchy and authority, the progressions of technology, the human condition. "In the traditional organization, the division of learning lent credibility to the legitimacy of imperative control. In an informated organization, the new division of learning produces experience that encourage a synthesis of members' interests, and the flow of value-adding knowledge helps legitimate the organization as a learning community."[58] Terms like 'value-adding knowledge', 'learning communities', 'informated organizations' take us far from the fields of reality in which work and labor operate today. Zuboff recognizes this when she indicates that the "language of work" in today's world remains incarcerated by the terminologies of a past and quickly passing industrial era. "We remain. . . ," she laments, "prisoners of a vocabulary in which managers require employees; superiors have subordinates; jobs are defined to be specific, detailed, narrow, and task-related; and organizations have levels that in turn make possible chains of command and spans of control."[59] Her complaint takes aim against the symbolic regimes that guide and help to organize the outmoded conceptions of work. "The guiding metaphors are military; relationships are thought of as contractual and often adversarial. The foundational image of work is still one of a manufacturing enterprise where raw materials are transformed by physical labor and machine power into finished goods. However, the images associated with physical labor can no longer guide our conception of work."[60] In the end, Zuboff employs the language of hope: "empowerment, commitment, and involvement." This language is framed by the possibilities of social reconstruction grounded in a constructivist pedagogy, one that conceives of power as the capacity of those who work to learn and through learning to shape the conditions which — partially and recursively — define their lives.

Conclusion

At this point, teachers might be tempted to delve into one of two ideal worlds, both of which are ideal precisely because they eliminate the contorted realities of human, in particular, capitalist, self-interest. The first is the idealized Marxian vision of the perfect socialist order. Here surplus value is channeled not into the crucibles of private property and class exploitation, but into the coffers of publicly owned and publicly controlled institutions. The second ideal vision derives from formal ethical theory. The most compelling of these in recent years is that proposed by John Rawls. The veils of ignorance fall down upon the face of self-interest in the name of justice. But teachers interested in linking the ideal to the real world may prefer to investigate how exploitation arises within specific settings or systems to explore with their students how the forms and mechanisms of exploitation constitute injustices against the backdrop of culturally relevant normative standards, standards which assume the moral autonomy of agents even under structural conditions of injustice.

The charge of injustice must be posited within contexts that assume choice and choice cannot exist without an assumption of agent autonomy. **No choice but to lose as one earns given the alternatives** refers not only to access to work and labor through labor markets, it also refers to control within the labor process, control that either reinforces or erodes managerial and capitalist extraction of surplus value. In real, rather than ideal situations, workers and laborers, those said to be exploited, possess, as Paul Thompson and others discussed above suggested, a range of devices to limit, undermine, obstruct, the devices of exploitation that demean them. Any fully fleshed normative theory of justice as applied to the real world and made relevant to a constructivist pedagogy must, therefore, examine these choices within the labor process itself in order to strengthen the theoretical links between structural explanations of exploitation, on the one hand, and normatively grounded applications of standards of justice, on the other. This linkage cannot occur meaningfully in frames of analytical reference that ignore the intermediaries of culture or the role that culture plays in any economy. The study of political economy thus requires due appreciation of cultural exchange.

Thus, teachers pursuing a constructivist strategy designed to introduce formal or ideal-world perspectives on justice in order to have students apply them to real-world contexts related to work and labor, might refer to such texts as that of R.G. Peffer's *Marxism, Morality and Social Justice*.[61] Peffer revises Rawls' original framework in the following way in order to enunciate a theory of social justice relevant to work and labor. Such an approach may be especially useful to some teachers wishing to introduce normative approaches to justice but from the perspective of political economy.

A sample of Peffer's formulations especially relevant to constructivism and to constructivist perspectives on pedagogy and teaching in political economy are as follows:

- Everyone's security rights and subsistence rights shall be respected.

- There is to be a maximum system of equal basic liberties, including freedom of speech and assembly; liberty of conscience and freedom of thought; freedom of the person along with the right to hold (personal) property; and freedom from arbitrary arrest and seizure as defined by the concept of the rule of law;

- There is to be (a) right to an equal opportunity to attain social positions and offices and (b) an equal right to participate in all social decision-making processes within institutions of which one is a part.

- Social and economic inequalities are justified if, and only if, they benefit the least advantaged, consistent with the just savings principle, but **are not to exceed** levels that will seriously undermine equal worth of liberty or the good of self-respect.[62]

Peffer's fourth principle, based on the Rawlsian conception of 'just savings', confronts the issue of private property and privilege generated intergenerationally. Thus we see a linkage between distributional and structural concepts reflective of the debates discussed above. But the major import of Peffer's reformulation of Rawls relates to the issue of choice and opportunity in the workplace and thus to standards of justice based upon meaning and meaningfulness in work. This is directly reflective of constructivism and could easily lend itself to a constructivist mode of instruction. Of particular interest in this regard is Peffer's reference to Kai Nielsen's 'radical egalitarian theory of social justice'.[63] Nielsen's proposition identifies "equal right to equal opportunities for meaningful work" as the ultimate standard for the just society. If constructivism and the debate over exploitation encourages students to learn, the purpose of such learning must include coming to understand the importance of access and choice in the workplace. **No choice but to lose as one earns** given the absence of alternatives represents a standard which students might adopt to examine the degree to which a society provides its workers with choice — not to lose — but to gain through work.

Labors Lost, Labors Gained

The message teachers might wish to adopt as they develop a constructivist pedagogy linking political economy and normative philosophy might well stress the availability of meaningful work and labor. Students might wish to examine capitalism, even, precapitalism, past and present, according to how such modes promote meaningful work, work that does not demean, work that edifies as well as sustains. The normative grammars of both teachers and students must become extended to accommodate to the new realities of the working world and thus to new possibilities of human relations at the workplace. Constructivism in teaching political economy calls both teacher and students to arms in a new manifesto of solidarity and commitment, one aimed at the construction of a new normative and social order built upon the premises of justice.

From the instructional point of view shaped by constructivism, therefore, the real world in which exploitation and injustice arises is a world of autonomous beings, autonomous beings who work and who labor within concrete cultural settings. These settings may guide, shape, and mold the character and meanings of work and labor, but they also reflect the response of such autonomous agents to the working conditions of their labor. If choice and autonomy are thus to serve as the conceptual core of constructivist pedagogies relevant to political economy and normative philosophy, teachers must raise the standard issues of justice and exploitation in the context of choice and autonomy. Such a pedagogical program would then require students to consider the following sets of questions and issues:

A Constructivist Program of Political Economy

- As a way of examining exploitation, students must seek to explore how system and structure limit or expand labor market opportunities in any social context and, additionally, they must identify the ways in which labor and work as processes, particularly, in capitalism, consistently advantage and consistently disadvantage certain classes and segments positioned by the relations of capital to labor; in other words, students should be required to seek to determine how systems that structure access or opportunity as well as systems that structure work, the labor process, and accumulation, intrude upon, protect, or expand the choices available to workers and laborers, positioned within the class structure by shifts in production modes;

- As a way of examining of injustice, students must assess the comparative conditions and the relative degrees of exploitation under different modes of production and under different regimes of accumulation; they should be required to examine exploitation in historical perspectives in order to ascertain how and in what ways social, economic, or political development or growth fosters new or greater forms of exploitation; they must also examine exploitation comparatively to determine how and what ways certain modes and regimes exploit in relation to alternatives;

- As a way of examining the conceptual/normative linkages between exploitation and justice, students must consider not only if or how socio-economic structures impose themselves upon workers in exploitative ways, but how individuals respond to such exploitation within specific cultural and social formations; students should be required to undertake a semeiotic study of the symbols of exploitation to interpret the meanings of injustice as narrated by different cultures; they must try to formulate a language of injustice relative to particular cultures, especially where the marriage between Western capitalism and non-Western traditions or modes of production is the conjugal force giving birth to exploitation; such instruction and learning entails a careful appreciation of how individuals view their traditional roles, how they perceive change, how they regard their relation to the newly derived forms of work, labor, or extraction; such constructivism in the classroom also recount the forms and methods of resistance by those who assert moral autonomy even in the face of compressed latitude and tightened extraction.

That the language of justice must be relativized against the background of universal standards of justice represents, therefore, the critical measure in determining the extent to which constructivist pedagogical categories inform the instructional project of any teacher of international and world political economy.

Notes

1. Margaret S. Archer, "Theory, Culture and Post-Industrial Society," *Theory, Culture & Society*, 7, (1990), pp. 97-119.
2. Archer, p. 111.
3. Archer, p. 111.
4. Archer, p. 113.
5. Archer, p. 113.
6. Archer, p. 117.
7. Nicholas Greenwood Onuf, *World of our Making: Rules and Rule in Social Theory and International Relations* (Columbia, SC: University of South Carolina Press, 1989).
8. Onuf, p. 1.
9. Onuf, p. 46.
10. Onuf, p. 40.
11. Onuf, p. 40.
12. Onuf, p. 41.
13. Onuf, p. 42.
14. Onuf, p. 43.
15. Onuf, p. 43.
16. For an elaboration of this theme, see Denis Goulet and Charles K. Wilber, "The Human Dilemma of Development," in Charles K. Wilber and Kenneth P. Jameson, eds., *The Political Economy of Development and Underdevelopment* 5th ed., (New York: McGraw-Hill, 1992).
17. Charles Taylor, "Philosophy and Its History," in Richard Rorty, J. B. Schneewind, and Quentin Skinner, eds. *Philosophy in History: Essays on the Historiography of Philosophy*, (Cambridge: Cambridge University Press, 1984), p 21.
18. Henry Bernstein, "African Peasantries: A Theoretical Framework," *The Journal of Peasant Studies*, VI, No. 4, (1979), pp. 421-43.
19. Bernstein, pp. 421-43.
20. Bernstein, p. 437.
21. Bernstein, p. 437.
22. Bernstein, p. 433.

23. Bernstein, p. 430.
24. Bernstein, p. 437.
25. Bernstein, p. 425.
26. Bernstein, p. 427.
27. References above are to James C. Scott's *The Moral Economy of The Peasant: Subsistence and Rebellion in Southeast Asia* (New Haven CT: Yale University Press: 1976); *Weapons of the Weak: Everyday Forms of Peasant Resistance* (New Haven CT: Yale University Press, 1985); and *Domination and the Arts of Resistance: Hidden Transcripts* (New Haven CT: Yale University Press, 1990).
28. Judith Carney and Michael Watts, "Manufacturing Dissent: Work, Gender, and the Politics of Meaning in a Peasant Society," *Africa*, 60, No.2, (1990), pp. 205-241.
29. James C. Scott, *Weapons of the Weak*, p. 241.
30. Scott, p. 236.
31. Scott, pp. 184-85.
32. Scott, p. 197.
33. Scott, p. 199.
34. Scott, p. 350.
35. Reference is to Harry Braverman, *Labor and Monopoly Capital: The Degradation of Work in the Twentieth Century* (New York and London: Monthly Review Press, 1974).
36. Paul Thompson, *The Nature of Work: An Introduction to Debates on the Labour Process*, 2nd ed., (London: Macmillan, 1989).
37. Thompson, p. 104.
38. Thompson, p. 107.
39. Thompson, pp. 107-108.
40. Michael Storper and Richard Walker, *The Capitalist Imperative: Territory, Technology and Industrial Growth* (New York: Basil Blackwell, 1989).
41. Storper and Walker, p. 155.
42. Storper and Walker, p. 166.
43. Manuel Castells, *The Informational City: Information Technology, Economic Restructuring and Urban-Regional Process* (New York: Basil Blackwell, 1991).
44. Castells, p. 228.
45. Castells, p. 191.
46. Castells, p. 189.
47. Castells, p. 188.
48. Shoshana Zuboff, *In the Age of the Smart Machine: The Future of Work and Power* (New York: Basic Books, 1988).
49. Zuboff, p. 393.
50. Zuboff, p. 393.
51. Zuboff, p. 393.
52. Zuboff, p. 393.
53. Zuboff, p. 394.
54. Zuboff, p. 394.
55. Zuboff, p. 394.
56. Zuboff, p. 395.

57. Zuboff, p. 395.
58. Zuboff, p. 394.
59. Zuboff, p. 394.
60. Zuboff, p. 394.
61. R.G. Peffer, *Marxism, Morality, and Social Justice*, (Princeton NJ: Princeton University Press, 1990).
62. Peffer, p. 418.
63. Of particular relevance is Kai Nielsen, *Equality and Liberty: Defense of Radical Egalitarianism* (Totowa NJ: Rowman and Allanheld, 1984), esp. pp. 48-9; see also pp. 423-29.

14

Creating a Pedagogy for Convivial Planetary Community: The Future Challenge of Political Ecology

Terrence S. Shea

Seeking a New Social and International Order

> ... these will hammer their swords into ploughshares,
> their spears into sickles.
> Nation will not lift sword against nation,
> there will be no more training for war. Isaiah 2.4

The close of World War II was a time for jubilation, a time for sober reflection. The people who gathered to write a charter for the United Nations knew well the scourge of war, the indignities suffered within oppressive political orders, the injustices of poverty, hunger, homelessness in economic systems run amuck, the indiscriminate terror and destruction of ever more powerful weapons. According to the 1945 charter of this new organization they hoped:

> To maintain international peace and security.... To develop friendly relations among nations.... To achieve international cooperation in solving international problems of an economic, social, cultural, or humanitarian character.... To be a center for harmonizing the actions of nations in the attainment of these common ends.
> Charter of the United Nations, Art. 1

While much has been achieved through the UN in the last 45 years, clearly we do not yet enjoy a new world order of justice and peace.

No sooner was the ink dry on the Charter then work commenced on an international bill of human rights to express more fully the Charter's mandate for the promotion of human rights and fundamental freedoms for all. Drawing upon mostly Western humanitarian traditions, and recognizing that concepts of human rights/dignity are the basis of all civilizations, the General Assembly proclaimed the Universal Declaration of Human Rights (UDHR) in 1948. Article 28 explicitly recognized all peoples' aspirations for a new world order of justice and peace: "Everyone is entitled to a social and international order in which the rights and freedoms set forth in this Declaration can be fully realized." The commission labored another eighteen years to transform the UDHR's principles into treaty provisions that establish legal obligations on the part of each ratifying state. Though the General Assembly adopted The International Covenant on Economic, Social and Cultural Rights, The International Covenant on Civil and Political Rights, and The Optional Protocol to the latter covenant on 16 December 1966, it was not until 1976 that the required minimum of 35 states ratified them to bring them into force. These three with the UDHR now constitute what is called the International Bill of Human Rights (IBHR).

The IBHR, with its focus on all persons as subjects with rights before and prior to their status as citizens, challenges nation-state political and economic systems to a radical reorientation. The human rights framework, which includes the IBHR and more than forty additional declarations, conventions and the like, brings critical emphases to an evaluation of social agency. Human rights proponents focus on those who are dealt the heaviest losses, and search out the possible systemic injustices responsible. They demand a *redistribution* of gains and losses in accord with basic principles of *solidarity* and *equality*.[1] They insist upon liberation from the insecurities of domination, subjection and exploitation. They enquire about political economic restructuring, pointing out that economic and class power constrain the realization of human rights in Latin America, North America, Eastern Europe, Africa, Asia, the Middle East and everywhere else.

Today, human rights activists predominantly perceive the various rights as interactive, and accept the idea of a certain hierarchy of rights only in relation to a general pattern of human and planetary life-development. The recent focus on the right to development is most indicative of this evolution in thought and action. The conceptual framework emerging within this dialectic of analysis and practice brings to the fore again the question about what is a good and legitimate society. As realists, they argue that the moral force of human rights claims is the eventual determiner of a government's legitimacy and security. They point to the growing masses who insist on greater participation and the equal validity of their experience for playing a part in decision making throughout the varied institutions and structures of political economy.

And from another perspective they highlight ecological imperatives that deny the rational legitimacy of any system dependent upon intensified commodity consumption in unlimited economic expansion fueled by unfettered exploitation of planetary resources. They proclaim that the only true measure of all economic and political systems is the well being of all human beings *with* their biological foundation — the living planet.

It is against these standards that we are asked to interpret and assess the rise and fall of both Mammon and Caesar in the great ideological contest of our century.[2] In the socialist movement to centralize all power in Caesar, especially the responsibility for planning a complex economy, we see a denial of democracy and radically inefficient and unresponsive management of the material affairs of peoples. And in the capitalist movement the reduction of all normative questions to Mammon, especially with an ever greater emphasis on the short-term bottom line, we see a mindless consumerism blinding any concern for meeting the civic and domestic needs of the greater part of the population.[3] The former crushes the present's dynamic insistence for extensive participation, freedom and honestly independent self-determination which is at the core of the basic human rights of all persons; the latter smothers the altruistic challenge to move toward equality in social life and responsibility for the well-being of future generations which similarly is foundational for any future global order of justice and peace. And both systems have imposed profoundly destructive costs on the environment. Despite the earlier promise of each framework, now there is a loss of hope in respect to both. In recognition of this, John Lukacs observes that "the twentieth century is over."

The multiple crises at hand confirm that we are at a certain 'dead end'. Class power, racism, sexism, hierarchical authoritarianism and ecosystem destruction are basic realities denying the realization of human rights around the globe. Individuals experience themselves as mere functionaries of efficiency and profit; they neglect personal, familial and societal needs while meeting the demands of competition. There is a fragmentation of roles and specialization with the consequent diminishment of personal responsibility, impoverishment of communications, narrowing of perspective, and increase of personal stress related illnesses. Our technologies enhance life expectancy for a portion of the species, allow us to communicate instantaneously around the world, and even put us on the threshold of acting upon the basic creativities and genetic process of life itself. But due to a mistaken priority of values, we seem incapable of recognizing proper limits; and unbridled hubris drives us to the boundaries of specicide by nuclear destruction and ecocide by mindless exploitation and despoliation. We, and our nation-states together, seem helpless in the face of international terrorism, ethnic tensions, nationalist separatism, religious fundamentalism, domestic violence, overloaded political systems, international traffic in drugs, migration of refugees, third world and domestic debt, and environmental deterioration.

Is there still hope for the future? Yes, because it is a step towards health/life to know and admit our illness. Most human rights activists and theorists now see their respective areas of concern not as discrete and separate realities but as integrally interrelated in a complementary holistic fashion.[4] They agree about the need to integrate all our efforts in the search for economic well-being and security. This requires inquiry and discussion of the values and norms that pertain to a humane or moral ordering of relations between us as members of one species within a single planetary life system. Neglecting this pedagogical mandate in recent centuries, we constructed organizations and technologies rooted in alienating ideological and 'scientific' claims that in turn served to protect and enforce their validity and control in the face of mounting evidence as to their profound destructiveness of persons, communities and planetary vitality. Now their pathological disorders stand exposed.

A sign of health and coherence emerges in the recent focus on the right to *development*. Although there is some debate whether the right to development constitutes a 'new right' or rather a 'synthesis right', there is significant consensus about its following elements:

- the development of persons and the maintenance of the planet's ecosystems are the proper measures of political and economic systems;

- personal development and dignity can be realized only when integrated with the well-being of the community;

- human development requires the satisfaction of interdependent material and non-material basic needs;

- the poor and the vulnerable have a special moral claim on the successful and powerful members of the group;

- participation and degrees of individual and collective self-reliance must be integral parts of all social institutions and processes;
- moral responsibility for enhancing human dignity and protecting human rights rests interdependently with private and public actors.

Nevertheless, to date the universal scope and applicability of the human rights framework has not really succeeded in becoming ". . . the newly conceived supreme fiction of our time that can make our lives meaningful".[5] The more recent claims of solidarity and collective rights of peoples "are largely a contribution of the developing world, in which Asian countries with their holistic, consensual and communal traditions that emphasize duties and obligations to the collective and social harmony, have frequently been in the forefront."[6] The immediate gain many of these other sociocultural traditions bring to the human rights movement is the addition of guarantors of human rights that are potentially more rich and powerful than formal constitutional forms and procedures.[7] This is not to claim that these more communal and social relational patterns have prevented abuses of human rights. Rather, it suggests that we have every prospect of gain as we identify and affirm the varied social customs and institutions that can promote the respect for and guarantee of human rights. Nevertheless, it seems that an anthropocentric paradigm for human rights is an insufficient pattern for the crises at hand. And it is the concerns and claims emerging on behalf of the planet that may present profoundly new common ground/ foundation for constructing "a social and international order in which the rights and freedoms set forth in this Declaration can be fully realized" (UDHR art. 28).

Seeking a Global Ethos for Planetary Survival

> In this world there is nothing softer or thinner than water. But to compel the hard and unyielding, it has no equal. That the weak overcomes the strong, that the hard gives way to the gentle — this everyone knows, yet no one acts accordingly. Lao-Tse

Two earlier revolutions evoked major shifts in the dominant social paradigm for human culture. They indicate the appropriateness of hope amidst difficulties in times of profound change. We know that the whole life style of our species changed about 10,000 years ago as our defining pattern shifted from that of nomads to agriculturally based communities. And then there was a second, a mere 400 years ago, with the reorganization of our major productive and political systems around nation-state industrialized communities. Each of these new levels of complexity embodied remarkable growth of information and reflexive consciousness, just as foreshadowed throughout the entire evolution of the planet's emerging life. The planetary and human crises of today are drawing us forward again into a more complex system in which the explosion of new information and required patterns of behaviors must find synthesis in a new world culture with transformed vision and social institutions.

The 'truth' of our present paradigm rests with an appropriate insistence on a certain separation of the individual from the clan, nation, etc., grounded in each person's dignity and right to self-realization; the 'falsity' rests with its negation of an essential union with others and with nature and the necessary relationship between personal development, bioregional authenticity and socio-cultural transformation. The new polar values are already identifiable — ecological health and universal human rights. These correlative values entail both an ethical and an aesthetic perspective embracing the need: a) of conversion, to be freed from the death dealing forces dominating the old patterns, institutions, etc.; b) of emancipation-liberation, to enter upon restructuring through transcending activities rooted in deeply personal and social behaviors focused upon choosing life linked to bioregional and ecological wholeness.

Human rights and ecological advocates heighten our consciousness about the moral imperative inherent in human agency to reconstruct global political economy in a more just and humane fashion. In both areas they frequently appeal to the symbol of 'community' as embodying the order and values of a more just political, economic and ecological order. The fundamental question of what properly constitutes or defines a community is ancient. But current questions and issues of human social agency, accented by today's crises of specicide and ecocide, refocus our examination on a sustainable, planetary, humane community and the virtues most central to it. While it is the sense of injustice that provided the foundation for human rights advocates calling for liberation from the present pseudo-communal, and illegitimate structures, it is a new sense of justice presaged in the human rights and ecosystems appreciation that offers the most instructive prospectus for creating a planetary community based on distributive justice and ecological wholeness. The proposals for alternative future world orders and transition paths to new types of global human communities entail a transcending of the political economics of sovereign statism and the global production system. They provide a powerful impetus for democratizing and ecologically harmonizing the global political economic and cultural order.

A full generation has passed since Rachel Louise Carson published *Silent Spring* in 1962. And in 1990 the 20th anniversary of the first 'earth day' was celebrated by peoples in almost all parts of the globe. No matter what the culture, what the degree of industrialization and incorporation into a global economy, peoples' thought and action is increasingly related to environmental concerns. While not yet to a sufficient degree, modern human societies are learning to include the earth community — the atmosphere, soils, waters, flora and fauna — in their value systems. We are witnessing the first steps in breaking out of our anthropocentric moralities and ethics and in moving into a new planet-become-conscious-whole-directing-itself value framework. This new common holistic consciousness with a simultaneous respect for its non-reducible bioregional differences is instructive for enhancing a framework of universal human rights with the simultaneous celebration of non-reducible cultural peculiarities. This change in consciousness in the latter half of the 20th century finds expression in a distinctive phenomenon in the realm of social organization. Starting from points around the earth a growing network of international institutions emerges to facilitate common understanding and insight and to coordinate complementary actions among peoples and their governments.

The insight linking human survival to planetary wholeness of life-health breaks forth at varied levels. Perhaps one of the earliest expressions is found in the Antarctic Regime established in 1959. Certainly a forceful drive along this line emerged from the 1972 Stockholm conference which established the United Nations Environmental Program. Principle 21 of the Stockholm Declaration dramatically confronted traditional nation-state prerogatives of independence and autonomy by insisting that they had a responsibility to regulate internal affairs in such a way as to prevent any damage to the ecosystems beyond their own national jurisdiction. In 1982 the Law of the Seas convention profoundly challenged modern conceptions of state and private ownership with its provisions around the 'common heritage of humankind'. But the 1983 UN Charter for Nature is possibly most significant for addressing the issue of the 'rights of nature'. which radically challenges dominant anthropocentric moral and ethical frameworks. Successive movements — the 1985 Helsinki protocol on sulphur reduction targets, the 1987 Montreal protocol on CFCs, the 1989 Basle Convention on shipping hazardous wastes — all serve to underscore the growing sense of urgency in responding to global problems. In 1989 the Convention on the International Trade in Endangered Species (CITES) was invoked to ban the international trade in ivory, successfully linking the critical area of international trade with limitations for the sake of ecosystems. And it is anticipated, despite U.S. foot dragging, that the United Nations Conference on Environment and Development (UNCED) in Brazil, 1992, will further solidify a global consensus about the primacy of the earth's health in evaluating the 'success' of our political, economic and social institutions. It should also advance our learning curve in formulating new instruments of international law and in designating new institutional authorities responsible for the integral rights and health of the planet.

We are in the early stages of a radical paradigm shift, one that entails the creation of new, voluntary, non-violent, participative and autonomous groups/actions for repossessing and humanizing ourselves and our social reality in harmony with the demands of planetary life. If true to earth-life, this can be neither monocratic nor uniaxial in its development and execution. But facing the global challenge will, of necessity, require a planetary society or culture at some level. Minimally, this would involve a common vision of what is constitutive for balanced planetary life and new institutions with some degree of planetary focus and authority. Cross cultural and critical care must be taken lest the rhetoric of new global and planetary language co-opt these visionary ideals and produce a new ideological veneer in defense of old interests. The style of the emerging world community must be that of radically simple and common folk, not that of another oligarchy of elites such as dominates in structures like the UN Security Council, the International Monetary Fund, the Group of Seven (G7), and the General Agreement on Trade and Tariffs club.

We are faced today with the need for an artistic and altruistic refounding of our mythic story within a new paradigm of earth-life and human-life mutuality and reciprocity. The worldwide new economics movement, dubbed The Other Economic Summit (TOES) at its annual meetings, provides a good example of work underway. Laying these foundations represents the essential challenge before teachers of world politics. At the core there is a shift from Newtonian politics and economics based on a mechanistic understanding of science and culture to political economies based on systems in dynamic tension representing metaregimes of transformation and liberation. Authority, information and power will not have fixed, unidirectional flows, but multidirectional and multivalent exchanges. New images and symbols will emerge as the old story becomes increasingly inadequate, even dysfunctional. Peoples in all lands are concerned about what type of world their children and grandchildren will inherit. History shows repeatedly — whether it is called 'common sense', '*intentio populi*', 'prophecy' or the 'hidden meaning of life' — that a foreknowledge of things not yet but that could be comes to play in tearing down and building up sociocultural realities. For the first time, this centering of human eruption, this focus of human dwelling is on a planetary scale. There is a gathering sense of wholeness, of responsibility to act in concert for life tomorrow.

The term 'convivial planetary community' comes to mind for this new pedagogical vision emerging around the core values of universal human rights and ecologically sustainable civilization.[8] And tolerance is the primary virtue requisite for implementing this vision. This is a critical tolerance suffused with both ethical and aesthetic perceptions. It matures in knowing and appreciating the beauty of other cultures, in recognizing the mutualism and reciprocity of all human and earth life. It affirms that there is direction within evolving life, even plan and order, though in the last analysis we again confront mystery. We experience awe and reverence. Consequently, in looking forward to constructing a 'convivial planetary society' three norms seem fundamental: a) differentiation respecting the uniquely creative efforts of the entire earth-life process; b) subjectivity and interiority as the locus where the all-pervasive numinous quality of life is operative; c) intercommunion to be deepened at and between all levels of reality. 'Convivial planetary community' is a dialectically developing symbol or design for a metaregime of balanced transformations of all sociocultural-earth realities. The vision itself is directive of and subject to social criticism based upon a praxis model of learning, teaching and reflection. As an evolving symbol it embodies our on-going self-interpretation and creating of earth-life. While teachers and students alike continue to study, analyze, experiment and revise, we can all fully enter into earth-life only by obedience to and contemplation of its rhythms and harmonies.

Creating the Myth for a Convivial Planetary Community

> Teach your children what we have taught our children, that the earth is our mother. Whatever befalls the earth, befalls the children of the earth. . . . We did not weave the web of life; we are merely strands in it. Whatever we do to the web, we do to ourselves. Chief Seattle

We are at a profoundly new point in human history. It is the first time that the physical survival of all humankind is at stake, and is so immediately and on such an extensive level confronting us with the necessity to choose life. The coalescence of concerns reveals that the search for progress and liberation without concern for the earth is shortlived, and seeking care and protection of the planet without concern for justice and peace is futile. As we first grapple with this insight, many experience a deep sense of spiritual inadequacy for meeting this crisis. Neither our political and economic ideologies, nor our religious creeds, are sufficiently robust to embrace the vulnerability required for reconstructing beliefs in accord with this new experience and knowledge. Consequently, the unique human capacity to invent and embrace a new order is paralyzed with anxiety. And this is the worst state, ". . . for the present anxiety kills the future before it is born."[9]

The disappointment experienced in the failure of both dominant ideologies in the 20th century and the new sense of responsibility and care for the planet converge in human rights claims of solidarity and collective rights and claims of intergenerational equity. Students are beginning to understand that every set of economic and political institutions, every cultural system, will flourish only in so far as it is aligned with the ground truth of the planet's way of life. For a period of time 'false' patterns can proceed and gather great force either by exploiting life from some other sector of the planet's resources, or from some other time, past or future, of the planet's bounty. But as our density both in numbers and impact bears ever more heavily on the planet, there is less possibility of simply exploiting another region, or mortgaging the future without irreparable harm and diminishment of life. Furthermore, the unavoidable fact of the present is that our species today tends to its basic human needs and wants through globally interdependent economic systems that are inseparable from the planet's global and bioregionally interrelated ecosystems. In these realities we are discovering a new, undeniably common ground. While there can be cultural and bio-regional differences within certain limits, none can any longer continue or proceed as if absolutely discrete from all the other cultures and the great unitary ecosphere of earth-life.

This new 'discovery' of the earth as a single life-dynamic presents us with many questions. What is the extraordinary or peculiar meaning of our species? How does this further modify our self-understanding of Enlightenment rationality, Freudian questions about consciousness, Marxian interpretations of human conflict, Einstein's and Heisenberg's insights about causality and objective reality? The immediacy and scope of the earth-life issues confronting us in all of our different locations today are directing us toward an appreciation of the common 'balance wheel' that tests both the parts and the whole of our species' actions, hopes, dreams. With this recognition it seems reasonable to hope that we can discern our way toward a global ethos which, like the unitary earth it is based upon, will at the same time accommodate a remarkably rich diversity of unique but interrelated and symbiotic sub-systems. But its possibility depends upon whether we human persons can/will lovingly embrace the whole of life. To advance this cause gives special significance to the teaching of world politics, international relations and related fields.

There is a new sense in which the earth is becoming a true center and measure of all that we do. This is not in the false Ptolemaic view that it is the center of all the universe. Indeed, as we discover additional galaxies and begin to peer into even more remote regions of the universe, that sense of 'place' is dead. But earth as 'center' and 'place' is more than ever *our* 'measure' today because of its defining peculiarity: life. And that brings with it a significantly changed sense of moral responsibility for 'earthkeeping'. We can no longer speak so simply of 'holding the earth in trust' or acting as 'earth's stewards'. It is far more complex. We begin to see that the earth is our steward, that its life exigencies largely define our life fabric, our human reality and potentiality. This might be humbling for some; for many it brings a reverence that embraces an even more precious humanity: not one that is unto itself, but one that is profoundly in and of service to 'another'.

The authors in this volume have continually reminded us of the necessity for examining the roots of myths, civilizations and cultures throughout the world if we are ever to build a consensus with enough defining power to effect a just and peaceful world order. Action will flow toward this end only insofar as there is a guiding passion, a moral vision, within which we can weave an epic pattern out of the diverse threads of our experience. Dangerous as the expression may seem, mounting evidence indicates that what we seek is a universal religious catharsis. But it is not of religious movements that seek to dogmatize persons' experience. Rather, as Moltmann writes, it is the religious experience of persons and communities who are willing to remain pilgrims.[10] This passion for earth-life cannot be fixed, stopped in time or place, but urges us on to deeper experiences and new discoveries. Our cultures, our political, economic, social institutions become successive moments of quasi-transcending understanding and praxis; they remain pliable and open.

Rooted in the common understanding of our planet's origins and development, the symbols of this earth-life will disclose the underlying ground of our myths and cultures. Guiding us back to a common starting point now formulated in a language and understanding that is truly transcultural, we will be reestablished in a genuine and integral solidarity. At the same time, our shared, emerging understandings of the ways of the cosmos as embodied in the day-to-day specificities of our planet's life will establish new common eschatological symbols for this earth-myth. The power of such symbols is to "invite people to break away from the same old thing and to a new experience of new life. As signs of the change, they are themselves changeable signs of a journey which does not turn back."[11]

Such an earth-myth could ground us once more in the hope that overcomes paralyzing anxiety. This hope rests not simply in human inventiveness, rationality and altruism, but in the irrefutable evidence of planet-life transcending improbabilities, unfathomably rich in its inventiveness and creativity, and its infinite potential toward the fullness of life. We are speaking of religion here as a moral ecology and as a moral pedagogy which reminds us of the interrelated parts of nature as well as our species' interdependent existence within the whole movement of life. It evokes awe and reverence. It reminds us that there are 'rules' proper to a humane and planetary social order. It calls for a habit of virtues which entail the interactions constitutive of community.[12] It is essential for refounding our mythic story:

> ... to know who we are, where we came from, and where we are going, to discover what our initial story is — our personal story as well as the story of our own society. Then we can come to understand it and to ask if it still makes sense to live this story, or to find another.[13]

This new 'earthkeeping' tradition involves symbolic complexes and represents multiple levels of information affecting our practices, our theories, and our critique of both. As in all religions, this sacred tradition calls us to cherish life and to enter in with all our life to help the birth of that which is ready to be born. In fidelity to the emerging life of the planet, this pedagogical ethos draws teachers into the dynamic life-flow continually refreshed and reconstituted by successive, participating generations. In such a dwelling, teachers join others as social artists at work on the directionality of the planet. The arts and sciences of earth-life must inform our political and economic teaching, indeed, all of our sociocultural endeavors. Teachers work not from simple, isolated standpoints of inevitability. They educate out of moral choice relevant to students but on behalf of the convivial planetary community as a whole.

Notes

1. Edmond N. Cahn, *The Sense of Injustice* (New York: New York University Press, 1949), p. 49.
2. Robert Heilbroner, "The Triumph of Capitalism," *New Perspectives Quarterly* 6, 4 (Fall 1989), pp.4-10.
3. Lewis Mumford, *The Human Prospect* (Boston MA: Beacon Press, 1955), pp. 288-289.
4. Michael Albert *et al.*, *Liberating Theory* (Boston MA: South End Press, 1986), pp. 1-3.
5. June K. Burton, "The Universal Declaration of Human Rights and Beyond," *Essays in Arts and Sciences* XII, 2 (May, 1983), p.102.
6. Achal Mehra, "Civil and Political Rights in Asia," paper read at Second Annual Conference in the Pacific Interest, Wilamette University, Salem, Oregon (February, 1990), p. 4.
7. Mehra, p. 9.
8. Ivan Illich, *Tools for Conviviality* (New York: Harper & Row, 1973), p. 11.
9. Jurgen Moltmann, *On Human Dignity: Political Theology and Ethics* (Philadelphia: Fortress Press, 1984), p. 166.
10. Moltmann, p. 181.
11. Moltmann, p.181.

12. Roberto M. Unger, *Knowledge and Politics* (New York: Macmillan/Free Press, 1975), p. 261. See also Hannah Arendt, *The Human Condition* (Chicago IL: University of Chicago Press, 1958), p. 207.

13. Alasdair MacIntyre, *After Virtue: A Study in Moral Theory* (Notre Dame: University of Notre Dame Press, 1981), pp. 219-220. See also Samuel S. Kim, *The Quest for a Just Social Order* (Boulder CO: Westview, 1984), p. 19.

For Product Safety Concerns and Information please contact our EU
representative GPSR@taylorandfrancis.com
Taylor & Francis Verlag GmbH, Kaufingerstraße 24, 80331 München, Germany